ROUTLEDGE LIBRARY EDITIONS:
INTERNATIONAL BUSINESS

MULTINATIONAL SERVICE FIRMS

MULTINATIONAL SERVICE FIRMS

PETER ENDERWICK

Volume 16

Routledge
Taylor & Francis Group

LONDON AND NEW YORK

First published in 1989

This edition first published in 2013
by Routledge
2 Park Square, Milton Park, Abingdon, Oxfordshire OX14 4RN

Simultaneously published in the USA and Canada
by Routledge
711 Third Avenue, New York, NY 10017

First issued in paperback 2014

Routledge is an imprint of the Taylor and Francis Group, an informa company

British Library Cataloguing in Publication Data
A catalogue record for this book is available from the British Library

ISBN: 978-0-415-64319-1 (Volume 16)
ISBN: 978-0-415-75201-5 (pbk)

Publisher's Note
The publisher has gone to great lengths to ensure the quality of this reprint but
points out that some imperfections in the original copies may be apparent.

Disclaimer
The publisher has made every effort to trace copyright holders and would
welcome correspondence from those they have been unable to trace.

Multinational
Service Firms

Peter Enderwick

ROUTLEDGE
London and New York

First published in 1989 by
Routledge
11 New Fetter Lane, London EC4P 4EE
29 West 35th Street, New York NY 10001

Typesetting by Gilfillan Ltd, Mitcham, Surrey
Printed and bound in Great Britain by
Biddles Ltd, Guildford and King's Lynn

British Library Cataloguing in Publication Data

Multinational service firms.
    1. Service industries. Multinational
companies
    I. Enderwick, Peter
    338.4

ISBN 0-415-00395-4

For Geoff Gravil, an exemplary teacher

Contents

Preface

Few, if any, edited collections are likely to satisfy all potential readers. Differences in scope, style and approach, as well as problems of overlap and inconsistency, serve to detract from overall coherence. These shortcomings are inevitably present in this volume. The subject matter, service-sector multinationals, is one many would concede as significant, indeed of rapidly growing significance, yet this importance has not been reflected in its past treatment.

The purpose of this collection of original essays is to review multinational operations in a number of important service industries and source nations. The relative neglect of this aspect of international business means that contributions have been commissioned from researchers in a number of disciplines resulting in some diversity of approach and treatment. Thus, while a number of authors have made contributions to the theory of the multinational enterprise others are experts on specific industries or source nations. Inevitably, this will be a source of dissatisfaction for some readers. This is unfortunate, but at this stage probably unavoidable. The growing importance of service industry multinationals and their cursory treatment to date outweighs the likely resultant limitations. Hopefully, the present collection will spur further work in this field.

The papers fall into four broad parts. The first comprises two introductory chapters. Chapter 1 surveys some of the most significant features of service-sector trade and investment. Existing data allow only indicative estimates of the size and growth of such trade and investment. More detailed data covering US service trade and investment are used to explore the distinctive features of service-sector MNEs. The usefulness of the prevailing eclectic theory of the MNE in explaining the operations of service firms is also assessed. This approach seems to offer a powerful explanatory framework.

Chapter 2, by Markusen, argues for a broadening of the concept of a service MNE. For Markusen all MNEs, irrespective of their industry origin, are engaged in service transactions. This occurs because the MNE is an institution engaged in the international sale of both final, and more significantly, intermediate services. Such sales represent the transfer and utilisation of the firms' competitive assets (technology, management, reputation, accumulated consumer and market information etc.). This conception of the service MNE has a number of very significant implications for both theory and analysis. Data limitations will be exacerbated under such a definition. Also problematic will be the terms of exchange as services are priced and transferred internally. Markusen explores these and other issues in his paper.

Part Two provides studies of four service industries. These are confined to what might be termed 'business services', currently the most dynamic and rapidly developing area of private sector services. Coverage includes those industries which have been subject to considerable research in the past (multinational banking) as well as areas relatively unexplored (multinational contracting, international news agencies). All are characterised by high levels of multinational production. These chapters offer a fascinating picture of internationalisation and highlight considerable variation in both operational forms and strategy.

These industry reviews which focus primarily on multinationals from the advanced Western economies are complemented in Part Three by studies of direct investment from both the Eastern bloc and the less developed economies. Malcolm Hill (Chapter 7) discusses the sizeable and long established investments made by Soviet and Eastern-bloc nations particularly in the fields of banking and trading. Complementing recent studies of the growth of overseas investment by less developed nations (Lall 1983; Wells 1983) is Chapter 8 by Donald Lecraw who considers the non-manufacturing investments made by these countries. Third World based multinationals provide an interesting challenge for theories of international business.

Part Four offers a comprehensive review of policy issues raised by international trade and investment in services. This topic forms part of the current GATT round and although there is considerable pressure for an easing of restrictions little progress has been achieved to date. The final chapter attempts to draw out some of the most significant findings of the collection as well as highlighting areas where further research is required.

In the final analysis this collection represents very much a starting point for work on what many feel will be one of the most fundamental issues in the international economy of the coming decades. This book is presented in the hope of stimulating such work.

Contributors

Oliver Boyd-Barrett is Lecturer in the School of Education, The Open University, Milton Keynes, England.

Peter W. Daniels is Reader in Geography, The University of Liverpool, England.

Peter Enderwick is Lecturer in Economics, the Queen's University of Belfast, Belfast, Northern Ireland.

Herbert G. Grubel is Professor of Economics, Simon Fraser University, Burnaby, British Columbia, Canada.

Malcolm R. Hill is Senior Lecturer in the Department of Management Studies, University of Loughborough, Loughborough, England.

Donald J. Lecraw is a Professor in the School of Business Administration, University of Western Ontario, Canada.

A. Leyshon is attached to the Centre for the Study of Britain and the World Economy, Department of Geography, University of Bristol, England.

James R. Markusen is a Professor of Economics, Department of Economics, University of Western Ontario, Canada.

Nigel J. Thrift is Reader in Geography, Department of Geography, University of Bristol, England.

Acknowledgements

I would like to acknowledge the work of The Queen's University Secretarial Centre in the preparation of this book, in particular Mrs Cobie Moore and Mrs Amanda Latimer. The bibliography and a number of tables were prepared by Georgina Holmes and Carol Richmond in the Department of Economics.

Abbreviations

AFP	Agence France Presse
ANA	Arab News Agency
ANEX	Asian News Exchange
AP	Associated Press
ANIS	Action by National Information Systems
BOI	Board of Investment
BOP	balance of payments
CAD	computer-aided design
CAM	computer-aided manufacture
CD	certificate of deposit
CMEA/COMECON	Council for Mutual Economic Assistance
DBS	direct broadcast satellite
DPA	Deutsche Press Agentiv
EC	European Community
EEC	European Economic Community
ECGD	Exports Credit Guarantee Department
FDI	foreign direct investment
FSA	firm-specific advantage/asset
FTE	foreign trade enterprise
FTO	foreign trade organisation
GATT	General Agreement on Tariff and Trade
GDP	gross domestic product
GNP	gross national product
ILO	International Labour Organisation
IMF	International Monetary Fund
IPTC	International Press Telecommunications Council
IRM	Institute for Research and Information on Multinationals
ISDN	Integrated Services Digital Networks
KMG	Klynweld Main Geordler
LAT-WP	*Los Angeles Times-Washington Post* news service
LDC	less developed country
LSA	location-specific advantage
MNE	multinational enterprise
MFN clause	most favoured nation clause
MOFA	majority owned foreign affiliate

NNA	Nigerian News Agency
NPA	Newspapers Publishers' Association
NTP	non-tariff barrier
NYTNS	*New York Times* news service
ODA	Overseas Development Administration
OECD	Organisation for Economic Co-operation and Development
OPEC	Organisation of Petroleum Exporting Countries
PA	Press Association
PANA	Pan-African News Agency
PTT	(Ministries of) Post, Telephone and Telegraph
R&D	research and development
SWIFT	Society for Worldwide Interbank Financial Telecommunications
TASS	Telegrafnoye Agentsvo Sovietskovo
TWMs	Third World multinationals
UNCTAD	United Nations Conference on Trade and Development
UNESCO	United Nations Educational, Scientific and Cultural Organisation
UPI	United Press International
UPITN	United Press International Television News

Part One

1

Some Economics of Service-Sector Multinational Enterprises

Peter Enderwick

1.1 INTRODUCTION

The continuing growth of literature on both theoretical and empirical aspects of multinational enterprises (MNE)[1] has enabled considerable progress to be made in understanding the dynamics of international business. With minor exceptions, the emphasis of this research has been on manufacturing enterprises. Several factors account for this selectivity. First, the post-Second World War growth wave of foreign direct investment (FDI) was dominated by the internationalisation of manufacturing industry. For example, the 180 largest US-based manufacturing corporations added 6,879 manufacturing affiliates to their parent systems between 1951 and 1975 (Curhan, Davidson and Suri 1977).

Second, early theoretical analyses of the MNE (Kindleberger 1969; Vernon 1966) stressed the need for overseas-based firms to possess some form of 'compensating advantage' if they were to compete successfully with indigenous companies familiar with the local market. Subsequent analyses stressed the significance of advantages in technology (Johnson 1970) and marketing skill (Caves 1971). Generalisation and empirical testing of these ideas (Buckley and Casson 1976) has concentrated on manufacturing industry.

Third, policy analysis has focused on manufacturing MNEs. This has been true for FDI source nations concerned with the substitution of overseas for domestic production and the restructuring of industry, and host nations seeking employment and export creation. Evaluation of these policy concerns is easier in the case of material producers where, for example, employment effects and the substitutability of overseas production for

3

exports are more readily identifiable.

The increasing proportion of national income and employment accounted for by the service industries within most advanced industrial economies and the apparent de-industrialisation of some (Blackaby 1979; Bluestone and Harrison 1982) have elevated both the domestic and international role of non-manufacturing industries. Interest in international trade and investment in services has been further stimulated by their balance-of-payments contribution, particularly for economies like the United Kingdom; the slowing down in rates of growth of foreign investment in manufacturing (OECD 1981) with concomitant implications for host-nation job creation; as well as rising concern over the stability of such investments as manufacturing organisations have striven to restructure and relocate their activities in response to a highly competitive world market (Ballance and Sinclair 1983).

In addition to these discernible trends, the maturing theory of international production associated with the work of Dunning and others has increasingly been applied to non-manufacturing industries and enterprises including international tourism (Dunning and McQueen 1982), international banking (Yannopolous 1983), office location (Dunning and Norman 1983) and export commodities such as bananas (Read 1983). These and other studies have provided a fragmented literature which suggests the general applicability of such an approach.

The balance of this chapter offers the background and framework for understanding the dynamics of service-sector multinationals. The following section describes the growing importance of the tertiary sector within the advanced industrial economies. Section 1.4 examines the significance and pattern of international trade and investment in services. The general paucity of data on these topics means that we are forced to place considerable reliance on evidence from the United States where such questions have been subject to more thorough investigation. The chapter concludes with an application of the theory of the MNE to service industries and offers some likely contrasts with manufacturing MNEs.

1.2 GROWTH OF SERVICES IN THE ADVANCED ECONOMIES

The analysis of service-sector activity presents considerable difficulties of both a conceptual and empirical nature. Categorisation of service-sector output distinguishes two related dichotomies: that between the private and public sectors and that between the marketed and non-marketed sectors. The complementarity of these categories is apparent. The first is concerned with the ownership of the means of production while the latter is based on the distribution of output. Since our primary interest lies in the internationalisation of service industries, the focus here will be upon private, marketed services.

Attempts to define service output follow two basic methods. The first emphasises the nature of service output, particularly its intangibility and frequent impermanence. The second approach focuses on the method of production defining service output as the residual not accounted for by agriculture, mining or manufacturing activity. Both approaches leave much to be desired. The first is overly restrictive excluding those activities which result in material goods e.g. construction, while the residual approach fails to specify the particular characteristics of service production. These problems of definition are compounded by the heterogeneity of the service sector. Even within the subgroup of industries concentrating on marketed services diversity is evident in the source of demand for such services. Thus, there are those industries such as transport and communication providing predominantly producer services and others supplying final or consumer services. A number of industries offer 'mixed' output marketing both final and intermediate services. This is the case within the distributive trades with component industries of wholesale and retail trade.

The relative importance of an economy's tertiary sector is closely correlated with its degree of economic development. Increasing development and maturity are associated with a rising proportion of employment and GNP accounted for by the service sector. Cross-section studies suggest that the increasing importance of the tertiary sector is at the expense of the primary sector during early stages of development (Gemmell 1982) but with industrial maturity the rising service share may be associated with a declining manufacturing sector (Kenward 1983). This structural view of a gradual shift towards a post-industrial economy must be interpreted with caution. First, there are cases like the Republic of Ireland (Norton 1984) which do not fit the general pattern. Second, such an approach implies

5

the gradual supplanting of manufacturing industry by service-sector activity. However, where a significant proportion of tertiary-sector output takes the form of intermediate or producer services there is likely to exist a limit to the degree of displacement between the two sectors and indeed the relationship appears more one of complementarity. Third, the structural transition view gives insufficient consideration to the relative price elasticities of demand between the service and non-service sectors. If, for example, productivity growth in services is below average then, all other things being equal, the price of services will rise relative to other commodities. This is likely to induce substitution effects i.e. alternative means of fulfilling the functions of service output, with concomitant implications for service activity and employment (Gershuny 1983).

The distinction between consumer and producer services provides a useful basis for examining the sources of growth of demand for service-sector output. Increased demand for final or consumer services is related to growth of real incomes i.e. the demand for final services is income elastic. Although cross-sectional analysis does, in general, support this relationship its robustness over time has been questioned by both more recent studies (Gershuny and Miles 1983) and estimates of income elasticities (Fuchs 1968).

Three principal factors account for the growth of producer services. First, the extension of the inter-industry division of labour has resulted in the expansion of industries such as distribution, banking, insurance and finance serving the needs of material producers. Second, occupations such as technologists and managers have grown as organisations pursuing geographical and industrial diversification have faced increasingly complex problems of administration and control. This changing intra-industry division of labour has been reinforced by corporate restructuring policies evident in the last few years. One effect of this has been a more dichotomised work-force with major employment losses occurring amongst subordinate primary jobs (Gordon 1979). Production processes are increasingly characterised by the application of proportionately more unskilled blue-collar and highly skilled white-collar labour (Noyelle 1983). Finally, the increasing importance of product differentiation as a competitive strategy in the last decade has resulted in the growth of market segmentation. Differentiation is increasingly based on the conjunction of material and non-material goods e.g. computer hardware and software. The complementarity of goods and service functions is again evident.

Whilst there is considerable variation between nations in both the relative importance of final and intermediate service production and their comparative growth rates, one study of five European Community nations concluded that around 50 per cent of marketed-service demand is intermediate rather than final (Gershuny and Miles 1983). Other studies (Momigliano and Siniscalco 1982; Norton 1984) tend to confirm these estimates.

Measurement of the significance of service-sector output raises additional problems. The first is the difficulty of isolating the 'pure' service component from that of goods in the valuation of tertiary output. Clearly, the majority of cases involve joint production. Measures based on the deflated money value of output face problems of identifying a valid price index for joint output.

Second, assessment of the importance of tertiary activity for a particular country appears sensitive to the measure selected. The two most widely adopted measures are service-sector share of GNP and of total employment. While these two measures are broadly correlated, there is some tendency for employment shares to lag output shares (Baer and Samuelson 1982). As Table 1.1 highlights, by the late 1970s the majority of advanced nations would be considered 'post-industrial' where more than 50 per cent of GNP is generated by service-sector activity. Although the two measures, relating to GNP and employment, are not strictly comparable since they refer to different years, they do give a broad impression of the significance of the tertiary sector. Excluding government services, private sector service output still accounts for around 40 per cent of GNP for most advanced economies. The countries considered in Table 1.1 cover almost all the major source and host nations for FDI, certainly in the case of manufacturing investment.

The final measurement problem relates to the reliability of the two measures over time. More specifically, there are grounds for caution in interpreting the trend of service sector employment share. The problem is that of comparative productivity growth. If productivity growth is below average in the tertiary sector then growing demand, even if spread equally across all sectors of the economy, would result in a rising service-sector employment share. Whilst empirical estimates of tertiary productivity

7

Table 1.1: Service industry GNP and employment as a percentage of total for selected OECD nations 1978 and *circa* 1970–5

Country	Service-sector proportion of GNP 1978		Percentage of total employment 1970–5	Approximate percentage change in employment 1900–75
	Total	Excluding government services		
Austria	48.4[a]	36.0	45.2	14
Belgium	57.7	43.6	55.6	16
Canada	55.2	39.9	63.8	35
France	52.7[a]	41.0	45.6	21
Great Britain	53.2	40.8	52.4	15
Italy	50.9	39.1	40.5	19
Japan	56.8	48.3	50.0	35
Netherlands	53.8[b]	39.6	52.0	15
Sweden	51.6	29.7	56.3	37
USA	63.6	50.9	61.2	27
West Germany	28.9	17.2	44.6	19

Notes: (a) 1977; (b) 1976
Sources: Columns 1 and 2 OECD (1980); columns 3 and 4, Pollard (1979)

growth offer no definitive answer to this question (Smith 1972) there are grounds for believing that productivity growth in services is lower than that of manufacturing. This conclusion follows from the above average rate of price increase of services which, by and large, has not been reflected in rising quality of such services. These trends are consistent with poor productivity growth (Gershuny and Miles 1983).

1.3 EXTENT OF WORLD TRADE AND INVESTMENT IN SERVICES

Table 1.2 which provides a breakdown of world trade by main category gives a broad impression of the importance of trade in invisibles.

Table 1.2 indicates that invisibles account for around one-quarter of non-governmental international payments. In turn, the category 'Other services',[2] which incorporates those service industries most likely to exhibit multinational organisation,

Table 1.2: World trade by main category 1960, 1970 and 1982 ($m)

	1960		1970		1982	
Visible trade	Receipts	Payments	Receipts	Payments	Receipts	Payments
Merchandise	101,700	100,800	274,700	281,400	1,687,000	1,692,600
Non-monetary gold	1,100	200	1,600	700	12,100	7,000
Invisible trade	31,400	30,500	92,770	93,380	602,300	709,000
Transport	9,900	10,600	25,900	28,325	126,400	163,600
Foreign travel	6,100	5,700	20,700	18,285	97,300	96,200
Investment income	8,800	8,200	26,570	28,200	227,800	330,200
Other services	6,600	6,000	19,600	18,570	150,800	119,000
Total (excluding government and transfers)	134,100	131,500	369,070	375,480	2,301,400	2,408,600
Invisible trade as % total trade	23.4	23.2	25.2	24.9	26.2	29.4
Other services as % invisible trade	21.1	19.8	21.1	19.9	25.0	16.8

Source: Committee on Invisible Exports (Various years), *World invisible trade* Committee on Invisible Exports, London.

constitute one-fifth of all payments for invisibles. Invisible trad appears to be growing faster than trade in visibles, with th share of invisibles in total trade rising from 23.4 per cent in 196(to 26.2 per cent in 1982.

The contribution of invisibles to international receipts and as a proportion of GNP displays considerable variation by nation as Table 1.3 illustrates.

Table 1.3: The importance of invisibles for selected nations

Country	% of world total receipts from invisibles	Invisible receipts as % of total receipts	Invisible receipts as % of GNP
	1982	1982	1982
Canada	1.9	13.9	3.9
France	10.6	41.4	12.1
Italy	4.3	26.4	7.7
Japan	5.5	19.4	2.9
Netherlands	4.5	30.8	21.5
UK	7.7	32.3	10.6
USA	19.7	35.9	3.9
West Germany	6.5	18.4	5.8

Source: Committee on Invisible Exports (1983)

The eight major countries considered above accounted for nearly two-thirds of all world trade in invisibles. They display consider-able diversity in both the importance of invisibles in total foreign earnings and as a percentage of GNP. The two most important source nations for exports of services are the US and France, together accounting for nearly one-third of the world total. Other countries for which invisibles provide a significant proportion of total international receipts include the UK, Italy and the Netherlands. Invisible earnings are far less important for Canada, Japan and West Germany. The importance of invisibles in total international earnings is closely correlated with the probability of a surplus on invisible transactions as Table 1.4 highlights.

For the industrial economies as a whole a current account trade deficit of $14.6 billion in 1982 was substantially offset by earnings from services and private transfers. The exceptions to this generalisation were Canada, Japan and West Germany where strong trade balances were partially offset by deficits in invisible

Table 1.4: Current account balance of payments summaries for major industrial countries 1982 $ US bn

	Current account balance on		
	Trade	Services and private transfers	Current account excluding official transfers
Canada	14.9	−12.7	2.2
France	−15.9	6.5	−9.4
Italy	−7.9	3.0	−4.9
Japan	18.1	−10.0	8.1
UK	3.9	6.5	10.4
USA	−36.4	30.6	−5.8
West Germany	26.3	−16.4	9.9
Other industrial countries	−17.5	3.3	−14.2
Total industrial countries	−14.6	11.0	−3.6

Source: International Monetary Fund (1983)

earnings. These figures suggest that strong trade performance in merchandise does not necessarily translate to an equally strong performance in invisible trade. Furthermore, the stability of countries' positions in terms of their net balance on invisibles suggests that comparative advantage (or disadvantage) in invisibles is relatively unaffected by short-term considerations (Griffiths 1975).

More restrictive estimates of the importance of international services are provided by data relating to 1974 contained in a US Department of Commerce study. These data are summarised in Table 1.5.

The estimates contained in Table 1.5 reveal a number of important insights. First, international service sales are of relatively limited significance, certainly in relation to domestic service-sector output or total US trade. Second, trade in services (exports and imports) account for a very small proportion of international activity. The predominant form of market servicing is through overseas affiliates. In the above table of the estimated $50 billion of services sold overseas by US companies, $43 billion (86 per cent) were attributable to affiliate sales. The importance of affiliates is also apparent in the case of non-US service

11

Table 1.5: Estimated service sales for US industries in overseas markets and non-US based industries in the US market 1974 $bn

From the US	$bn	To the US	$bn
Total foreign sales of which:	50.0	Total sales to US of which:	28.8
exports	7.0	US imports	7.9
overseas affiliate sales in:	43.0	affiliate sales in US in:	20.9
banking	12.0	banking	4.4
insurance/other finance	2.1	insurance/other finance	6.9
wholesale/retail trade	6.4	wholesale/retail trade	6.6
advertising	3.4	advertising	0.1
franchising	1.5	franchising	–
transport, communication and utilities	2.7	transport, communication and utilities	1.8
other	14.9	other	1.1
Service sales as % of goods sales	12.1	Service sales as % of goods sales	24.8

Source: US Department of Commerce (1976)

companies supplying the US market where 73 per cent of sales were through affiliates. The importance of overseas production in comparison to exporting is much greater for service industries when contrasted with goods producing industries. Indeed, these figures understate, if anything, the significance of affiliate activity. Thus $3.1 billion of the $7 billion worth of service exports from the US in 1974 was attributable to ocean and air transport services. Excluding these services from US service imports yields the finding that 92 per cent of total foreign service sales in the US were accounted for by affiliates. The widespread use of service subsidiaries reinforces the case for examining the activities of MNEs in the world market for services.

Third, while international services in aggregate are of minor significance in comparative terms, the contribution of overseas earnings is sizeable for particular services. For example, overseas affiliate revenues within the advertising industry are equivalent to almost 13 per cent of US domestic earnings. The comparable figure for banking is nearly 20 per cent. Clearly in these cases the economic well-being of the source-nation industry is closely related to its performance in overseas markets (United States Department of Commerce 1976).

A broader perspective on the importance of service sector direct investments is provided in Table 1.6.

Table 1.6: Service sector direct investment abroad as a percentage of total stock of direct investment

Country	Year	Services as a percentage of direct investment		
		All	Of which in: developed economies	developing economies
Canada	1974	28.7	–	–
Italy	1976	38.2	89.3	10.7
Japan	1974	38.8	65.3	34.7
UK	1974	26.8	80.2	19.8
USA	1976	28.7	68.3	31.7
West Germany	1976	22.4	59.4	40.6

Source: United Nations (1978), Table III-38

These data covering the major FDI source nations indicate that on average service industries accounted for 28.5 per cent of the total stock of foreign investment in the mid-1970s. Direct investments in services were particularly significant for countries like Italy and Japan. In the case of Japan considerable investments in commerce and other services are trade related, that is they are in support of Japanese exports or exports sourced from newly industrialising countries (Franko 1984). Table 1.6 illustrates the concentration of service-sector investments in the advanced economies which account for an average of almost 70 per cent of the total stock of service investment. In fact, for selected service industries like retail trade or communications, very little investment occurs outside the most advanced economies. Part of the explanation for the importance of developing countries as hosts to service investments is that the figures include banking and insurance much of which tends towards the tax haven and offshore banking sectors of the developing nations.

The use of measures such as proportion of total stock of FDI accounted for by service industries tends to overstate their relative importance. This problem arises because assets per employee tend to be much higher in the service sector than the average of all industries. The problem is compounded by the fact that the difference is solely attributable to the very high assets per head figure for the non-banking finance industry. A alternative measure of international investment in servic industries is provided by employment statistics. An Internation; Labour Organisation (ILO) estimate for the mid-1970s suggeste that non-manufacturing multinationals employed some 1(million world-wide (International Labour Organisation 1981).

1.4 GROWTH OF WORLD TRADE AND INVESTMENT IN SERVICES

Evidence in Table 1.2 shows that world trade in invisibles appears to be growing more rapidly than visible trade. The share of world trade taken by invisibles has risen by 6 per cent between 1960 and 1982. This increasing significance of invisible earnings does not appear to hold for the United States where service earnings as a percentage of all export earnings declined from 35.3 per cent in 1970 to 35.0 per cent in 1980. Furthermore, over the same period the most rapid growth in service earnings occurred in government transactions and investment income, private miscellaneous services grew at an average annual rate of 15 per cent, well below the 22 per cent annual growth of investment income (Dilullo 1981). However, turning to affiliate sales it is apparent from Table 1.7 that US service affiliates (excluding trade and banking) are increasing their share of sales relative to manufacturing.

Table 1.7: Sales of manufacturing and non-manufacturing affiliates of US MNEs for 1966, 1970 and 1977

	Value of Sales $bn		
	1966	1970	1977
Manufacturing	47.4	77.0	246.3
Non-manufacturing (excludes mining, petroleum, trade and banking)	5.6	10.2	51.7
Non-manufacturing as a % of manufacturing	11.8	13.3	20.9

Source: United States Department of Commerce (Various years) *Survey of current business*, Washington.

A number of factors appear to explain this dynamic growth. First, service-sector multinationals began to enter world markets later than manufacturing companies. Late entry coupled with low penetration rates facilitate rapid sales growth. In 1974 non-petroleum US goods producing affiliates had overseas sales equal to 16 per cent of goods production in OECD nations with the exclusion of the US. The comparable figure for private marketed services supplied by US affiliates was 3 per cent. Second, the changing forms of international involvement, particularly minority participation, joint ventures and management contracts which are of increasing importance, encourage the export and overseas supply of service functions as a source of earnings and control. Appropriation increasingly occurs through the engineering of technological indivisibility and overspecification. Control lies in ownership of the product or technology rather than the producing entity. As manufacturing and extractive MNEs have turned to these novel forms of ownership and control so the demand for contractual, technological and other service activities has increased (Hoogvelt 1982). Income received in these forms passes through the invisible balance. Third, service sales have grown as non-service companies have diversified into non-traditional industries, and as services not widely marketed e.g. franchising have increased their share of world sales. Furthermore, service-sector MNEs have turned to new market segments (e.g. governments) and new geographical areas (e.g. OPEC nations) in an attempt to boost sales.

Table 1.8 separates the growth of US MNEs into that occurring within the US parent and that within allied affiliates. Figures are presented for the three major service-sector industries: trade, finance (excluding banking) and other industries. For comparative purposes comparable figures for manufacturing are also presented.

Table 1.8: Growth of total assets of US parents and allied foreign affiliates 1966–77 by industry

	Compound annual growth of total assets	
	US parents	Allied affiliates
Manufacturing	10.5	13.1
Trade	14.7	16.0
Non-bank finance, insurance and real estate	8.3	16.3
Other industries	10.7	15.7

Source: Howenstein (1982)

15

Two important points emerge from Table 1.8. First, no manufacturing MNEs appear to have grown more rapidly tha manufacturing companies over the period 1966–77 (with th exception of US parents in finance). Second, affiliate growtl rates invariably exceeded those of their US parents. The differential growth rates were most apparent in service industries. There are some notable limitations which attach to these estimates, particularly in the case of overseas affiliates. Whilst faster economic growth outside the US would encourage rapid asset growth, the monetary value of such assets reflects differential inflation rates. In general, inflation rates in other advanced nations exceeded that of the US in this period. Further escalation of the value of affiliate assets is likely to have occurred in the translation of asset values from host-nation currencies to US dollars. The overvaluation of the dollar, certainly until 1971, favoured market servicing by foreign investment rather than exports further encouraging overseas asset formation. However, some reassurance for these estimates can be drawn from a comparison of affiliate growth rates in assets and employment as shown in Table 1.9.

Table 1.9: Growth in the total assets of allied affiliates and employment in majority-owned affiliates of US MNEs by industry and area of affiliate 1966–77

Industry		Annual growth rates of: allied affiliates total assets	MOFA employment
Manufacturing	Developed countries	12.4	3.5
	Developing countries	13.6	7.6
Trade	Developed countries	17.0	10.0
	Developing countries	13.7	2.8
Finance etc. (except banks)	Developed countries	15.4	5.3
	Developing countries	26.1	7.5
	Developed countries	14.7	5.7
Other industries	Developing countries	8.9	2.7

Source: Howenstein (1982)

Four important conclusions follow from this table. First, asset growth rates invariably exceed increases in employment. Second, service affiliates have been growing faster than manufacturing affiliates on both measures, certainly in the case of investment in other developed countries. Third, unlike manufacturing investment, service industries (with the exception of finance) are overwhelmingly attracted to the developed countries. Finally, the service sector disaggregated even to the extent shown in Table 1.9 exhibits considerable heterogeneity with regard to growth rates and preference for particular types of host country. Thus, non-bank finance has grown spectacularly in the developing nations, unlike other industries which have grown much more slowly in the developing world.

1.5 SERVICE INDUSTRIES AND THE THEORY OF THE MULTINATIONAL ENTERPRISE

Theoretical explanations of the MNE are dominated by the eclectic approach associated, in particular, with the work of Dunning (1981b). According to this model three related factors determine the incidence of FDI and the emergence of MNEs.

The first is that potential investors must possess firm-specific advantages (FSAs) which allow them to compete successfully overseas against indigenous firm's enjoying familiarity with the local market environment. Second, the overseas transfer of FSAs must occur within the organisation, that is to be internalised. Imperfections in or absence of external markets in FSAs encourage their internal exploitation. Where FSAs are internalised across national boundaries the MNE is created. Multinational production requires the fulfilment of a third condition, that FSAs be combined with location-specific advantages (LSAs) implying production outside the source nation.

When applying this model to service-sector industries three aspects require particular consideration. The first is that identification of FSAs may be difficult in industries traditionally seen as being of low technological complexity as this concept is normally understood. Second, 'non-equity' forms of foreign involvement, for example, licensing, management contracting and franchising, are widely used in some service industries. These forms of involvement based on market exchange may have significant implications for the role of internalisation in the theory of the MNE. Third, the difficulties of defining and categorising

17

service-sector output are compounded in the international context. Particularly relevant for a discussion of multinational production is the degree to which services are internationally tradable. Attempts to classify types of international services have focused on locational mobility (Daniels 1982) and the interaction of location and source of demand (Gray 1983). A useful starting point is provided by Boddewyn, Halbrich and Perry (1986) three-fold distinction between:

i.   Foreign-tradable services which create a commodity distinct from the productive process itself and which lend themselves to exporting;
ii. Location-bound services that necessitate a foreign presence, generally because consumption cannot be separated from production e.g. hotel accommodation; and
iii. Combination or 'mixed' services where locational substitution is possible.

1.6 FIRM-SPECIFIC ADVANTAGES AND THE SERVICE MNE

It is widely accepted that foreign-owned firms are at a competitive disadvantage when competing against indigenous enterprises familiar with the local market environment. To compensate for this MNEs require internationally transferable competitive advantages.

There are three principal sources of such advantages. The first arises where the firm enjoys exclusive or privileged access to competitive assets. The second derives from ability to better manage complementary assets under single ownership (so called economies of common governance). The third occurs where agglomerative economies enable existing firms to offer innovative or complementary services reinforcing their competitive position.

In the case of the former we may identify five principal types of ownership advantage. The first is the existence of goodwill or brand names. Since all services are embodied either in goods or people, their quality displays more variation than that of 'pure' goods. Similarly, many services are 'experience' commodities whose performance can only be assessed after consumption. For these reasons branding may form a powerful competitive weapon conveying, as it does, valued information to potential buyers. A variety of evidence is supportive of this expectation.

MNEs in retailing (Hollander 1970) and international tourism (Dunning and McQueen 1982) tend to concentrate on higher quality segments of the market. Product differentiation and non-price competition are particularly widespread within industries such as multinational banking (Rabino 1984). Similarly, branding among services has lent itself to international franchising e.g. fast goods. In a number of service industries producers have highlighted the problems they face in protecting brands and trademarks e.g. automobile leasing (United States Department of Commerce 1976).

The generation of goodwill and corporate identity is encouraged by the product specialisation characteristic of many service firms. Even where a policy of diversification has been pursued this tends to focus on related business areas. Where corporate skills relate to commercial know-how (banking, finance) and close contact with turbulent market environments (news agencies, international financing) their defining characteristics include opportunities for economies of learning and doing, their tacit or uncodified form (Teece 1981) and the importance of quality maintenance. The role of economies of learning and doing are particularly important in multinational services like banking (Yannopolous 1983) and process plant contracting (Barna 1983) where success in gaining contracts is, in many cases, tied to previous experience in similar technologies. Similarly, in their study of multinational business services, Dunning and Norman (1983) identify experience in the home (US) market as a major source of FSAs available to US-owned affiliates operating within Europe. Product specialisation and the diffusion of corporate identity is particularly valuable in industries characterised by supplier–client confidentiality e.g. auditing, consultancy and banking. However, the product specialisation of some service industries has created problems for the participant firms. In international news the traditionally poor return earned on mainstream business has forced some agencies to diversify e.g. Reuters expansion of financial and economic news. Often this diversification has been undertaken reluctantly since it may threaten the objectivity and legitimacy of mainstream business i.e. spot news. In this industry extreme product specialisation is seen as a source of competitive strength (Tunstall 1981).

The second principal type of ownership advantage is innovation as a competitive factor. In many cases innovations which form the competitive advantages of service MNEs are relatively unsophisticated, certainly in the sense of the technological achievements of some manufacturing firms, and typically incremental. For example, the multinational retailer Carrefour has applied overseas the concept of hypermarkets; within international medical services corporate chains have achieved a competitive edge based on the application of modern managerial methods to an area traditionally lacking in commercial acumen. In other cases significant innovations based on the conjunction of goods and services have provided a competitive edge. Examples abound in the fields of manufacturing systems, computer-aided design, data transmission and entertainment services.

The third source of ownership advantage is to be found in differential access to, and ability to process and apply, information. Information has a number of significant economic characteristics. It often requires considerable investment in indivisible assets; offers considerable economies of learning, scale and scope in its production; and lends itself to specialisation and economies of integration in the different stages of production. The existence of such economies in the production and processing of information suggests first-mover advantages. There may also be an interaction between multinationality and the establishment of competitive assets. That is, multinationality achieved on the basis of advantages of differential access to information is likely to reinforce such advantages creating barriers to competitive entry and allowing incumbents a considerable degree of immunity from competitive threat. This phenomenon is apparent in multinational banking (Yannopolous 1983).

Fourth, the widespread existence of government restrictions in the area of services provides a variety of opportunities for creating competitive assets. Regulation not only encourages foreign investment by restricting international trade but also creates opportunities for those enterprises located in unrestricted regions, for example international banking and shipping. Similarly, differential regulation may generate advantages. For example, until 1978 foreign-owned banks operating in the United States were exempt from restrictions on interstate banking which inhibited the growth of their indigenous competitors. The dynamism of government regulation (and increasingly deregulation) has served to create competitive advantages which may be successfully applied overseas.

A good example of this fourth characteristic is provided by international hospital chains (Salmon 1984). The injection of competition into the US health-care market has fostered the development of large, concentrated, for-profit corporate hospital chains. These institutions have attained a strong domestic position by the application of modern management methods, the achievement of huge purchasing economies and the development of arrangements with commercial insurance companies which have yielded financial and policy-formulation strengths. As privatisation and liberalisation of medical services has proceeded in countries like the United Kingdom, US-based chains have launched themselves overseas from the basis of their domestic consolidation. Of the 7,600 private beds in the UK health system some 1,132 (15 per cent) are under the ownership of US corporations (Mannisto 1981).

A fifth source of ownership advantage is provided by the growing importance of economies of scale and scope in services. Scale economies are particularly significant in those sectors characterised by high fixed costs and comparatively low variable costs of operation such as shipping and data transmission. In banking and finance large size bestows advantages of risk spreading and arbitrage. Economies of scope, which are a function of the spread rather than the scale of a firm's activities, may provide competitive advantage. While apparent in areas such as retailing, banking and brokerage services they are becoming increasingly important in a number of business services. The spate of mergers and take-overs apparent amongst accountancy firms, advertising agencies and management consultants is partly driven by the search for scope economies.

Economies of common governance arise from the efficient integration of economic resources with a concomitant reduction in transactions costs as exchange is hierarchically managed. In the service sector such economies may be considerable. They arise because of the high costs of market transactions in information. Again, the reasons for this are to be found in both the nature of services as economic commodities and their markets. Services are characterised by considerable quality variation; they may require significant customising; and much knowledge is tacit and non-codifiable. The markets for services are often segmented and there may be difficulties in protecting core knowledge. For all these reasons there are significant incentives to the internalisation of markets for services. Differential performance in the management of these hierarchies provides opportunities for competitive advantage.

The final source of competitive asset is that derived from economies of agglomeration. Where a number of competitors are spatially concentrated there may arise opportunities for the provision of innovative new services that can be supplied only because of the degree of market development. Good examples are provided by international banking where the concentration of several similar competitors in major financial centres may allow the creation of an interbank market. Here incumbent firms enjoy a clear competitive advantage over non-participants.

The strategy implications of this discussion should be clear. Contrary to the widely held view that geographical dispersion, small firm size and market fragmentation apparent within many domestic services prevent the erection of significant barriers to entry, the international case appears untypical. Here the returns to quality maintenance and branding as well as the benefits of incumbency suggest that established firms may enjoy significant advantages over newcomers.

1.7 INTERNALISATION AND THE SERVICE MNE

In serving overseas markets firms have a choice of three principal modalities: exporting, direct foreign investment and a variety of non-equity arrangements including licensing, management contracts etc. There is considerable evidence that the importance of overseas production in comparison to exporting is much greater for service industries when contrasted with goods-producing industries (see Table 1.5).

A number of factors explain this predisposition towards overseas production within services. First, there is widespread agreement that restrictions on free trade in services are pervasive. Such market imperfections discourage arms-length trade and encourage overseas production. Second, for some services a local presence is a prerequisite and exporting is never a viable alternative.

Whilst barriers to trade explain why service exports are relatively unimportant they cannot account for the apparent preference for direct investment as opposed to non-equity arrangements. In a number of service industries there are strong incentives to overseas-market servicing through affiliate production. Information-intensive industries such as banking and business services generate considerable knowledge which is better protected and more profitably applied within the organisation. Within construction, car rental, advertising and some business services horizontal integration occurs as firms seek to maintain quality and protect investments in goodwill. For service establishments complementing goods production, wholesale trade, market research, product servicing etc. there are obvious economies of common governance encouraging direct investment.

Joint-ventures and non-equity agreements do exist in a number of sectors. They are of particular appeal where services require customisation to suit local preferences e.g. financial and legal services; where risks must be shared e.g. insurance, banking; where complementary assets are required e.g. local business knowledge; or where investing firms are too small or too immature to undertake the investment single handedly. An advantage of such arrangements is that they may help in off-setting risk. For two principal reasons risk is high in many service industries. First, the nature of service output does not lend itself to gradualism in overseas operations. Service firms are often unable to gain experience of overseas markets by initial servicing through exports or licensing. This factor may be compounded by the need to establish strict, and immediate, quality standards for many service products. The second element of risk refers to the high rates of expropriation occurring in services. A United States Department of State (1971) study reported that the financial sector, particularly banking and insurance, was second only to the extractive sector in the incidence of expropriation.

In the case of knowledge-based innovatory services there are further incentives to internalisation. When innovators must undertake market-making expenditures, demand creation and diffusion require buyer education. Innovators, often with unique knowledge of their services, may be the best equipped to undertake buyer instruction. This suggests at least vertical integration of production and sales (Burstein 1984). That the decay in the proportion of benefit innovators can appropriate as diffusion occurs implies the need to provide potential innovators with some form of protection. A widely adopted solution is the issue of patents. One of the drawbacks of a patent system is the incentive it provides for premature innovation i.e. rushing of Research and Development (R & D) to ensure initial registration.

For those service activities where quality considerations are paramount, alternatives to patents may be necessary if services of the requisite quality are to be developed. Contractual solutions to the problem of premature innovation exist in vertical integration and brand-name promotion (Yu 1984). Both arrangements assure potential innovators of marketing commitments. It is noteworthy that in these cases internalisation is an economically efficient solution. Since simple patents are unlikely to cover the nebulous knowledge released by diffusion, property-rights protection may need to be extended to higher-order product-spaces (Telser 1979). Such extensions manifest themselves in the forms of tied sales (Burstein 1960a), full-line forcing (Burstein 1960b) and resale price maintenance (Telser 1960): business practices widely viewed as anti-competitive.

These incentives to the internalisation of exchange are reinforced by the high frequency of exchange for services of an intangible or transient form, serving to offset the formation costs of overseas affiliates. Evidence of dynamic economies of transfer (Davidson 1980; Teece 1977), whereby transactions and production costs are reduced with repetitive transfer of the same technology, encourages the retention of such benefits within the organisation. A further advantage of a significant overseas presence is the possible strengthening of protection over intangible assets e.g. trademarks and copyright. The example of publishing is illustrative here. The inability of many publishers to protect copyright of their works and to prevent pirating in the developing nations may be related to their preference for appointing overseas agents or representatives as opposed to creating subsidiaries.

Internalisation of service outputs may also bring advantages to potential buyers. Multinational branding of services conveys valuable information about the quality and performance of services. Similarly, existing customers in one market face lower search and transactions costs if they wish to purchase the same service in a second market where this market is serviced by an MNE. Furthermore, service MNEs may offer facilities for ordering the commodity in one location for supply in another e.g. hotel accommodation, car rental, or air travel. Such a facility will be valued by buyers who benefit from the lower international transaction and communication costs enjoyed by multinational sellers (Casson 1982b).

Licensing is discouraged by a number of facets of service-sector activity. There are problems of separating out the technology package of many services. Studies of insurance and retailing suggest that effective transfer necessitates the sharing of experience and provision of on-the-job training. The product specialisation of many service firms creates problems of small numbers exchange as potential licensees are limited. This problem is exacerbated in the case of developing countries since there is evidence that dissimilarities between the licensor and potential licensees raise transmittal and assimilation costs. Support for this contention is provided by international news agencies who engage in regular exchange with national agencies, both receiving valuable information from national agencies and in turn supplying them with global spot news. This barter of information is generally supplemented by a relevant cash adjustment (Boyd-Barrett 1980a). The transactions costs of this exchange (clearly fraught with tremendous problems of quality control) are presumably lowered by institutional similarities. For novel or differentiated service outputs, valuation differences between buyer and seller will raise the costs of market exchange and discourage licensing.

For differentiated and branded quality services there is a danger of underperformance by potential licensees which imposes potential costs on licensors. This problem arises from the inseparability of inputs supplied by the licensor and licensee and is significant in construction (see Chapter 6) and international business services (Dunning and Norman 1983). Some licensing occurs for certain technologies (particularly those which have matured) within construction, professional services and consultancy, and advertising.

Table 1.10 provides a comparison of the relative importance of technology receipts and direct investment income. Three points are particularly noteworthy. First, licensing income is considerably more important for manufacturing industries than it is for trade, banking and finance. Second, for all industries licensing income is far less significant in the case of developing countries. These findings are very much in line with our expectations. Third, there appears to be considerable use of licensing within the other services industry, particularly in relation to the advanced economies. Inability to disaggregate this industry and assess the role of licensing for specific products prevents a full explanation for this. However, it is likely that certain technologies (particularly those which have matured) within construction, professional services and consultancy, and advertising, may lend themselves to this form of trade. It is also likely that technology transfer within some services will take the form of franchising, a variant of licensing which allows the franchiser to retain a greater degree of control over service and system inputs facilitating quality maintenance. Management contracts are also prevalent in a number of service sectors including international medical services, hotel management and process plant contracting.

Table 1.10: Technology receipts in relation to direct investment income from affiliates for US parents by industry 1977 ($m and %)

	Manufacturing	Trade	Banking	Non-bank finance	Other industries
All countries					
(receipts)	2,907	512	188	107	644
(income)	6,655	2,041	1,819	2,220	1,102
Receipts as % of					
income	43.7	25.1	10.3	4.8	58.4
Developed countries					
(receipts)	2,674	449	111	89	467
(income)	5,428	1,556	587	1,187	625
Receipts as % of					
income	49.3	28.9	18.9	7.5	74.7
Developing countries					
(receipts)	234	63	78	17	17
(income)	1,227	485	1,232	1,033	463
Receipts as % of					
income	19.1	13.0	6.3	1.6	38.2

Source: United Nations (1983), p. 385, Annex Table IV.12

Rapid changes in both technology and the economic environment are shifting the balance between direct investment and non-equity agreements. Direct investment is encouraged by the growing liberalisation of policies towards inward-investment in a number of countries. Advances in information technologies are broadening the managerial and spatial encompass of the modern multinational. On the other hand, such advances reduce both market imperfections and the cost of communications infrastructure facilitating joint-ventures and non-equity agreements. The future is likely to witness both a growth in traditional investment as well as the development of a plethora of alternative arrangements. The choice of modality will be determined by a complex interaction of service characteristics, market and government requirements and organisational capabilities.

1.8 LOCATION-SPECIFIC ADVANTAGES AND THE SERVICE MNE

Locational considerations for multinational services vary with the type of service. For location-bound services where consumption and production are spatially and temporarily inseparable a foreign presence is inevitable. For such services growth may be based on multiple representation. Location choice is considerably greater for foreign-tradable services. In this case the existence of a viable market is likely to encourage an overseas presence. The number of overseas affiliates is likely to vary inversely with the ability to service a regional market through exports, the importance of internal scale economies and the extent to which the affiliate can eschew localised external and agglomeration economies (Dunning and Norman 1983).

While for many service firms production economies of scale may be relatively unimportant, greater reliance may be placed on economies of agglomeration. For services heavily dependent on specialised information sources and specific skills, location may be dictated by such considerations. For financial services like insurance and banking a central business district location within the major city is often a prerequisite (Dunning and Norman 1983). There are some grounds for believing that, compared with national firms, multinational affiliates may be less dependent on agglomeration effects. This follows from both their larger than average size which allows the internal exploitation of economies previously consumed as externalities and their privileged access to parent services.

In addition to relative concentration of location, predominantly within the developed countries, the growth of service firms is likely to be based on the development of multiple outlets (Doyle and Corstjens 1983). The synergy of a concentrated presence stems from economies of regional promotion and the reinforcement effects of multiple representation. A number of industries including banking and retail trade typically adopt this growth path. These considerations suggest that service sector FDI will exhibit considerable geographical inequality, multi-location affiliate formation and the predominance of sales for local market servicing. Some relevant evidence on these questions from US MNEs is presented in Tables 1.11 to 1.13.

Table 1.11: Concentration of foreign affiliate employment for US MNEs 1977

| | Per cent of employment accounted for by largest | |
	Four countries	Eight countries
All industries	44.4	64.7
Manufacturing	46.8	67.8
Selected services		
Wholesale trade	50.2	65.3
Retail trade	72.0	89.7
Finance		
(except banking)	69.9	85.0
Insurance	68.9	79.5
Real estate	68.9	84.8
Transport,		
communication		
and public utilities	69.5	80.3
Services	44.7	60.3

Source: Whichard (1982)

Table 1.11 indicates that most multinational service industries display marked geographical concentration, with the four major host countries (typically Canada, France, United Kingdom and West Germany) accounting for nearly 70 per cent of overseas employment. Exceptions to this are provided by wholesale trade and other services where geographical dispersion is as great, if

Table 1.12: Percentage of affiliates having operations at 1, 2–5, 6–10 or 11 or more physical locations 1977 by industry of affiliate

| | Percentage of affiliates with: | | | |
	1 location	2–5 locations	6–10 locations	11 or more locations
All industries	61.5	27.6	5.0	5.9
Manufacturing	57.3	32.4	5.6	4.7
Selected services				
Trade	64.1	24.9	4.7	6.2
Retail trade	38.0	26.6	7.2	28.3
Finance				
(except banking)	78.5	13.5	3.3	4.6
Insurance	63.5	21.5	6.2	8.8
Construction	57.3	33.3	5.5	4.0
Services	65.7	24.1	4.6	0.5

Source: Barker (1981)

Table 1.13: Destination of sales of majority-owned foreign affiliates of US companies 1976 (%)

	MANUFACTURING			TRADE			OTHER INDUSTRIES		
	Local sales	Export to US	Export to other foreign countries	Local sales	Export to US	Export to other foreign countries	Local sales	Export to US	Export to other foreign countries
Canada	73.6	21.1	5.3	69.8	19.8	10.4	96.9	2.2	0.9
Europe	69.5	2.1	28.4	56.0	1.2	42.8	83.6	1.7	14.7
Japan	86.9	2.1	11.0	74.0	D	D	98.3	D	D
Other developed countries	94.5	0.4	5.1	98.2	D	D	77.1	D	D
All developed countries	72.9	7.2	19.9	62.1	6.1	31.8	88.3	2.1	9.6
Latin America	93.6	2.4	4.0	63.8	7.2	29.0	77.5	8.1	14.4
Other Africa	81.8	7.5	10.7	93.1	–	6.9	92.3	D	D
Middle East	72.4	1.4	26.2	68.6	–	31.4	100.0	–	–
Other Asia & Pacific	78.5	8.3	13.2	39.6	4.8	55.6	98.8	D	D
All developing countries	90.6	3.5	5.9	53.5	5.8	40.7	86.8	5.0	8.2
International and unallocated	–	–	–	1.3	0.3	98.4	82.5	14.0	3.5
All countries	75.6	6.6	17.8	59.6	5.9	34.5	87.5	3.6	8.9

Notes: D: suppressed to avoid disclosure of data of individual reporters
Source: Chung (1978)

not greater, than that of manufacturing. Geographical concentration appears to be coupled with multi-location affiliates as Table 1.12 highlights.

These data relate to the number of separate physical locations where business is conducted by a particular affiliate. There is considerable support from these tables for the view that a regional multi-locational growth path is one likely to appeal to a number of service industries, notably retail trade and insurance. Again, major exceptions exist, particularly in trade and non-bank financing.

Evidence for the destination of sales of US majority-owned foreign affiliates is presented in Table 1.13. The picture is a little less clear-cut here where aggregation difficulties allow only a separation of trade and other industries within the service sector. For the developed countries non-trade service output is destined primarily for the local market; there is very little in the way of service exports. The picture for the developing countries is obscured by the importance of finance capital within Latin America and other financially attractive areas. These international finance centres are involved in extensive movement of financial claims. The clear exception to this reasoning is obviously trade where there is evidence of considerable re-export to third-party nations. The geographical dispersion and limited role of multiple outlets in wholesale trading (Tables 1.11 and 1.12) suggests the use of regional market servicing by these affiliates. Again, we note the heterogeneity of experience within the service sector highlighting the dangers of generalised statements concerning these industries.

1.9 SOME CONTRASTS BETWEEN MANUFACTURING AND SERVICE MNEs

There are likely to be significant differences in both structure and strategy between service-sector multinationals and their manufacturing counterparts. Some of the differences may be accounted for by the nature of products e.g. product standardisation may be less prevalent in services, or by the conditions of production e.g. many services such as banking and finance depend on economies of agglomeration. Furthermore, the relatively recent take-off in service-sector FDI implies that these firms may not have yet reached the multinational maturity characteristic of many manufacturing enterprises.

In this section a number of likely contrasts are highlighted and, where possible, pertinent empirical evidence is presented. Any notable differences are important since they would imply a challenge for theoretical explanations of foreign investment with any claim to generality and could raise unexpected issues for a policy framework heavily orientated to extractive and manufacturing multinationals.

The first notable contrast relates to differences in size and scope of activities. For a number of reasons service-sector multinationals are likely to be smaller than their manufacturing counterparts and display greater product specialisation. Production economies of scale appear to be less important for service firms. The immobility of many services implies that concentration of production and dependence on mass distribution is not a viable growth strategy for much of the service sector.

Table 1.14: Mean number of affiliates and employees and degree of multinationality of US MNEs by industry of parent 1977

Industry	Mean number Affiliates	Average employment US parents	Affiliates	Affiliates as a % of MNEs worldwide		
				Assets	Sales	Employees
All industries	7	6,175	348	24.1	31.5	27.6
Manufacturing	8	6,406	514	29.0	28.7	31.1
Trade	4	6,609	180	18.4	19.7	15.5
Finance (except banks) Insurance and real estate	3	3,533	91	10.4	17.3	33.3
Other industries	5	6,779	228	25.2	20.1	18.0

Source: Barker (1981)

Small size is also likely to be related to the relative immaturity of many service MNEs. In industries such as retailing the degree of multinationality is widely considered to be low (White 1984). Relevant empirical evidence on this question is presented in Tables 1.14 and 1.15.

Table 1.15: Percentage of US MNEs having affiliates in various numbers of countries 1977 by industry of US parent

Industry of US parent	% of MNEs having affiliates in:				
	Only 1 country	2–5 countries	6–10 countries	11–20 countries	More than 20 countries
All industries	49.2	30.6	9.6	6.6	4.0
Manufacturing	39.8	33.8	12.0	9.1	5.3
Trade	59.0	30.1	6.4	3.7	0.8
Finance (except banks), insurance and real estate	77.2	18.3	2.5	0.5	1.5
Other industries	46.2	31.8	11.6	7.4	3.0

Source: Barker (1981), p. 39.

The tables offer considerable support for the view that service MNEs are both smaller and of lower multinationality than manufacturing corporations. Table 1.14 makes it clear that the lower world-wide employment size of service MNEs is the result of their operating, on average, fewer affiliates of well below average size. US parent size is only significantly below average in the case of non-bank financial MNEs. The smaller mean number of affiliates operated by service MNEs is reflected in the lower percentages of assets, sales and employment accounted for by affiliates of service MNEs. As Table 1.15 indicates service-sector MNEs display a lower probability of having affiliates in more than ten overseas countries.

Indeed, 62.9 per cent of service MNEs have affiliates in only one country compared with 39.8 per cent in the case of manufacturing MNEs. The limited use of exporting by service industries suggests other areas where experiences will diverge. There is likely to be a much lower degree of locational substitutability between source and host-nation facilities for service MNEs, reducing the probability of them being charged with the exporting of jobs (Enderwick 1985: Ch. 3). The comparatively late take-off and considerable cross-investment in services suggests that acquisition may be a preferred form of entry for many firms. Analysis of inward investment in the USA suggests that acquisition is a widely adopted strategy for service MNEs (Belli 1981) allowing both more rapid entry and the achievement of a critical mass which may be considerable in industries characterised by multiple outlets. Furthermore, we would expect to observe considerable variety in the forms of overseas representation adopted by service MNEs. As changing conditions have forced many manufacturing (Oman 1984) and extractive (Ozawa 1982) MNEs to accept non-majority ownership positions, service MNEs with their more recent take-off and heterogeneity of output reveal considerable flexibility of organisation (Advertising Age 1984; Salmon 1984; White 1984).

1.10 CONCLUSIONS

In conclusion, first, our discussion has made clear the considerable heterogeneity of the service sector, as this is generally understood. There are notable behavioural and structural differences between the various industries normally subsumed within the services sector. These differences are most apparent in the case of wholesale trade. This heterogeneity reinforces the case for analysis at the level of the individual service industry.

Second, our analysis has placed considerable reliance on data relating to US-based MNEs. Generalisation of our findings to encompass the behaviour of non-US service MNEs may be unwarranted. This is particularly likely to be the case with Japanese service investments which are often trade supporting. Considerable work remains to be undertaken with regard to Japanese and European service firms. Similar limitations attach to the application of our findings to Third World service MNEs.

Third, motives for overseas service investment appear to be considerably more complex than the simple following of, and support for, manufacturing MNEs. Undoubtedly some service firms in financial and professional services have internationalised in an attempt to retain the patronage of nationally-based manufacturing MNEs. However, many examples including hospital services, retailing and news agencies do not fit this pattern. The growth of both final and intermediate demand for services suggests that the dependence of service MNEs on their manufacturing counterparts is less than complete. Similarly, evidence on the possession of firm-specific advantages within many service industries implies that service firms may undertake foreign investment for offensive i.e. profit-seeking motives. The apparent relationship between domestic industry strength and international success in world services suggests the existence (and maintenance) of country-specific ownership advantages (Shelp 1981).

Finally, our search for the compensating advantages likely to be held by service MNEs highlighted their tacit and often incremental nature. Indeed, in some instances service investments have undoubtedly been achieved in the absence of such compensatory factors. This is likely to have been the case for British and European banks operating internationally during the nineteenth century and is true for contemporary international news agencies. In these cases there is no question of the foreign-owned facilities facing any indigenous competition and hence subsidiaries are not regarded as being at any competitive disadvantage. In these examples of specialised intermediate service supply the parent organisation enjoys systemic synergy; that is the role of individual affiliates is judged on the basis of their overall contribution rather than component performance. The success of both nineteenth-century wholesale banking and current international news services depend on efficient collection, interpretation and application of information within extremely turbulent and fragmented markets. Informational economies and the need for critical mass involvement overseas implies that ownership advantages may be generated by overseas representation i.e. advantages accruing to incumbent firms rather than the possession of such advantages being a necessary condition for overseas production. This in turn has implications for the generation of dynamic barriers to entry by established producers enjoying economies derived from incumbency and experience. This is an area where further work is warranted.

NOTES

1. An MNE is defined here following Casson (1982a) as a firm which owns outputs of goods or services originating in more than one country. This creation of value may affect the quantity, quality or availability of goods and services.

2. Other services comprises primarily insurance, banking, construction and consultancy, advertising and other professional services.

2

Service Trade by the Multinational Enterprise[1]

James R. Markusen

2.1 INTRODUCTION

Important differences in the degree of multinational activity across industries have long been observed. In some industries, multinational enterprises (MNEs) account for a major share of total output while in other industries this share is minor. It has also been shown consistently that the degree of multinationality in an industry is closely related to such variables as R&D expenditure as a percentage of sales, marketing expenditures as a percentage of sales, and the ratio of white-collar workers to total work force (e.g., Caves 1982).

These explanatory variables give rise to the concept of knowledge-based, firm-specific assets (FSAs). These are proprietary assets of the firm embodied in such things as the human capital of the employees, patents or otherwise exclusive technical knowledge, copyrights or trademarks, or even more intangible assets such as management 'know-how' or the reputation of the firm. There are two good reasons why these knowledge-based assets are more likely to give rise to foreign direct investment (FDI) than physical-capital assets. First, knowledge-based assets can be transferred easily across space at low cost. An engineer or manager can visit many separate production facilities at relatively low cost. Further, knowledge often has a jointness or 'public-goods' characteristic in that it can be supplied to additional production facilities at very low cost.

Blueprints (a knowledge-based asset) for new products or production processes can be provided to additional plants without reducing the value of the blueprints to the initial plants.

Blueprints are thus a joint input into all plants. Trademarks and other marketing devices also have this property. Assets based on physical capital such as machinery tend to not have this property. That is, physical capital usually cannot yield a flow of services in one location without reducing its productivity in other locations.

The joint-input characteristic of knowledge-based assets has important implications for the efficiency of the firm and in turn for market structure. These implications are summarised in the notion of economies of multi-plant production. These are defined to be a situation where a single two-plant firm has a cost efficiency over two independent single-plant firms. The multi-plant firm (i.e., the MNE) need only make a single investment in R&D, for example, while two independent firms must each make the same investment. The latter industry structure therefore involves the duplication of FSAs. Cost efficiency will then dictate that MNEs (multi-plant firms) will arise as the equilibrium market structure in industries where FSAs are important.

The converse proposition should also be emphasised. Scale economies based on physical capital intensity do not in general lead to FDI. This type of scale economy implies the cost efficiency of centralised production rather than geographically diversified production. Of course, some industries with a high physical-capital intensity may also be industries in which FSAs are important. This often occurs with respect to the marketing and servicing of output. Many Japanese 'multinationals' in manufacturing industries in fact do little manufacturing in North America, preferring to concentrate this phase of their operations in Japan. Their subsidiaries in North America are largely and often exclusively involved in wholesaling, marketing and servicing the firms' products. Thus knowledge-based scale economies (multi-plant economies) may dominate in certain phases of operation while plant scale economies dominate in other phases.

Let us therefore assume for the remainder of this chapter that MNEs are firms which possess, in at least some of their operation, FSAs. What then is the real trade flow across borders that is generating a stream of returns for the MNE? The latter is observable while the former generally is not (in some cases the MNE does of course supply financial capital to the foreign subsidiary). In essence, MNEs are in the business of supplying the services of the firms' FSAs to foreign subsidiaries. These services include management, engineering, marketing, and financial services which are based on human capital. They also include the services of patents and trademarks which are other knowledge-based assets. Subsidiaries import these services in exchange for repatriated profits, royalties, or direct service charges.

At this point, it is important to note the distinction between trade in services by MNEs and MNEs in service industries. Note that the service flows referred to in the previous paragraph make no reference to the industry into which the firm is classified. The final business of the firm could be manufacturing or the provision of services. The above argument applies to both. This is of some importance in so far as much of discussion about liberalising trade in services (arising primarily in the US) actually seems to be about improving foreign market access for MNEs in service industries. These industries include banking, finance, and insurance. It is important to make clear that the foreign sales by MNEs in these industries do not constitute trade in services but foreign production in service industries. Similarly, it is important to understand that MNEs in manufacturing industries are indeed involved in trade in services.

An understanding of the nexus among FSAs, MNEs, and trade in services also involves the key concept of internalisation (Rugman 1981, 1985, 1987; Casson 1987). Internalisation is the notion that, for a firm to engage in FDI, it must perceive that the costs of doing so are less than the costs of an arm's-length transfer of its FSAs through a licensing or franchising agreement. For a firm to choose FDI over licensing, there must exist transaction costs with the latter mode such that the firm chooses to internalise through FDI.

If the ownership advantages that a firm wishes to exploit abroad are knowledge based, it is easy to imagine important transactions costs associated with arm's-length agreements. Perhaps the most obvious is that the same jointness or 'public-good' property that gives rise to the efficiency of foreign production implies that the value of the firm's FSAs can be easily dissipated. If engineers can supply technology to a branch plant at almost zero cost, so can a licensee pass on the technology to third parties at essentially zero cost. Marketing assets such as a reputation for quality can similarly be dissipated by a licensee who shirks on quality for short-run profits. This (potential) ability of licensees to dissipate knowledge-based assets leads to the firm internalising the problem through FDI. The same problem does not occur with physical-capital assets and thus we have a second reason why MNE activity tends to be concentrated in industries in which knowledge-based assets are important. The implication that MNEs are heavily involved in trade in the services of such assets follows directly.

If we accept the notion of FSAs as the cornerstone of the theory of the MNE, several implications for the balance-of-payments (BOP) accounts and our qualitative understanding of trade in services follow directly. This theory implies that a major component of the trade between parent firms and subsidiaries is management, engineering, marketing, and financial services along with the services of other assets such as patents, trademarks, and reputations. If these assets were traded at arm's-length, they would be classified in the BOP statistics as trade in producer services. When producer services are traded intra-firm by the MNE, payments by subsidiaries to parents for these services can be classified in different ways. They can be classified as fees and royalties, and indeed much of this category in the BOP statistics does turn out to be intra-firm charges. But payments for services can simply be lumped in with general returns to FDI as if they were returns to capital invested. Except for possible tax considerations, MNE's are under no incentive to provide detailed accounting classifications for their payments from subsidiaries. We thus do not have an idea of how the category returns to FDI breaks down into returns for capital invested, payments for producer services, monopoly rents etc. The BOP statistics are, in other words, kept on the basis of the mode of transaction (arm's-length versus intra-firm) rather than on the basis of the economic content of the transaction. While this is certainly appropriate for some purposes, it is not helpful for understanding the content of real trade flows. Some attempt at inferring trade in producer services from payments for FDI would be most useful. Among other things, such statistics would show that trade in producer services is of far more quantitative importance than we currently realise.

The outline of the remainder of the chapter is as follows. In the next section, a simple model of the MNE based on FSA is presented and its implications for trade in services are given. This model is a much shorter and technically simplified version of Markusen (1987), and the interested reader is referred to that paper for a more rigorous and comprehensive treatment. (For the less technically-minded this section can be omitted without loss of continuity). Section 2.3 presents a non-technical discussion of the main implications of the model. Following that section, is a review of some of the literature on the MNE to help justify the importance of knowledge-based assets. Section 2.5 presents some evidence on the quantitative significance of trade in business services versus payments for FDI and presents the main policy implications. Section 2.6 contains a brief summary.

2.2 FIRM-SPECIFIC ASSETS AND MULTI-PLANT ECONOMIES

This section presents a greatly simplified version of the model from sections 2–6 of Markusen (1987). Two goods (X and Y) are produced from a single factor, labour (L), which is in inelastic supply at any point in time ($L = L_X + L_Y$) and internationally immobile. Y is produced with constant returns by a competitive industry and units are chosen such that $Y = L_Y$. Y is used as the numeraire so that the wage rate in terms of Y is equal to 1. To begin producing X, a firm must incur the once-and-for-all sunk costs of F (firm-specific cost) and G (plant-specific cost) in terms of Y (or L). Additional plants may be opened for the cost of G only. F is thus intended to represent the knowledge-based capital that is a joint-input or 'public good' within the firm. F could be thought of as an R&D investment necessary to design a product or a production process. Once the design is produced, it can be costlessly incorporated into additional plants. This leads to multi-plant economies of scale in that a two-plant firm only incurs F once, while two one-plant firms must each incur F. The fact that the services of F can be costlessly extended to additional plants does not, of course, imply that these services are of no value to the additional plants.

The economy is represented in Figure 2.1, where *YGFX* is the country's production frontier. *Y* is the maximum feasible production of Y. In order to begin production of X, a firm must invest the fixed costs G (given by the distance *YG* in Figure 2.1) and F (given by the distance GF in Figure 2.1). After investing the fixed costs, X can be produced at a constant marginal cost in terms of Y which gives us the linear segment F*X* in Figure 2.1. This linear segment has slope m if m is the marginal cost of X in terms of Y.

39

Figure 2.1

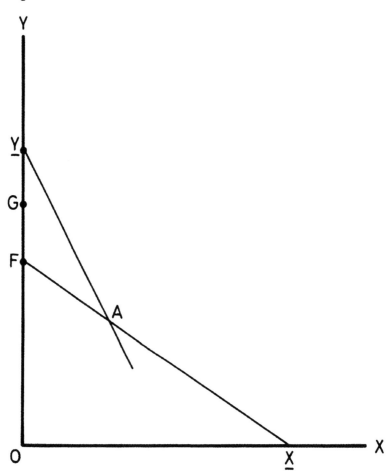

Because of the fixed costs, average cost exceeds marginal cost and hence the price of X in terms of Y must exceed the marginal cost m if the firm is to make non-negative profits. The average cost of producing X in terms of Y is given by the simple formula

(1) $Ac_X = L_X/X = (L - L_Y)/X = (Y - Y)/X$

Consider point A in Figure 2.1. The average cost of producing this amount of X is, from (1), simply the slope of the line passing through Y and A. Average cost is everywhere decreasing in X. The non-negative profits constraint implies that the price ratio at a point like A must be at least as steep as the average-cost line YA.

Figure 2.2

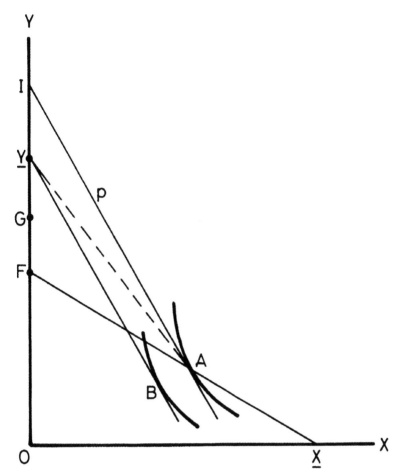

Figure 2.2 shows an equilibrium in which the firm producing X is making positive profits. Equilibrium production is at A and the equilibrium price ratio is p. A community indifference curve is shown tangent to p at A. The point I in Figure 2.2 gives total income or GNP in terms of good Y. But total labour income in terms of Y is simply $L_X + L_Y = Y$ in Figure 2.2. Total income (IO) thus divides into profits (IY) plus labour income (YO). The budget line for labour is the line through Y with slope p. The indifference curve tangent at B in Figure 2.2 thus represents the consumption bundle and welfare level of labour, with the difference between B and A being consumption out of profits.

41

The division of total output between labour income and profits is just a distributional issue in the closed economy, but becomes an issue of GDP (the value of domestic output) versus GNP (the income of domestic citizens) if a foreign-owned MNE is producing X and repatriating profits.

Figure 2.3

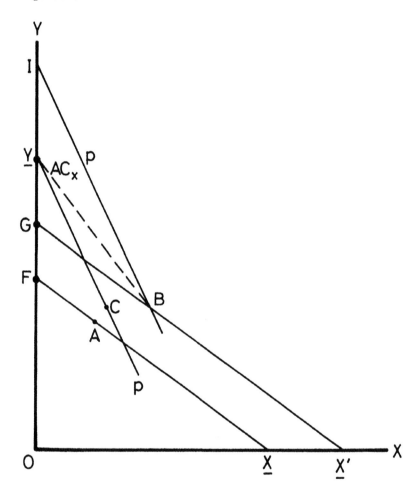

Figure 2.3 shows one of many possible outcomes when the country is host to a foreign MNE. Because this firm has already invested F, production in the host country does not require this initial investment. Thus the production frontier is now YGX which is like a technical improvement over the autarky frontier YFX. The value of the imported services, measured in terms of opportunity cost, is the distance GF. In Figure 2.3, it is assumed

that the MNE maximises profits by producing at point B at price ratio p. I is total GDP, but the amount IY is repatriated as profits by the MNE, leaving labour income YO as the GNP of the domestic citizens. This allows the latter to reach consumption bundle C in Figure 2.3. This consumption bundle is shown to be above the autarky bundle A and thus playing host to the MNE generates a welfare gain.

Three important points should be noted. First, the outcome shown in Figure 2.3 is somewhat arbitrary. The figure could have been drawn so that the amount of repatriated profits IY was either larger or smaller in relation to the value of service imports GF. Various extreme outcomes are presented in Markusen (1987), including the case where zero profits are repatriated and a case where profit repatriation is so in excess of the value GF that the country actually loses from trade. In other words, the welfare effects of MNEs on host country are a trade-off between the technical benefits of 'free-riding' on the MNE's firm-specific assets versus the loss of rents due to profit repatriation.

Second, note that there is an alternative scenario under which the economy reaches point C in Figure 2.3. Suppose that there were no multinationals but that the country could trade Y for X in world markets at price ratio p. In that case, the country would gain relative to the autarky equilibrium at A by specialising in Y (producing at Y) and trading at price ratio p to reach the optimal consumption point C. In this sense, imports of goods and imports of producer services via the MNE are substitutes. In one case we import X, and in the other we import the services of the firm-specific asset F and produce X domestically. In the former case, we pay for the imports by exporting Y, while in the latter we pay in some combination of X and Y that is repatriated by the MNE as profits. Although the production bundles are very different, the consumption bundles could in principle (but in practice only by chance) be identical.

Third, note that the foreign country, which we have not shown explicitly, must be better off given the equilibrium shown in Figure 2.3. It is costless for the foreign country to supply F, yet it is shown as earning the positive return IY in Figure 2.3. This latter amount is thus a pure return earned on the MNEs FSA. Indeed, it could be the case that we initially had two identical countries. One, by chance, becomes the home country of the MNE. Both countries can make gains from the asymmetric industry structure even though the countries are identical. This bilateral gain is captured by sharing the returns to capitalising on the joint-input character of the FSA and eliminating duplication of this asset in the two countries.

2.3 IMPLICATIONS OF THE MODEL

The joint-input described in the introduction and developed formally in the preceding section has a number of implications that can be summarised in relatively non-technical terms. First, when the MNE enters the host country by capitalising on its FSA, it does indeed supply the host country with a very real service even though nothing physical may cross the border. Further, a very real value can be put on that service flow. This is the opportunity cost that would have to be incurred for the host country to create those assets itself. The value to the host country of the management and engineering services supplied to a subsidiary is the opportunity cost that would have to be incurred to accumulate the human capital necessary to supply those services domestically. If these services were purchased from foreign companies rather than transferred internally through the MNE, the transaction would be classified as trade in producer services. Indeed, by itself Figure 2.3 gives no clue as to whether it is describing a MNE or an arm's-length sale of the FSA for the amount IY. In terms of economic content, the two are equivalent.

But while the value of the service imports can in principle be identified in terms of opportunity cost, the second point is that this value may differ dramatically for the price actually paid. This arises for two reasons. One is that MNEs are typically found in oligopolistic industries in which firms have some measure of market power. Repatriated earnings by MNEs may therefore contain monopoly profits as well as payments for the services supplied. The other element is the joint-input notion, which was taken to the extreme in the previous section by assuming that the FSA could be supplied to a foreign plant at exactly zero marginal cost. If there was competition for entry that drove prices down to marginal cost, it would therefore follow that the host country receives the services of the FSA for free, a price obviously far below the opportunity cost of developing it at home. Combining the market-power and joint-input characteristics thus implies that the profits repatriated by a MNE can substantially overestimate (market power dominates) or underestimate (competitive pressures dominate) the value of the producer services supplied to the host country. Payments for FDI are not a reliable measure of services rendered.

A third point is that there are potential welfare gains to both home and host countries through FDI. Even if countries are absolutely identical, the joint-input or 'public-goods' characteristic of knowledge-based assets allows bilateral gains from trade. Each country 'free rides' on the R&D and other knowledge capital created by the other country's MNEs (subject to the caveat about market power just mentioned). This free-rider argument stands in contrast to the argument often heard that a host nation may lose (relative to some unspecified alternative) when foreign MNEs producing locally do their R&D at home.

Fourth, the model suggests how trade in services through the MNE and trade in commodities are substitutes. We showed in the previous section how the host country could either import X directly or import the services of the FSA through the MNE and produce X at home. In the two cases, the production pattern and industry structure of the host country are quite different. Yet at the same time, the actual consumption levels and income of domestic citizens might be very similar. In one case the country pays for X through exports in arm's-length markets while in the other, X is paid for in repatriated profits. The fact that the host-country industry is partly controlled by foreigners in the latter case makes the country no less dependent than in the case of gaining access to X through imports.

The substitutability of trade in goods and trade in producer services is not of course always the case. FDIs that are simply distributing/marketing/servicing facilities are complementary to imports of manufactured goods. If computer companies were not allowed to establish training and servicing facilities in a country, for example, they would probably be much less likely to attempt to export to that country than if there were no such restrictions.

A final point, related to the bilateral gains discussion, is that from a strategic/competitive point of view, the host nation might wish to help domestic firms become MNEs, at least in those industries in which knowledge-based assets are important. In these industries, foreign operations are low marginal-cost investments which substantially help the firm spread the high fixed costs of R&D investments etc. over larger total sales. The knowledge that a firm can successfully penetrate foreign markets through branch-plant production may lead the firm to undertake investments at home that it could not otherwise afford.

2.4 EMPIRICAL EVIDENCE

The purpose of this section is to present an informal review of extensive empirical work on the MNE in so far as it is relevant to the question of intra-firm service trade by the MNE. Rather than attempt to be comprehensive, only a few recent works will be mentioned, since each of these builds upon and incorporates large bodies of earlier work. Readers desiring more extensive evidence are referred to these authors and to the extensive bibliographies contained in their publications.

4.1 Industry studies

An excellent survey and synthesis of a huge volume of literature is presented in Caves (1982). Particularly relevant for the purposes of this chapter is the discussion of extensive evidence on the determinants of multinationality of an industry. The percentage of production accounted for by MNEs in an industry is a statistic that varies widely across industries. Caves notes that studies have consistently shown that such things as R&D expenditures as a percentage of sales, advertising expenditures as a percentage of sales, and non-production (white-collar) workers as a percentage of total work force are excellent predictors of the degree of multinationality of an industry. That is, industries that have higher values of those variables have a higher degree of multinationality.

While these variables are instrumental variables that do not directly test the notion of FSAs or intangible assets as Caves often calls them, they are generally regarded as good proxies. High levels of R&D suggest technological advantages, whether embodied in human capital, patents, or in more intangible forms. Technological advantages are in the terminology of this chapter knowledge-based intangible assets. Accordingly, the high correlation between R&D and multinationality supports the view that many MNEs are supplying the services of these knowledge-based assets to their subsidiaries.

Similar comments can be made with respect to advertising variables and white-collar work-force variables. High levels of the former suggest assets in the form of product differentiation, brand identification, and reputation. The latter variables are of course partly correlated with R&D and advertising, but probably also capture managerial intensity and expertise. Again we have the strong suggestion that multinationality and knowledge-based assets are highly correlated. Finally, in so far as R&D, marketing, and management are concentrated in home countries, we have good reason to suppose that MNEs are indeed heavy exporters of the services of knowledge-based assets.

2.4.2 Firm studies

In a recent study Beaudreau (1986) used a very large firm-level data set (US-based MNEs) to examine the dependence of multi-nationality at the firm-level on a number of explanatory variables. These included again such things as R&D and advertising intensity. As in the case of industry studies, these variables proved to be excellent predictors of multinationality.

The advantage of the firm-level data set was that Beaudreau was able to test multinationality against such variables as the life span of the firm and its accumulated production experience. Both variables proved to be excellent predictors of multi-nationality. Firms with a long history in terms of time and/or accumulated production experience had significantly higher foreign taxes paid as a percentage of all taxes paid. This is a far from perfect variable, but it would seem to proxy foreign operations (as opposed to export sales) in an acceptable way.

The historical variables are also proxy variables for the human and other intangible capital held by the firm. The idea is of course that knowledge capital is accumulated through time and production experience. To the extent that this is true, Beaudreau's results add support for the notion the MNEs are firms possessing knowledge-based firm-specific assets. Other evidence points in the same direction. Davidson and McFetridge (1984) examine international transfers of technology that take place internally (i.e. by FDI) versus those that take place at arm's-length through licensing. Evidence shows that newer and technically more sophisticated products are more likely to be transferred internally. Studies by Teece (1977), Mansfield and

Romeo (1980) and Wilson (1977) arrive at much the same conclusions although the data sets and dependent/explanatory variables are somewhat different.

It is reasonable to suppose that newer and/or more complex products are correlated with the existence of knowledge-based assets. They may embody non-standard production 'know-how' that cannot be easily transferred at arm's-length. Moreover, the firm may wish to keep this know-how secret, and transferring the knowledge internally helps safeguard against loss of this proprietary knowledge (dissipation of the FSA through agent opportunism) relative to transferring the knowledge at arm's-length through a licensing agreement.

This last point relates to the extensive literature on internalisation by the MNE (Rugman 1981, 1985, 1987; Casson 1979, 1987). This literature sees the MNE arising because of transactions costs associated with the use of arm's-length markets. It is reasonable to conjecture that these transactions costs may be particularly large when the firm is transferring knowledge-based assets. These assets, precisely due to their public-good property discussed earlier, can be easily dissipated by agent opportunism. Other evidence supports this point. Studies by Caves and Murphy (1976) and Nicholas (1983) show that firms have problems with licensees or franchisees with respect to quality control. In so far as a reputation for quality is a FSA of the firm, this is another small piece of evidence that suggests that MNEs and the existence of FSAs are closely associated.

2.4.3 FSA versus trade barriers

A popular explanation of MNEs has long been that trade barriers induce firms to 'jump the tariff wall' and build branch plants in foreign countries with protected markets. There is however one theoretical problem with this argument which suggests that tariff/transport costs by themselves are not sufficient to generate MNE activity. This is that trade barriers can indeed induce domestic production of a good, but there is no reason why that production should be by foreign firms instead of domestic firms. Indeed, if there are arbitrarily small costs to doing business abroad, the production will be by multi-plant economies of scale and trade barriers. Unfortunately, the multi-plant economies part of this statement often seems to get lost. In John Dunning's (1977, 1981) terminology, a MNE needs both an ownership advantage (FSAs or multi-plant economies) and a location advantage (trade barriers) if it is to produce abroad. It is thus important to note that the tariff-wall explanation is not a competitor to the FSA hypothesis, but rather that they are complementary.

Quite apart from this theoretical point, tariffs and transport costs have never performed well as an explanation of multi-nationality. Explanatory power in regression analysis is low and often has the wrong sign. A good summary of this literature is found in Beaudreau (1986). Variables which proxy FSAs have much greater explanatory power and generally have the right sign. While not particularly relevant to this chapter, there are several possible explanations of the empirical failure of the tariff argument. One is the endogeneity of tariffs. Once branch plants are in place in a country, tariffs may be lowered in subsequent negotiations. Second, many MNEs are in service industries (e.g. hotels) in which the final output is non-traded. Third, a good part of the MNE activity observed in the manufacturing sector is actually just wholesaling/marketing/servicing activities that have little to do with trade barriers.

2.4.4 High tech versus low tech

A number of recent studies have shown that foreign control of manufacturing is much higher in high-tech industries than in other manufacturing industries (Dunning 1985). For example in the case of Canada, Conklin (1987) notes that 'foreign-controlled establishments accounted for 37 per cent of employment in manufacturing in 1981. The percentages are much higher in the high-tech industries, ranging from 52 to 82 per cent' (Conklin 1987). Nioisi (1985) finds that most MNEs are found in industries where R&D and technological barriers play the largest role. This evidence is once again consistent with the notion that multinationality is related to the existence of knowledge-based assets. R&D and technological sophistication are probably excellent proxy variables for the stock of knowledge capital possessed by a firm.

Referring to results of Mansfield, Romeo, and Wagner (1979), Conklin notes that returns to R&D are positively related to the extent of foreign operations. This is consistent with the notion that the output of R&D is knowledge that can be incorporated into additional plants at very low cost. Adding foreign operations allows the cost of R&D to be spread over larger output while at the same time the larger output does not affect that cost. These and other studies (e.g. Caves 1982) also confirm that MNEs do most of their R&D in the home country, again reinforcing the notion that MNEs are the exporters of the services of knowledge-based capital.

2.4.5 Returns to FDI

While accepting that MNEs are major traders of the services of FSAs it does not follow that payments by subsidiaries to parents are closely linked to the 'value' of the services supplied. On the one hand, since MNEs tend to be in oligopolistic industries, repatriated earnings may include returns to market power and thus may overestimate the value of services provided to the subsidiaries. On the other hand, competition among MNEs may drive the returns to FSAs down to the marginal cost of providing them, which is zero in the extreme case presented in sections 2.2 and 2.3 above. Higher transactions costs of doing business abroad might also erode a large part of the returns to FSA.

Some light is shed on this issue by Grubel (1974, 1977). Grubel provides data on rates of return to US investments abroad and compares them to domestic rates of return. He finds little evidence that the two differ in any systematic fashion. In other words, Grubel is inclined to conclude that returns to FDI can be largely explained in terms of returns to capital invested. Returns to FSAs are either very small or are fully accounted for by payments listed as such (e.g. fees and royalties).

We would argue very strongly that one should not conclude from this that MNEs are not trading the services of FSAs. Rather, we would offer three alternative explanations. First, as we noted earlier, it is perfectly consistent with the model developed in sections 2.2 and 2.3 for the return to FSAs to be very small. As we have just noted, this can occur when competition drives the return to these assets down to the marginal cost of providing them, which is small or in some cases zero. Second and closely related, the higher transactions cost of doing business abroad may largely offset the returns to FSAs as we also noted (this explanation was suggested by Alan Rugman).

Third, firms probably apportion fixed costs, including those generated by the creation of knowledge-based assets (e.g. R&D), over all production facilities, home and abroad. Thus domestic and foreign operations tend to show the same rate of return to knowledge-based assets. It is unlikely that a firm would charge all R&D and related firm-specific costs against domestic operations only (or against one domestic plant only). We are inclined toward this third explanation of Grubel's results, while also accepting the view (suggested by Grubel) that competition drives the rate of return to FSAs to their marginal costs in the long run and Rugman's suggestion about the higher transactions costs of doing business abroad.

Let us conclude with an observation that is of some significance from a welfare point of view. If competition does on average drive the returns to FSAs to marginal cost, then FDI is in general of substantial benefit to the host countries. These countries are receiving the services of the FSAs at substantially less than the average cost that would necessarily be incurred by producing these assets domestically. Host countries are in other words 'free-riding' on the services of the knowledge-based assets created in the home countries. We would tend to support a weaker version of this argument as suggested by Grubel's data. That is, host countries tend to pay the average cost of FSAs, but this cost is averaged over all sales and countries in which the MNE operates. This 'world' average cost will be less, and for small host countries substantially less, than the average cost of developing the FSAs for an individual host country. Host countries benefit from this difference in cost.

2.5 IMPLICATIONS FOR THE BOP ACCOUNTS AND FOR PUBLIC POLICY

2.5.1 The quantitative importance of trade in producer services

A principal point of this paper is that MNEs management, engineering, marketing, financial and accounting services engage in intra-firm trade in what would be classified as producer (or business) services if the trade was conducted at arm's-length. MNEs supply their subsidiaries with management, engineering, marketing, financial and accounting services as well as the services of assets such as trademarks and reputations. Some, but probably far from all, of these service flows are invoiced and recorded in the BOP statistics as such. The balance-of-payments accounts treat produced services and returns on FDI separately, so that returns to knowledge-based assets and investments listed by firms as simply repatriated earnings are classified quite separately from trade in producer services. The BOP accounts are thus kept on the basis of the mode of international transaction rather than on the basis of the economic content of the transaction. Essentially the same point is made by Rugman (1987).

It is of course true that returns on FDI include payments for items other than intra-firm service trade. A significant part is certainly returns on financial capital invested, although often the MNE provides for most of its requirements from local (host-country) capital markets. From this point of view, to impute returns to FDI as returns to FSAs would be to overestimate trade in the latter. On the other hand, a substantial portion of earnings by MNEs in Canada are retained and re-invested in Canada. Canadian accounting conventions (unlike those in the US) are such that these retained earnings do not show up in the BOP statistics. Recorded returns to FDI thus significantly underestimate the true combined returns to both FSAs and financial capital invested.

For the sake of argument, let us make the extreme assumption that retained earnings are closely related to financial capital invested for foreign MNEs operating in Canada and Canadian MNEs operating abroad. We thus assume that returns to FDI are entirely composed of payments for producer services. Table 2.1, derived from Rugman (1987) illustrates the implications. In 1984, Canada exported a little less than 4.5 billion dollars of producer services and imported slightly over 6.6 billion. The corresponding figures for returns on FDI are 1.1 billion of exports and 2.9 billion of imports. If we add these two categories together, we get combined exports of 5.5 billion and imports of 9.6 billion.

Row 4 of Table 2.1 shows the total service sector (excluding interest payments) exports of 15.2 billion and imports of 21.5 billion. Row 6 then shows that the combination of producer services and returns to FDI are 36.2 per cent and 44.6 per cent of service imports respectively. When this combination is taken as a percentage of 'other' service trade (i.e. total service trade minus (PS + FDI)), it amounts to 56.6 per cent of exports or 80.5 per cent on the import side. Row 8 of Table 2.1 gives total

Table 2.1: Canada's trade in services – 1984
(millions of Canadian dollars)

	Exports	Imports
1. Producer services (PS)	4,486	6,667
2. Returns on FDI	1,011	2,900
3. Combined PS + FDI	5,497	9,583
4. Total service trade (excluding interest)	15,200	21,489
5. 'Other' service trade (4 minus 3)	9,703	11,906
6. PS + FDI as a % of total service trade	36.2	44.6
7. PS + FDI as a % of 'other' service trade	56.6	80.5
8. Total trade (merchandise, services, interest)	131,900	130,700
9. PS + FDI as a % of total trade	4.2	7.3

Source: Derived from Rugman (1987) Table 3

exports (merchandise plus services plus interest) and imports in 1984, and row 9 then gives the combined total of producer services and returns to FDI as 4.2 per cent of total exports or 7.3 per cent of total imports.

Accepting the assumption that payments for producer services and returns to FDI have much the same economic content, the result of Table 2.1 suggests that this category of trade may be much more important than is generally realised. A large percentage of the service account and a non-trivial percentage of the total trade account (PS + FDI) are involved. An export percentage of 4.2 per cent seems small, but it rivals such categories as wheat or minerals. The import percentage of 7.3 per cent is large relative to the imports in some commodity categories normally thought of as much more important. These data suggest the need for a reassessment of the trade account.

2.5.2 Growth in exports of producer services, exports of FDI

A recent publication, Statistics Canada (1986) provides a great deal of documentation about trade in services. Payments for foreign direct investment are, unfortunately, excluded from the definition of trade in services, something to which the argument of this chapter is strongly opposed. This publication documents the fact that trade in producer services has been growing, certainly in (real) absolute amounts, but also as a percentage of the service account. The statistics reveal that exports of producer services rose from 20.0 per cent of service exports in 1969 to 31.6 per cent in 1984. The growth in the import percentage was less dramatic, growing from 30.0 per cent in 1969 to 35.9 per cent in 1984 (Statistics Canada 1986, Table 1). Exports of producer services were 48.3 per cent of imports of producer services in 1969, growing to 67.3 per cent in 1984.

Other publications have documented the tremendous growth in outward FDI from Canada over the last two decades, and show that the stock of Canadian FDI abroad has grown from about 18 per cent of foreign FDI in Canada in 1960 to about 35 per cent in the early 1980s (Markusen and Melvin 1985).

While it is always dangerous to extrapolate statistical trends, these figures at least show an increased competitiveness on the part of Canada in the related areas of producer services and FDI over the last two decades. Deficits remain in both areas, but the movements certainly do not suggest a declining Canadian performance in these categories. One policy implication is that it may be time for Canada to stop thinking of itself entirely as a host nation for these activities and formulating its policies accordingly. Canada should not approach negotiations on trade in services or on liberalisation of foreign investment codes from the strictly defensive point of view of an importer.

2.5.3 The factor intensity of producer services, FDI

The traditional view of services seems to be that they are intensive in the use of unskilled labour and thus not something that the government should be particularly concerned to develop. While there is little systematic evidence on the factor intensity of the service sector, those services which enter into traded producer services and those that are traded intra-firm by the MNE can hardly be termed intensive in the use of unskilled labour.

Statistics Canada (1986) data for 1984 show that the top categories of exports of producer services were: (1) consulting and other professional services; (2) transportation related services; (3) commissions; (4) tooling and other automotive charges; and (5) insurance. On the import side, the top five categories were: (1) royalties, patents and trademarks; (2) management and administrative services; (3) transportation-related services; (4) financial services; and (5) research and development. None of these would seem to fit the category of being intensive in the use of unskilled labour. There is of course no good data on intra-firm service trade by the MNE, but if such data were available, it would show a related pattern. Particularly important categories would include management services, consulting services, R&D, and financial and advertising services.

Again, there appears to be no systematic information on the factor intensities of these service categories, but we conjecture that an analysis would show that they are all quite intensive in the use of human capital. If one objective of government policy is to encourage the development of human-capital intensive industries, then the producer service and FDI sectors should not be overlooked. A movement of our thinking away from the manufacturing sector is long overdue.

2.5.4 Trade in services by the MNE versus MNEs in service industries

A few words on this topic are appropriate in this policy section. This chapter is about intra-firm trade in services by the MNE. That is, it is concerned with the economic nature of the things that cross international borders between parent and foreign subsidiary. Yet it could be argued that this is not necessarily the policy issue. There is an impression that the US government in particular is concerned about foreign rights of establishment for its MNEs in service industries. The US wants increased access for its MNEs in the insurance, finance, banking, and related industries.

Most of the content and arguments in this chapter have little to do with the industrial classification of the firm in question. Nevertheless, this distinction is vital in clarifying the policy debate.

2.6 SUMMARY

This chapter is concerned with intra-firm trade in services by the MNE. Perhaps its most basic point is that a major activity of MNEs is the export from parent to subsidiary of what we would call producer (or business) services if the same transactions were to take place in arm's-length markets. These services include management, engineering, marketing and financial services along with the services of such assets as patents, trademarks and reputations. Payments by subsidiaries to parents are in large part payments for producer services.

This is supported by extensive empirical evidence which has been summarised above. Studies consistently support the view that MNE activity is highly correlated with the existence of knowledge-based firm-specific assets. This makes a great deal of sense from the theoretical point of view as well, since the services of knowledge-based assets (unlike physical capital) can be supplied to distant subsidiaries at a very low marginal cost. MNEs are thus firms intensive in knowledge-based assets and are thus engaged in trade in the services of these assets.

The current balance-of-payments accounting methods do however keep separate accounts of producer services and payments for FDI. Some intra-firm trade in producer services is so classified in the BOP statistics if it is invoiced as such (e.g. fees and royalties). But our conjecture is that much of the returns to knowledge-based assets are simply classified as returns to FDI and thus classified separately from trade in producer services. The BOP accounts are thus structured more on the basis of the mode of transaction rather than on the basis of the economic content of the transaction.

Returns to FDI certainly includes payments for things other than the services of knowledge-based assets, especially returns to financial capital invested. Thus to assume that all payments for FDI are payments for producer services would be to over-estimate trade in the latter. Balancing this (at least for Canada) is the fact that substantial retained earnings do not show up as returns either to knowledge-based or to financial capital. Although immense practical difficulties thus exist in attempting to calculate returns to FDI and in retained earnings, it would in principle be very desirable to try to do so and then combine this estimate with recorded trade in producer services.

In this chapter, we gave an example of this under the extreme assumption that all payments for FDI are payments for producer services (alternatively, retained earnings approximately equal payments for financial capital invested). The consequence of this is that trade in this expanded category is by far the dominant category in the service trade account. Further, the combined total is not an insignificant component of the overall current account. Other evidence was presented to show that exports in this expanded category were growing significantly in real terms and growing significantly relative to imports under the same definition. It was also conjectured that the types of services that enter into trade in this category do not fit the traditional view of services as intensive in the use of unskilled labour, but are probably very intensive in the use of skilled labour. As such, they should be of interest to public policy.

A caveat was offered that we should be careful to distinguish between trade in services by MNEs and MNEs in service industries. The former is the subject of this paper, but the latter seems to be the focus of much of the policy debate.

NOTES

1. The work reported in this chapter was funded under a grant from the Fraser Institute of Vancouver, Canada as part of a much larger study on service industries and trade in services. With minor differences, this paper is also being published by the Fraser Institute. Helpful comments by and discussions with Herbert Grubel and Alan Rugman are gratefully acknowledged.

Part Two

3

Multinational Banking

Herbert G. Grubel

3.1 INTRODUCTION

Banks have always engaged in international business. They have
dealt in foreign exchange, extended credit in connection with
foreign trade, traded and held foreign assets and provided
travellers with letters of credit. Historically, the banks have
carried out all this and some other types of business from their
domestic locations. There was no need for a physical presence
abroad. Business that could not be carried out by mail or telecommunications was handled by correspondent banks abroad.

Some banks began to establish a physical presence abroad in
the late nineteenth and early twentieth century. This move
abroad mostly was part of colonialism. Under the umbrella of
the home country's colonial government, banks from Britain
opened branches in the Indian subcontinent, Africa, Hong Kong
and Singapore; European and North American banks moved
into the Caribbean and Latin America. These banks provided
modern banking services to economies which previously had no
or only a relatively rudimentary financial industry.

Multinational, also sometimes called transnational, banking
is of relatively recent origin. Its development coincided and
accelerated with the technological improvements and cost-
reductions in international travel and communications in the
post-war period. This type of banking involves the physical
presence of a bank abroad. The most prevalent and versatile
legal form of this presence is a branch, which uses the home-
country bank's name and organisation. It is usually an
independent corporate entity with limited liabilities, whose
shares are owned by the parent. Other legal forms used in foreign

physical presence are agencies and representative offices, which have limited legal operational authority but also limited liabilities. Subsidiaries are used if ownership is shared with other firms or individuals, mostly residents of the country hosting the foreign bank. These subsidiaries are mostly corporations with limited liability. In addition, of course, banks have maintained networks of correspondent banks for doing business in locations where they have no physical presence.

The theory of multinational banking explains why these banks find it profitable to have a physical presence abroad. The theory takes as given the most fundamental and important reason for any foreign investment: it raises the risk-adjusted rate of return to capital invested in the firm. The theory then develops explanations of the sources of comparative advantage, which allows a bank abroad to compete effectively with domestic banks. These domestic banks would be expected to be more familiar with local customs, laws, governments and business firms and to have other cost advantages. For example, their managers are locals who do not have to be paid a premium salary to persuade them to work in a foreign and sometimes relatively unpleasant environment. They do not have to coordinate business across borders and spend extra money on legal, translation and communication services.

The theory of multinational banking addresses the same question as the theory of multinational enterprise generally. It is therefore no surprise to find that there is much overlap between the two theories. Both rest on the proposition that modern business generates certain assets for which there is no market except inside the firm. To maximise the value of these assets, therefore, the firm must operate abroad once it has expanded to fullest extent domestically. Through these foreign operations it increases the return to its domestic capital above what it would have been without this move abroad. Assets giving rise to this motive are marketing and managerial know-how and information about home-country multinational manufacturing firms and tourists. Other important motives for multinational banking are the avoidance or evasion of national taxation by customers and the escape from regulation and taxation by the banks themselves. There are also certain technical scale economies and benefits from the international diversification of business and portfolios.

In the following we discuss these motives for international

banking in greater detail and then use the ideas to speculate about the welfare effects it has had. But before turning to these topics, we present some empirical data about the magnitude of multinational banking.

3.2 SOME FACTS ABOUT MULTINATIONAL BANKING

Table 3.1 contains some information about the number of branches and representative offices which banks from different countries maintained in other countries and regions of the world in 1983. These data are presented here for the first time. They were obtained from the country pages of the *Bankers almanac and yearbook* (1983–4). The vertical list of countries is virtually complete in showing the countries of the world that have a foreign presence. The horizontal groupings were chosen in order to keep the size of the matrix manageable without loss of insights about the extent to which the world's banks have interpenetrated each others' territories.

The data show that all of the industrial countries have large numbers of branches and representative offices in other industrial countries, as well as in developing countries and the two major communist countries, the USSR and China. However, it is also noteworthy that the developing countries have banking presences in most of the industrial countries. In addition, they have networks within regions of developing countries, as in Latin America.

The United Kingdom is the home of the largest number of foreign banks, most of which are located in Africa. The United States is home to the second largest number of banks, followed by France. The latter country has a remarkably small number of foreign banks in its territory, given that it has such a large presence abroad. The Caribbean hosts the largest number of foreign banks, except for Africa, whereas the United States and the United Kingdom host a very large number of foreign banks. Remarkably large for the size of the territory and populations are the number of banks in Belgium/Luxembourg, Hong Kong and Singapore.

The growth of multinational banking may be judged by the fact that in 1968 the number of the same type of foreign banks was reported to have been 2,744 (Lees 1974). Since, according to Table 3.1, the 1983 figure was 5,814, there has been a growth

Table 3.1: The world matrix of international banks in 1983

Country of parent bank	Canada	USA	Carib-bean	Latin America	UK	France	Belg./ Luxem.	Nether-lands	Germany	Switzer-land	Italy
					Country or Region of Foreign Presence						
Africa		1			9	4			1	1	
Argentina		9	1	27	1	1			2		2
Australia		17	2		8				1		
Austria		1		1	2						2
Bahrain		1			1						
Bangladesh					7						
Belgium/ Luxembourg		9	1	40	4				1	2	4
Brazil	3	19	10	31	7	4	1	3	4	1	2
Canada		39	44	17	9	5	2	1	3	1	2
Chile		3		4	1						
China		3		1	3		1		1		
Columbia		2		1							
Denmark		4	14	2	1						
Egypt			1		1						
France	9	31		102	26		16	5	32	10	18
Germany	4	24	6	46	12	5	4				6
Greece	1	3			3			1	2		
Hong Kong		11	1	2	10	1		1	2	1	1
India	2	7	1	1	41		1		2		
Indonesia		1			1						
Israel	5	12	2	9	6		3	1	1	1	1
Italy	2	32	1	18	19	8	2		22	8	
Japan	2	65	2	71	24	6	1		26	2	2
Korea	2	10		5	7	2	1		6	1	
Lebanon					1					1	
Malaysia		2			1				1		
Mexico		4	5	1	4						
Netherlands		19		30	11		5		6	2	1
Pakistan		6	1		85		1	1	1		
Panama		1		5							1
Paraguay		1		5							1
Peru		1	1	1					1		
Phillipines	2	3			2			1	1		
Singapore					4						
Spain	1	24	7	109	20		4	4	17	10	5
Sri Lanka											
Switzerland	2	25	9	31	8		4	1	2		
Taiwan		2		2							
Turkey		4			4			4	25	4	
UAE		1			4						
UK	1	147	2					7			
Uruguay	1	6		15					1	1	2
USA	6		130	194	65		10	9	24	12	28
Venezuela		3		9	1			1	1		
Total	43	553	241	780	413	20	68	44	186	58	78

Notes: The regional groupings consist of the following: Latin America: Venezuela, Uruguay, Surinam, Peru, Paraguay, Panama, Mexico, Columbia, Chile, Brazil, Argentina; ASEAN: Phillipines, Malaysia, Indonesia; Other Western Europe: Turkey, Spain, Greece, Denmark, Austria; Caribbean:

64

Oth. West Eu.	Africa	Middle East	India Su.	USSR	China	Asia Pac.	Japan	Hong Kong	ASEAN	Singapore	Austra-lia	Total
		1						1				18
1							1					45
		1			2	1	5	2	3	5		47
		2					2	1		1		12
										1		3
		5	2									14
5		5		2			4	25		5	4	111
6	3	3					2			2	1	102
2	5	7	2			4	6	7	5	5	5	171
												8
					3			56		5		73
												3
2							3	2	1	1	1	31
		8										10
24	11	37	13	7	8	6	18	43	16	10	11	453
15	5	11	4	3	3	1	17	8	7	6	6	193
		2									2	14
		2	24		6	5	4		39	13	1	124
	11	11	6			2	3	14	3	7		112
							1		1	2		6
	2							1				44
13	1	13		4	2		5	5	1	4	3	163
9	4	19	5		13	17		30	30	23	23	374
2	1	2					9	8	2	7	2	67
		3										5
		1					1	3		30		39
3							2					19
7	2	8	7	1		3	7	13	7	1		130
	4	44	2		1		1	4	1	1		153
		2		1						1		11
		2		1						1		11
1												5
		2			1	1	2	3	1	2	1	22
					3	1	5	13	79		2	107
3		7		3			6	2	1	3	1	227
										1		1
3	4	10		1			8	10		7	5	130
						1	2			1		8
		2										43
	1	10	14				1	1		1		33
42	1,432	73									6	1,710
	1	1		1						1		30
42	17	30		2	4	45	45	12	44	29	24	772
												15
180	1,504	324	79	26	43	90	160	264	241	176	98	5,669

Cayman Islands, Bahamas; Asian Pacific: Taiwan, Korea, Guam; Middle East and Egypt: Bahrain, United Arab Emirates, Saudi Arabia, Lebanon, Israel, Egypt; Africa: Kenya and Republic of South Africa.

Source: Compiled from *Bankers almanac and yearbook*, 1983–4.

of 3,070, or 112 per cent in 15 years.

The importance of multinational banking can also be measured by the value of their assets and liabilities, both absolutely and in relation to those of the host countries and of the world as a whole. Unfortunately, data for the calculation of this measure are not available except for the United States. Here, the share of foreign banks' assets in the US total has risen from 3.6 per cent in 1972 to 9.5 per cent in 1978 (Goldberg and Saunders 1981). Since then, the share has continued to rise, but it is not certain by how much.

Finally, it is interesting that for some of the smaller countries that have become multinational banking centres, the industry has developed into a major contributor to GDP. In industrial countries, most of the banking services are attributed by national-income accountants as intermediate inputs into the production of consumer and investment goods because they are purchased by domestic firms. Therefore, the amount of GDP originating with consumer spending on banking services is only about 1 per cent. In small countries with a large multinational banking sector, on the other hand, most of the services of banks are exported and therefore enter GDP as such. They have been estimated to be as high as 15 per cent of GDP for Luxembourg and undoubtedly are of similar importance for Hong Kong, Singapore and some other such multinational banking centres.

3.3 RETAIL AND SERVICE BANKING

Some international banks have branches abroad that compete with the local banks for the traditional retail banking business. Thus, we find the large British banks in South Africa and Kenya; Canadian banks are in the Caribbean; banks from Britain and Japan are in California; US and French banks are in some Latin American and Caribbean countries. These banks often introduced modern banking to these countries at an early stage of economic development. Since the end of the Second World War and the growth of economic nationalism, these banks have been on the retreat. In some cases they were forced to close down by legislative actions. In others, more subtle tax measures were used to encourage the development of a competitive, domestically owned and operated banking industry, which reduced or ultimately drove out these foreign banks.

All this history has a simple analytical explanation. At an early stage of economic development local entrepreneurs did not have the technical know-how or human capital to establish and operate modern banks. The banks in the developed countries brought this know-how and human capital from their home operations, using well-established and proven managerial, marketing, accounting and other procedures. However, these sources of comparative advantage eventually became accessible to domestic entrepreneurs in the developing countries, either through education abroad, the imitation of foreign banks or purchase from consultants. At such a point, the innate advantages accruing to local entrepreneurs became dominant and it was natural that they should eventually come to dominate the industry. In the case of some British banks, their continued operations in countries like South Africa and Kenya are British only in name. They have almost complete local autonomy and are run predominantly by local people with very limited perspectives on the global maximisation of the parents' profits.

The growth of foreign retail banking in California in recent years has a slightly different explanation. Its origin stems from the ability of banks to offer differentiated packages of services appealing to specialised segments of consumers. Thus, Japanese banks in California appeal to Americans with Japanese backgrounds and others with similar tastes. In a sense, therefore, the new generation of foreign retail banks represent only an extension of the process of product differentiation which has characterised domestic banking in all Western countries. It is not likely to grow very much or become a strong force in international banking and finance.

3.3.1 Multinational service banking

In the postwar years international trade, direct foreign investment and tourism have grown at a very rapid rate, partly because of the overall growth in income and partly because of technological innovations which lowered the cost of transportation and communication and made possible the effective global control of business operations. Banks both followed and pioneered this internationalisation of business. As they followed firms and tourists, they offered services that their home-country customers had become accustomed to. In so doing they discouraged them from going to foreign banks and acquiring a preference for their services. Once abroad, banks also provided information to firms in their home countries about business conditions abroad and assisted them in starting operations in other countries.

The basic economic factor enabling banks to compete with foreign banks for this type of business is knowledge. For example, a US bank has daily operational contacts with a US manufacturing firm. It knows the most current status of its balance sheets and income statements. It has inside information about product development and the health of its chief executive officers. It collects this knowledge routinely as necessary input into loan and other banking decisions. This knowledge is needed in providing bank services to the foreign operations of the US manufacturing firm and has two important characteristics. First, the marginal cost of its use abroad is practically zero. Second, there is no market, where foreign competitors can buy it. For these reasons, the US banks abroad can service the subsidiaries of US-based multinational trading, manufacturing and service enterprises at a lower cost than their local competitors.

However, the US banks abroad also offer their US customers a special kind of attraction. US business men and tourists abroad find it more convenient and cheaper to deal with a bank that uses business practices with which they are familiar. The offices of American Express deliberately provide an environment that makes US tourists feel at home. No foreign bank can hope to compete with those efforts, which are almost legendary among American tourists.

The growth of this service business of multinational banks levelled off at the same time as the growth of international trade, tourism and investment stagnated in the early 1980s. It remains to be seen whether this development represents merely a recession rather than a more fundamental structural change.

3.4 TAX EVASION AND GLOBAL MONEY AND CAPITAL MARKET BANKING

The largest proportion of all foreign bank presences are not for participation in the local retail or the international service markets. They exist for two main reasons, the evasion of domestic taxes and regulations and the participation in global money and capital markets. It is a striking characteristic of banks in this type of business that they are often found in the upper floors of office buildings and have only very small areas for servicing customers through tellers and other typical retail banking facilities.

Through the 1960s there developed so-called paper banking centres. These are typically located on small islands with sovereign governments, such as Bermuda and the Cayman Islands. Favourable legislation encouraged foreign banks to open 'brass plate' offices, which establish nothing but a legal presence there. A foreign bank would buy a license for as little as $20,000 a year, hire a lawyer and rent a postal box. Local lawyers represent many banks in this fashion and signify their commitment by attaching brass plates with the banks' names outside their offices. From this practice stems the name of the undertakings.

Banks keep separate books on their paper-centre operations in their domestic offices. One advantage of doing this has been that the business escapes certain domestic regulations and taxes. It also assures depositors and lenders anonymity from domestic, legal and taxation authorities, which the banks cannot offer otherwise. The growth of this business has been curtailed sharply by legislation in the major industrial countries, especially the United States, which deliberately was aimed at closing these tax havens for ordinary business and the refuge possibilities for criminal dealings. Of course, it is not possible to legislate away all such activities, but the relative importance of paper centres has declined since the early 1970s.

3.4.1 Euro and Asian currency markets

The main business of multinational banks now consists of participation in global money and capital markets functioning in all of the traditional major industrial cities of the world such as New York, London, Paris, Frankfurt, Zurich, Milan, Tokyo and Montreal. It also functions in locations that do not have the rich industrial base of these cities, such as Panama, Luxembourg, Bahrain, Singapore and Hong Kong. Location of banks in all of these centres is a necessary condition for participation in capital-market transactions, where a physical presence at meetings, and proximity to transactions and the demanders and suppliers of funds generate substantial information and transactions economies.

The most successful multinational banking centres have attracted the international capital market business by providing an environment that is relatively free from taxation and regulation. The smaller centres without a large industrial base, in particular, have deregulated banking deliberately in order to create an environment attractive to foreign banks. The Singapore government, for instance, asked the large banks of the world to prepare a wish-list of regulatory and tax concessions needed to make them establish a presence there. After some bargaining and strategic decisions, many of these concessions were granted and Singapore today has a flourishing multinational banking industry where previously it had none. At a time when growth of the Singapore business was slower than had been expected, the authorities discovered that a certain local tax encouraged banks to take some of their business to Hong Kong. This offensive tax was promptly removed and growth resumed.

3.4.2 Deregulation

Probably the most important forms of regulation absent from these multinational banking centres are minimum reserve requirements. These requirements represent a fairly heavy, implicit tax on banking. Thus, consider a bank which obtains a $100 deposit. In the absence of a reserve requirement it can lend out, say $90, leaving $10 as a liquid, non-interest bearing asset. If the interest paid on the deposit by the bank is 8 per cent and it earns 10 per cent on its loan, the gross margin is $1 per $100 of deposits.

Now consider the margin of this bank when the government insists that out of every $100 deposit it diverts 5 per cent or $5 into a non-interest bearing deposit with the central bank. It still has to keep the same liquid safety margin of $10, so under these conditions it can make a loan of only $85. Assuming that the bank's lending and borrowing rates remain the same, the bank's income is only $8.50 and its interest costs are $8, leaving a margin of only $0.50. In other words, the innocent-looking 5 per cent reserve requirement results in reduction of the gross operating margin from $1 to $0.50. This is an implicit tax of 50 per cent. Now if $0.45 of the gross margin in the regulated situation is spent on labour, equipment and rent, the profit is

$0.05 per $100 of bank business. Under the assumption that the operating costs of the bank are the same in the regulated and deregulated environment, escape from the reserve requirement raises profits from $0.05 to $0.55, or by 1,000 per cent.

These simple calculations capture the essence of the reason for the growth of multinational banking since the 1960s. US and other banks moved to London and have been able to accept deposits and make loans in US dollars without having to maintain required reserves with either the US Federal Reserve System or the Bank of England. This has been so because traditionally, domestic monetary authorities have not required such reserves on deposits denominated in foreign currencies. These deposits have grown rapidly to a point where world-wide and in all currencies, they amounted to over $2,500 billion in 1985. They are usually referred to as Euro-currency deposits and Asian currency deposits, depending on the location of the banking centres. It is clear that more generally they should be referred to as geographic currency deposits, though another popular descriptive term is offshore deposits.

The growth of this business was caused by the ability of the multinational banks to offer somewhat higher deposit and charge somewhat lower loan rates on business transacted in these offshore banking centres. These advantages have not been great enough to attract retail and small commercial business. However, large corporations and financial institutions, as well as governments and quasi-government agencies have been able to take advantage of these favourable interest rates. The multinational banks in these centres developed to perfection the system of loan syndication in order to meet the needs of very large borrowers. These syndicated loans led to a diversification of loan risks that was very attractive to the banks. They were the vehicle by which the governments and other borrowers in developing countries were able to obtain loans so readily that they overborrowed and found themselves in the debt crisis, which rocked the world in the early 1980s.

Offshore banking was encouraged not only by the absence of reserve requirements, but also by other advantageous regulations and tax treatment. For example, withholding taxes on interest income earned by depositors is absent in all of the offshore banking centres. This gives the multinational banks in this business a big competitive edge over their domestic rivals. However, the very great importance of the reserve requirements may be judged from the fact that after the introduction of these requirements on foreign currencies in Germany, multinational banks in that country reduced their presence substantially and all of the Euro-currency business left the country.

3.4.3 Money market operations

However, statistics show that only about a quarter of the loans of the multinational banks are to ultimate borrowers such as governments and corporations. The rest at any given moment in time are very short-term interbank loans and deposits. This business parallels the Federal Funds Market of the United States and equivalent short-term inter-bank markets in other countries designed to make the most efficient possible use of the commercial banks' reserves with central banks. The multinational banks have extended this business around the world.

Money in this market moves at extremely narrow margins between lending and borrowing rates and in very short maturities, often just over night. The market takes advantage to some extent of the fact that the world has daylight and working hours at different periods of the 24-hour earth day. It is highly efficient because it involves banks that have close operating relationships, which assures up-to-date information about credit-worthiness and has led to procedures that minimise transactions costs. Thus, billions of dollars are lent and borrowed on the basis of agreement reached over the telephone.

International currency exposures are an important aspect of multinational banking. As it turns out, the banks have managed to deal with these risks very effectively by simply matching assets and liabilities by maturities in every currency in their portfolio. As a result, the losses from the devaluation of a currency held are exactly matched by gains on liabilities in that same currency. The multinational banks have also succeeded in protecting themselves against changes in interest rates by the adoption of floating rates on both assets and liabilities. To the extent that they deal in fixed rates they have also matched assets and liabilities. However, it has not been possible to protect the business against the risk of default. The international debt crisis of the 1980s has raised this possibility, though no actual defaults of really major borrowers have taken place. This has been achieved, at least in part, by re-scheduling of debt maturities, which in turn has increased the riskiness of the business above planned levels.

3.4.4 Other economic causes

The capital market business of multinational banks has been encouraged also by two other benefits. First, the multinational banking centres have made it possible to generate large economies of operation for the individual banks and for the industry through externalities in the generation of information and transactions costs. The banks in this business typically do not accept deposits smaller than $1 million and make loans only in large amounts, though the banks in Singapore and Hong Kong have attempted to tap a large market by accepting deposits as small as $50,000. They avoid the costs of dealing with retail customers, such as cheque-clearing, cash services and instalment loans (hire purchase agreements), which represent a large share of the cost of doing business for domestic banks. The capital markets in the multinational banking centres have become models of integration and efficiency, made possible by the intensive use of electronic equipment and the favourable legal environment. The centres have become the heart of a web of relationships with banks in the surrounding territory channelling funds back and forth and providing intermediation more efficiently than the regional banks ever could.

A second benefit from participation in multinational banking stems from the diversification of business and risks. The increased geographical spread of loans widens the types of influences affecting the banks' portfolios and since most of these influences are imperfectly correlated, they serve to stabilise earnings. It has been shown statistically (Rugman 1979) that the earnings of multinational banks are more stable the greater is their international involvement. As is well known, wealthholders like such stability and correspondingly bid up the share prices of these banks and permit them to borrow at a lower cost.

All of these benefits from participation in the multinational banking business raised the profits of these institutions during the 1970s and until the international crisis of the 1980s. As an example of such profitability and international market participation consider Canadian banks. During the 1970s the share of foreign currency assets and liabilities in the total rose from about 10 per cent to about 50 per cent. At the same time, profits attributable to foreign operations rose to about 60 per cent of the total (Grubel 1983). In the 1980s, however, the multinational banks found many of their foreign loans to be non-performing, that is, they received no interest and amortisation payments. Many should possibly be written off as non-collectable, but banks have been reluctant to take this step. Profits from foreign operations are down and many banks have withdrawn from offshore banking activities. A number of US banks have withdrawn from London, where probably they should never have been, given the existing US banking laws which severely restrict their basis of operation in the United States.

It may well be that the expansion phase of multinational banking and international capital-market participation has ended. Certainly, it has become more and more difficult for new banking centres to develop in competition with existing ones. Most locations with advantageous time zones and hinterlands have been occupied or their advantages have been pre-empted by economies of scale in others.

3.5 WELFARE EFFECTS

The beneficial welfare effects of multinational banking are as follows. First, the retail and service banking activities permitted the spreading of the fixed costs of investment in managerial control, marketing and other know-how over a broader base. It lowered the average cost of these investments to consumers in the home country. It also resulted in overall lower costs of banking to consumers in the host country. Therefore the productivity of investment has been raised in the world as a whole. In many countries domestic banking is oligopolistic and competes mostly through non-price mechanisms, such as product differentiation and tied-in sales. Through this mechanism oligopolistic rents are dissipated in real-resource expenditures and even though bank profits are normal only, consumers face a larger spread between lending and borrowing rates than they would under greater competition. Multinational retail and service banks entering a country typically are not members of the domestic cartel and therefore can compete on price. In doing so they bring pressures on the domestic banks to do the same and the result is a more efficient system for the benefit of consumers.

Second, the global network of multinational banks and centres has integrated the world's capital markets, assuring that savings generated anywhere in the world are more likely to be used most productively in another part of the world. In addition, by causing narrower spreads, they have encouraged some lenders who would otherwise have kept their funds idle to make them available for loans. At the same time, the lower borrowing rates have encouraged some borrowers from entering the capital market who would not have done so otherwise. Third, the benefits from diversification on the stability of bank earnings have raised the welfare of wealthholders. Fourth, the growth of multinational banking has forced governments to re-examine the merit of banking regulation and taxation. As a result, the regulatory and taxation system of a number of countries has been made more efficient and made consistent with the mandates of modern technology.

However, multinational banking has also had some negative welfare effects. These have arisen mainly as a result of the banks' escape from the regulatory environments that governments had established in the past for the protection of the public. Presumably, these regulations forced the internalisation of externalities and led to the creation of socially useful information. It has been argued that through this escape the banks engaged in unhealthy competitive lending to developing countries, which may yet disrupt the stability of the entire world's financial system. Imperfect information about the lending of subsidiaries abroad prevented domestic bank supervisory authorities from noticing that there had developed an unhealthy concentration of loans to a few borrowers and an excess of loans over capital that had been considered prudent in the past. Furthermore, the loss of revenue from the taxation of banking has required the raising of other taxes and possibly the development of new and more serious distortions in other sectors of the economy. Finally, the greater integration of the world's capital market means that the national monetary independence of countries has been eroded further. The multinational banking system has become a most efficient conduit for short-term capital flows which constrain national governments from pursuing monetary and fiscal policy for the benefit of their domestic economies. Moreover, short-term capital flows following speculative rather than real economic sentiments, have added to the instability of exchange rates and have made economic management more difficult.

A more subtle, rather technical criticism of the multinational banking system focuses on the fact that it makes private gains from the more efficient use of money, which in turn costs very little to produce. Therefore, banks waste real resources economising on the use of a commodity which governments can make available at practically zero cost by an increase in commercial bank reserves and the printing of notes. Increases in the velocity of circulation and of money multipliers of national money supplies represent a very dubious social benefit.

All of these costs, however, can easily be overestimated. New theories of regulation suggest that they have reduced welfare to the extent that regulatory authorities have been captured by interest groups representing the allegedly regulated. The market solution, while not costless, may in fact be more efficient than regulation perverted through interest group pressure. The transition from a regulated to a deregulated environment may have presented difficulties, which are likely to disappear in the longer run. The world's private banks have in fact already created the Institute for International Finance in Washington, which is charged with the task of gathering and disseminating information about loans made to individual borrowers. In the presence of such a system, a problem, such as overlending to developing countries, is unlikely to recur.

It is also worth remembering that the multinational banking system developed when the world went through a very severe economic crisis brought about by the oil price increases of 1974 and 1979 and the accompanying payments surpluses of the oil exporters and the deficits of many oil users. The banks recirculated these surpluses and probably prevented the crisis from becoming even larger than it was. Finally, the multinational banks probably added very little to the integration of the world's capital markets and therefore to the loss of national monetary sovereignty. These developments were dominated by the evolution of new technologies. The institution of multinational banking only made the new system somewhat more efficient.

3.6 IMPLICATIONS FOR PUBLIC POLICY

It is obvious from the preceding list of costs and benefits of the development of multinational banking that their impact is not easily quantified. It may take years for the final assessment of the costs of the international debt crisis. The evolution of new private institutions needed for the generation of information in a deregulated environment is not complete and should continue to evolve in response to new technologies and institutions. Judgements of the costs and benefits are also coloured by the analysts' faith in unregulated markets on the one hand and the ability of governments to improve welfare through regulation on the other. These characteristics of analysts are highly correlated with their political views. For this reason, the assessment of multinational banking, like that of most economic institutions, often has political overtones.

However, there is a technical and politically rather neutral policy issue concerning multinational banks. During the 1970s the US government initiated negotiations for the international, collective imposition of regulation of the industry, administered through the IMF, the Bank for International Settlements or a similar institution. These initiatives went nowhere, as most governments correctly judged that such regulation would push the banks into other countries, which would only be too glad to open their doors to them. There exists no conceivable, voluntary mechanism that could assure that such shifting of bank activities would not take place.

A more sensible policy for the control of multinational banking would be to eliminate the distortion caused by domestic reserve requirements. Not only do these requirements result in distortions in domestic financial markets, they also represent a strong incentive for moving banking operations abroad and into foreign currencies, as we noted above. The elimination of these incentives does not require the abandonment of reserve requirements. It would only be necessary to pay interest on the central bank deposits of the commercial banks. That this is so can easily be seen from the above numerical analysis.

The proposal has the support of a number of economists and research departments of central banks and international organisations. It has not been adopted because the interest which central banks would have to pay the commercial banks, under present arrangements would be lost to governments as general tax revenue. While opposition to the proposal based on these arguments is understandable from the point of view of democratic political systems, it is not warranted in the light of the fact that these revenues are very small as a proportion of total tax revenues. It also would require only a relatively simple education campaign to convince the public that such interest payments would raise the profits of banks just briefly. Competition would be certain to lead quickly to smaller spreads between lending and borrowing rates to the benefit of domestic consumers of bank services. And with the distorting incentive removed, multinational banking would find its reduced, efficient level.

4

Internationalisation of Professional Producer Services: Accountancy Conglomerates[1]

Peter W. Daniels, Nigel J. Thrift and A. Leyshon

4.1 INTRODUCTION

As internationalisation of services continues to gain momentum it poses some new research questions. These include its effects on, and contribution to, trade in services (Noyelle and Dutka 1986); its consequences for the division of labour (Bertrand and Noyelle 1986), for methods of delivery, and for access to the specialist knowledge embodied in many of these services. The spatial consequences of these processes are also important both at the global level (Dunning and Norman 1987; Noyelle and Dutka 1987) and within national space economies (Daniels, Leyshon and Thrift 1986), especially for the relative growth of the urban areas that are usually the focus of locational choice by services choosing to operate offshore. Such choices will clearly be associated with employment effects, the reinforcement of information and related linkages, and the stimulation of commercial office and residential property markets (see for example, Noyelle 1986, 1987).

Professional producer services are playing a leading role in the internationalisation process which is one of several significant trends in the recent development of large accountancy firms in the UK (Leyshon, Daniels and Thrift 1987). One of the key processes sustaining the concentration and to some extent the diversification of accountancy firms has been their growing involvement in overseas markets. An orientation towards offshore markets accounts for an increasing proportion of the output of UK-based financial and business services (Daniels, Leyshon and Thrift 1986) and, given the extensive involvement of accountancy firms in management consultancy or corporate finance advice it is inevitable that internationalisation has become essential to their competitiveness and survival.

This chapter outlines the modes of overseas expansion employed by accountancy firms and brings together some data on the geographical expansion of the international office networks of major UK-based accountancy practices. Most of these firms are arms of the world's largest accountancy firms. The information used has not always been complete and data-bank development is an ongoing activity. The collection of data on accountancy practices is not an easy task for a number of reasons. Firstly, partnerships are under no obligation to publish annual reports; secondly, some partnerships are more willing than others to reveal information about their staffing structure and distribution; and thirdly, the volume of retained information about their activities is greater for some partnerships than for others. The period between 1975 and 1985, upon which this research is focused, has been so dynamic that full records simply do not exist in some practices. What follows must therefore be viewed as indicative rather than conclusive evidence about the processes and the geographical consequences of internationalisation of major accountancy practices.

4.2 ORGANISATION OF WORLD-WIDE ACCOUNTING OPERATIONS

An analysis of data on the international expansion of accountancy practices is made more comprehensible if the modes of organisation that are commonly employed are identified. Unfortunately, none of the largest firms operate on an identical basis (Cairns, Lafferty and Mantle 1984) but Bavishi and Wyman (1983) have identified seven major types of organisational arrangement utilised by accountancy firms. Essentially these arrangements vary according to the relationship between the 'international firm' and the 'local' practices:

(i)   An *international name* occurs where an auditing firm uses its name to practise in a foreign country, e.g. Arthur Andersen in the UK and Price Waterhouse in Italy. These are sometimes referred to as 'World Firms'.

(ii)   A *combined name* arises where auditing firms combine their international name with names of local firms that are fully affiliated with them.

(iii)   A *local name* occurs where an international firm practises
         entirely under a local firm's name where the local firm
         is totally affiliated with the international firm.
(iv)   An *Association or Federation* is employed when an
         international firm is used mainly for coordination
         purposes among member firms.
(v)   *Correspondent status* is conferred in circumstances where
         an international firm is represented exclusively by a local
         auditing firm. In this case the local auditing firm will
         have clients that have not necessarily been referred to it
         by the affiliated international firm.
(vi)   Although not a significant category on a global basis it
         is also possible to have *multiple affiliation* where a local
         firm represents several international firms.
(vii)   Finally, *two or more names* may occur if an international
         firm practises under two or more national firm names.

These categories are not mutually exclusive since firms may
operate under more than one organisational arrangement
depending on the regulatory and other circumstances prevailing
in the country where they have offices. However, the
'international name' and 'association' forms are virtually
independent of one another, and are the dominant methods of
international operation (see Table 4.1).

The 'international name' organisational structure signifies
those firms that operate a 'world firm'. The world firm is a central
(controlling) body that plans and integrates the firm's flow of
international services. Each national firm uses a common name,
thus ensuring that the world-wide operations of the international
firm are closely identified with one another. Until relatively
recently, this has been the preferred mode of operation of the Big
Eight firms but attempts at cross-border litigation have
encouraged some firms to lower their transnational profile (see
Leyshon, Daniels and Thrift 1987). Of the Big Eight, only Arthur
Young has fewer than 50 per cent of its partners operating under
a common name. The world firm is most comprehensively
utilised by Arthur Andersen; 98 per cent of the partners operated
under the firm's common name in 1982 (Bavishi and Wyman
1983). A uniform transnational name is primarily used by
accountants to help promote their international identity and
status to clients (Cairns, Lafferty and Mantle 1984).

The 'association' is the second important organisational

Table 4.1: Organisational arrangement of world's largest international accounting groups

| Firm | Percentage partners by organisational structure | | | | | |
	Inter-national name	Com-bined name	Local name	Asso-ciation	Corres-pondent	2 + names
Arthur Andersen	99	–	–	–	1	–
Price Waterhouse	94	–	4	–	1	–
Peat Marwick						
Mitchell	93	1	3	–	3	–
Ernst & Whinney	89	–	6	–	5	–
Coopers & Lybrand	75	1	17	–	1	7
Deloitte Haskins						
& Sells	72	–	21	–	1	5
Touche Ross	58	2	33	–	–	7
Arthur Young	44	9	18	–	–	29
Horwarth & Horwarth						
International	3	–	–	72	18	7
Binder Djiker Otte	1	–	1	72	–	27
Grant Thornton						
International	–	–	–	99	–	–
Klynveld Main						
Goerdler	–	–	–	100	–	–

Source: Bavishi and Wyman (1983), Table 2.1

structure operated by the international firms and signifies those partnerships that operate within federated networks of national firms. Such groups operate without a common practice name. The largest and most successful example of federated organisation is Klynveld Main Goerdler (KMG) which came into operation in 1979 through the amalgamation of leading national firms outside the Big Eight.[2] These included Main Hurdman (United States), Thorne Riddell (Canada), Thomson McLintock (United Kingdom), Deutsche Treuhand (West Germany), Hancock & Offner (Australia), Fides Revision (Switzerland), Fiduciare de France (France), C. Jespersson (Denmark), Klynveld Kraayanhof & Co., and Pelson, Hauselberg, Van Til & Co. (Netherlands) (The Accountant 1979).

Although the world firm/international name and federation/association organisation forms are dominant operational modes, they are not exclusive of other structures. For example, several countries maintain anti-monopolistic legislative barriers (Cairns, Lafferty and Mantle 1984) to preserve the independence of national accountancy firms. In such instances those firms that operate as world firms are forced to enter into a different relationship with the national partnership. The usual practice is for the national partnership to retain its local name (see Table 4.1) but nevertheless be fully integrated at the international level (see Table 4.2).

Table 4.2: The ten leading accountancy firms in France, 1983

Firm	International affiliation	Turnover (FFm)	No. offices	Total staff
Fiduciare De France	KMG	835	184	3,000
Helios/Streco Durando	Arthur Young AMSA	159	9	530
Sofinarex	–	140	90	660
De Bois Dieterle & Ass. (BDA)	Touche Ross	90	4	310
Guy Barbier	Arthur Andersen	80[a]	2[a]	180[a]
Guffiet Et Cie	Coopers & Lybrand	73	3	200
Champagnie Gen-Fiduciare	–	70	32	399
Blachard Chauveau	Price Waterhouse	64	3	152
Eurex/Comp. Fid. Europeene	–	60	31	280
Audit Continental	Price Waterhouse	59	2	120

Note: (a) Estimates.
Source: International Accounting Bulletin (1984)

4.3 THE INTERNATIONAL EXPANSION OF LARGE ACCOUNTING FIRMS

Expansion of the UK operations of the leading accounting firms has been paralleled by a similar extension of their international activities. All of the major UK accounting firms now have the capability to serve clients on an international basis and are able to refer business between their own offices in different countries. They function as multinational service conglomerates (Clairmonte and Cavanagh 1984) with the leading 20 UK firms employing more than 300,000 people world-wide in 1986 (International Accounting Bulletin, 1986; see Table 4.3).

The internationalisation of these firms is not, however, a very recent phenomenon; it has developed over a considerable period of time. Some firms have indeed only established international links since 1975 but a number of others had gone multinational before 1900.

Table 4.3: The 20 leading accountancy groups world-wide, 1985

Firm	Fee income ($m)	No. countries	No. offices	No. partns.	No. Prof. staff[1]	All other staff	Total staff
Arthur Andersen	1,574	47	191	1,630	21,336	6,836	29,802
Peat Marwick Mitchell	1,445	89	335	2,533	20,482	6,849	29,864
Coopers & Lybrand	1,410	98	519	2,850	n/a	n/a	36,000
Price Waterhouse	1,234	95	378	2,113	20,656	7,603	30,372
Ernst & Whinney	1,185	77	359	2,199	17,201	5,600	25,000
Arthur Young International	1,060	68	370	2,560	17,640	6,600	26,800
Touche Ross International	973	90	463	2,550	17,500	5,950	26,000
Deloitte Haskins & Sells	953	63	433	2,125	16,621	5,266	24,012
Klynveld Main Goerdler	n/a[2]	73	487	3,215	19,300	12,817	29,766
Grant Thornton International	479	57	449	1,419	n/a	n/a	14,800
Binder Djiker Otte	450	50	310	1,150	7,500	2,500	11,150
Horwarth & Horwarth	807	72	233	915	4,930	2,455	8,300
Dunwoody Robson McGladrey & Pullein	282	51	393	1,118	3,822	1,340	6,280
Pannell Kerr Forster	240	75	215	700	3,300	2,500	6,000
Spicer & Oppenheim	189	40	200	672	3,935	1,503	6,110
Moores Rowland International	182	32	220	762	4,097	1,219	6,078
Moore Stephens	172	63	201	602	3,644	765	5,011
Deardon Farrow International	n/a	38	171	612	3,208	1,130	4,950
DFK International	130	35	166	525	2,090	885	3,500
Clark Kenneth Leventhal	145	24	137	466	n/a	n/a	3,749

Notes: (1) Excluding partners; (2) 1983 the income was estimated as $d1m.
Source: International Accounting Bulletin (1984)

4.3.1 Development of international office networks

It is therefore possible to distinguish two historical periods in the internationalisation of large UK accounting firms. These are most conveniently termed the 'early' and 'late' periods. The early period of internationalisation began in the 1890s and continued until 1939 while the second, 'late', period commenced in 1945. During the early period the impetus for the development of an international operating capacity came entirely from the UK as City-based accounting firms followed the movement of manufacturing capital into overseas markets. The later stage of internationalisation has involved a more structured build up of multinational activities through the formation of international partnerships. These have been predominantly between Anglo-American firms, although more recently associations on an international level have been formed between leading European partnerships which, for example, has led to the creation of major accounting groups such as Klynveld Main Goerdler and Binder Djiker Otte.

4.3.2 The early period of internationalisation from 1890 to 1945

The initial opening of overseas offices by UK accounting firms was stimulated by motives similar to those which prompted the development of their UK office networks, namely the ability to serve clients in specific locations. International expansion of accounting firms was client led as firms 'followed a parallel path to the evolution of the business which they served' (Jones 1981, p. 108). Three of today's leading firms – Touche Ross, Price Waterhouse and Deloitte Haskins & Sells – had opened their first overseas offices before the end of 1900 (Deloitte, Plender, Griffiths & Co. 1958; Richards 1950; Richards 1981). Indeed, the development of the overseas office networks of these firms preceded the opening of their regional UK offices as they aligned themselves with the movement of British industrial capital into overseas markets.

Within 20 years, the international capabilities of these firms were already substantial. For example, following the opening of an office in New York in 1890, Deloitte & Co. proceeded to construct a network across the Americas. Offices were opened in Buenos Aires (1895), Cincinatti (1905), Mexico City (1906),

Rio de Janeiro (1911), Montreal (1912), Tucaman (1912), Havana (1914), Rosario (1917) and Recife (1917). Meanwhile, offices were also opened in southern Africa; in Johannesburg (1904), Bulawayo (1905), Cape Town (1907), Durban (1908) and Salisbury (1910) (Deloitte, Plender, Griffiths & Co. 1958). The decisions to open all these offices were specifically guided by the requirements of individual clients. Those in South America were developed initially as a consequence of work undertaken for the London and River Plate Bank, although the provision of business services to railway construction companies later bolstered and encouraged further expansion of the office network. The Mexico City office was opened to handle the oil and railway interests of just one British company, while the South African offices were opened to deal with the growing volume of business resulting from the development of gold mining activities (Deloitte, Plender, Griffiths & Co. 1958).

Extensive overseas office networks were also being developed by the other firms that engaged in early internationalisation. For example, with offices in New York and Chicago by 1900, Price Waterhouse subsequently established eight overseas offices in seven different countries by 1920 (Price Waterhouse 1985). Similarly, Touche Ross opened a number of North American offices during the first twenty years of this century (Richards 1981).

The period leading up to 1939 saw a steady increase in the overseas representation of those accounting firms that had embarked upon early internationalisation. It was during this period that the first tentative links were made between City-based practices and leading national practices based in the United States, contacts that were later to have a dramatic impact on the international capability of the UK accounting firms.

4.3.3 The late period of internationalisation from 1945

The development of the overseas office networks of leading UK accountancy firms since 1945 has been heavily influenced by mergers at the international level between themselves and national US practices. A formal linking of international capability has occurred both between those UK and US firms that previously operated under the same names in both countries (for example, Price Waterhouse) and between formerly independent national practices.

The earliest merger between a leading UK and a US practice was that of Peats of London with Marwick Mitchell of New York in 1911 (Wise 1981). Before 1939, representational links between firms in the two countries were common; one firm would agree to act on behalf of the other in their particular spheres of interest. For example, Ernst & Ernst and Whinney, Sith & Whinney first entered into an agreement of this kind in 1918. It was not until after 1945, however, that these incipient international contacts were extensively strengthened by a series of mergers that created new Anglo-American firms. The purpose of each merger was to strengthen the overseas representation of the participants and to facilitate the penetration of hitherto unentered national markets. Thus, just as the development policies for regional offices in the UK switched from one of orientating offices to specific clients to one of orientating clients in general, increasing internationalisation of economic activity in general after 1945 encouraged accounting firms to increase their overseas representation. The increasing multi-plant, multinational tendency of large firms and the requirement for them to produce consolidated accounts based on returns from each of their operating units acted as a further encouragement for accounting firms to extend their international office networks in much the same way as it encouraged the expansion of their UK operations. By doing so, the large accounting firms increased their market share of the world accounting market.

The largest accountancy practice to establish a separate international firm on a world-wide basis through the integration of its existing national practices was Price Waterhouse in 1945 (Price Waterhouse 1985). This was facilitated by the fact that, even at this stage, virtually all of its international operations were carried out under one unifying name. In 1952, the UK firm Deloitte, Plender, Griffiths & Co., and the US national practice of Haskins & Sells merged at the international level to create Deloitte Haskins & Sells (Deloitte, Plender, Griffiths & Co. 1958). This had a dramatic effect upon the international capability of Deloittes and expanded its own substantial network of overseas offices from 41 to 87 in just four years immediately following the merger. A major part of the return included penetration of almost 30 US cities but also included Brazil, Peru, Venezuela, Colombia, Uganda and Japan, for example. In 1957, the UK practice of Cooper Brothers, the US firm Lybrand, Ross

& Montgomery and McDonald Currie & Co., Canada, formed the international firm of Coopers & Lybrand (C & L Journal 1979). Although Cooper Brothers had opened overseas offices in Africa, Europe, Australia and New Zealand prior to the merger with Lybrands (Table 4.4; Cooper Brothers & Co. 1954), the UK–US–Canadian merger enabled the firm to offer its clients services in Asia and North and South America for the first time. A similar Anglo-American–Canadian tripartite international merger was performed in 1960 between the perspective national practices of 'Touche' firms. George A. Touche in the UK, Touche Niven Bailey & Smart of the US and Ross Touche & Co., of Canada merged to form the international firm of Touche Ross Bailey & Smart (Trobas), later shortened to Touche Ross (Richards 1981). More recently, the leading firms of Ernst & Whinney and Grant Thornton were formed as a result of a formal merger between US and UK practices.

The merger of firms at the international level not only increased the overseas representation of the constituent firms, but provided the framework that enabled them to systematically enter previously unserved national markets. For example, Coopers & Lybrand has four key 'liaison' firms that assume responsibility for business within specific geographically defined areas. For example, following the formation of Coopers & Lybrand the UK arm was responsible for the British Commonwealth and Europe, the US arm for South America, Mexico, Central America, Japan and the Far East, while the McDonald Currie arm in Canada was responsible for coordinating business in Bermuda and the Caribbean. The other liaison firm, based in Australia, covered the South Pacific region. Each liaison firm is detailed to identify areas where it would be desirable for Coopers & Lybrand to be represented and then either to find a suitable local firm with which the international firm could enter into some form of association or merger or, alternatively, make arrangements for a new firm to be established. The success of this expansionist programme has seen the number of Coopers & Lybrand world-wide offices increase from 35 to 352 between 1950 and 1979 and total employment rising from under 1,000 to almost 22,500 (C & L Journal 1979).

Mergers at the international level have significantly increased the American influence in the leading UK accounting firms. For example, the Policy Committees of the international firms usually comprise more partners from the US arm of the practice

Table 4.4: Cooper Brothers international office network (1954) prior to merger with Lybrand, Ross & Montgomery

Country	Office	Date opened
Belgium	Brussels	1920
	Antwerp	1948
France	Paris	1930
Holland	Rotterdam	1949
South Africa	Johannesburg	1931
	Durban	1933
	Port Elizabeth	1942
	Cape Town	1950
Kenya	Nairobi	1947
	Mombasa	1947
Tanzania	Dar-es-Salaam	1947
(Tanganyika)	Moshi	1947
Uganda	Kampala	1947
	Jinja	1947
Zimbabwe	Salisbury	1947
(Rhodesia)	Bulawayo	1947
	Crwelo	1951
Malawi	Limbe	1951
(Nyasaland)	Kitwe	1954
	Ndola	1954
Nigeria	Lagos	1953
Zaire	Elisabethville	1953
(Belgian Congo)		
Australia	Sydney	1948
	Melbourne	1948
	Canberra	1948
	Perth	1948
	Brisbane	1948
New Zealand	Dunedin	1948
	Wellington	1948
	Auckland	1948
	Christchurch	1948
	Palmerston North	1951
Canada	Montreal	1936
	Quebec	1948[a]
	Ottawa	1948[a]
	Toronto	1948[a]
	Saint John	1948[a]
	Sherbrooke	1948[a]
	Vancouver	1948[a]
	Kirkland Lake	1948[a]
	Hamilton	1948
	Charlottetown	1948
	Edmonton	1948
United States	New York	1926
	Boston	1948[b]

Table 4.4: Cooper Brothers... Contd.

New Bedford	1948[b]
Springfield	1948[b]
Cleveland	1948[b]
Chicago	1948[b]
Philadelphia	1948[b]
New Haven	1948[b]
Syracuse	1948[b]
Detroit	1948[b]
Los Angeles	1948[b]
Buffalo	1948[b]
San Francisco	1948[b]

Notes: (a) Offices of associated national firm McDonald Currie & Co. (date indicates year of international agreement); (b) Offices of associated national firm Scovell, Wellington & Co. (date indicates year of international agreement).
Source: Cooper Brothers & Co. (1954)

than any other part of the firm. Two of the current leading firms, Arthur Young and Arthur Andersen, were themselves formed in the United States. Although Arthur Andersen is currently ranked as the world's largest accounting firm (International Accounting Bulletin 1984), its internationalisation developed appreciably later than that of the UK-based firms, since it was not until after 1918 that US capital began to flow abroad in significant volumes (Arthur Andersen 1963). Moreover, the extension of its international office network ultimately followed a different path to that of many of the current large firms. Prior to the Second World War, the firm had not opened any overseas offices in its own name but had preferred to enter into agreements with overseas practices that would represent them in particular countries and by 1939 Arthur Andersen had links with national practices in nine countries on this basis. In 1949, the firm established a joint firm with the London-based practice Turquands Yourn to coordinate the business of the two firms in continental Europe. However, rather than strengthening international links between the national partnerships as other firms were to do in the 1950s, Arthur Andersen instead gradually severed all its existing agreements with other national practices. This move was stimulated by a desire to maintain strong central control over accounting standards and procedures and led to an effective dissolution of the firm's existing international network of offices. Therefore it was not until 1955 that Arthur Andersen opened an overseas office in its own name but within eight years, 25 offices had been added to the new international networks achieved entirely by organic growth via a process of new start ups and completed buyouts of existing national practices (Arthur Andersen 1963).

4.3.4 Process of expansion

The closed centralised approach to expansion favoured by Arthur Andersen is not typical. Entrance into national accounting markets by the leading firms has generally been through mergers with established national practices. Touche Ross International, for example, admitted new firms to the international partnership in Barbados, Bolivia, Chile, Denmark, Greece, Canary Islands, Mexico, the Netherlands, New Zealand, Sweden, Switzerland and the USA (Accountancy 1980). In 1981 the firm merged with practices in Hong Kong, Belgium, Italy and Norway (Accountant 1981a, 1981b; Accountancy 1981). Such merger activity meant that between 1979 and 1983 Touche Ross International demonstrated substantial international growth; world-wide employment expanded from 16,000 to 20,000, the number of offices rose from 333 to 393 and the number of countries in which the partnership operated increased from 80 to 85 (Accountancy 1980, 1983).

The other large international firms have embarked upon a similar course of frenetic merger activity. This process has been driven by the larger accounting groups' desire to achieve comprehensive international networks (Cairns, Lafferty and Mantle 1984). But the merger is only one of the routes by which an international firm may establish a business capability in a new country. At the most limited level of involvement a firm may engage national firms as representatives or correspondents to act on their behalf. However, some representative firms may act on behalf of more than one large accountancy group and so the level of integration with the international firm is low. Successful relations between correspondents and international groups may eventually lead to a full merger when the larger group wants to increase its presence in particular countries. However, if no suitable national practice exists for merger then the international firm may be forced to establish an entirely new firm. When building up an entirely new practice in overseas markets, the large firms recognise that it is important to establish a high local staff content as soon as possible. Although expatriots will play a crucial role in the early establishment of an office, they will endeavour to ensure that the firm is locally run as soon as possible. This is because although large numbers of new offices are opened to serve particular clients, unless the office quickly builds up a local client base, the office may eventually struggle. Therefore, local staff are engaged to help merge the office into the cultural background of the area. The passing of control to the local office is entirely consistent with the profit-centre mode of operation practised by leading firms (see Leyshon, Daniels and Thrift 1987). The new partnership acts as a separate profit centre, which will be charged by other profit centres for work performed. Crucially, the new partnership provides the international firm with additional international capacity which it can present to clients.

4.3.5 Geographical expansion of world-wide office networks

In an attempt to monitor the increases in the international capability of the leading accounting groups, a cross-sectional analysis of the international office networks of the 20 leading accounting firms operating in the UK was performed for 1975 and 1985. Analysis confirms that these firms have greatly increased their international activities and between them more than doubled the number of offices operated world-wide (see Figure 4.1). The total number of offices operated by the twenty largest firms increased by some 115 per cent between 1975 and 1985, from 2,323 to 4,991. All the eight regions shown in Figure 4.1 experienced an increase in the number of offices operated. In both 1975 and 1985 the United States, Canada and Europe accounted for over two-thirds of the total number of offices operated world-wide but Europe now contains more offices in absolute terms than North America following a 160 per cent increase in the number of offices operated there by the leading twenty firms; more than 1,000 offices were opened in Europe by the twenty firms between 1975 and 1985. Some 32 per cent of the European office growth occurred in the UK and the Netherlands alone. Nevertheless, the USA was the location for almost 25 per cent of the total offices in 1985 and remained the nation with the largest number of accounting offices. The largest relative increase occurred in Asia (290 per cent) while those in Australia increased by some 138 per cent. More than 50 per cent of the new offices in Asia were located in Japan, Malaysia and the Philippines. The remaining regions experienced a decrease in their share of total offices.

Figure 4.1: Worldwide distribution of offices of the leading 20 accountancy firms in the UK

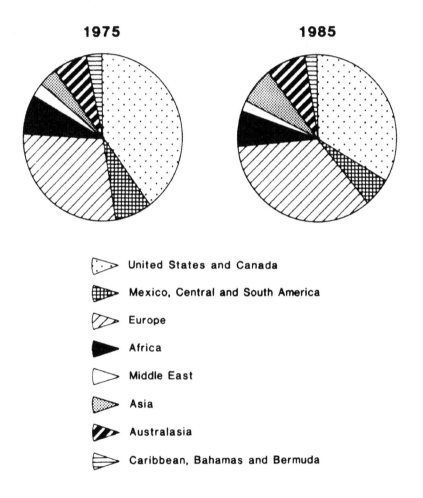

1975   **1985**

United States and Canada

Mexico, Central and South America

Europe

Africa

Middle East

Asia

Australasia

Caribbean, Bahamas and Bermuda

The growth in the number of non-UK offices operated by the leading twenty firms has been substantial; they increased at a rate proportionally greater than their domestic office networks and have expanded by some 122 per cent since 1975 (see Table 4.5). Expansion is attributable to the increasing penetration of new locations by the largest accounting groups and to the relatively late adoption of international status by some of the smaller firms. For example, of the twenty largest firms in the UK in 1985, three did not operate any international offices.

Table 4.5: International offices operated outside the UK by the leading 20 accountancy firms (UK 1985) 1975–1985[a]

UK Firm[b]	International firm	No. of offices 1975	1985	Increase 1975–85
Coopers & Lybrand	Coopers & Lybrand	262	472	210
Deloitte Haskins & Sells	Deloitte Haskins & Sells	206	418	212
KMG Thomson McLintock[c]	Klynveld Main Goerdler[d]	186	411	225
Arthur Young	Arthur Young	149	368	219
Touche Ross	Touche Ross International	207	363	156
Price Waterhouse	Price Waterhouse	230	326	96
Ernst & Whinney[e]	Ernst & Whinney	173	298	125
Grant Thornton[f]	Grant Thornton[g]	31	287	256
Peat Marwick Mitchell	Peat Marwick Mitchell	262	280	18
Robson Rhodes	Dunwoody Robson McGladrey Pullein[h]	104	258	154
Arthur Andersen	Arthur Andersen	94	181	87
Binder Hamlyn	Binder Djiker Otte[i]	19	161	142
Stoy Hayward	Horwarth & Horwarth International[b]	0	159	159
Deardon Farrow	Deardon Farrow International[b]	0	144	144
Spicer & Pegler	Spicer & Oppenheim[b]	23	81	58
Hodgson & Impey	Hodgson Landau Brands[b]	0	74	74
Moore Stephens	Moore Stephens	11	67	56
Clark Whitehill	Clark Kenneth Leventhal[b]	6	65	59
Pannell Kerr Forster	Pannell Kerr Forster	58	200	142
Neville Russell	Neville Russell	5	9	4
Total non-UK offices		2,026	4,622	2,596

Notes: (a) Not correspondent offices; (b) International firm was not in existence in 1975 and UK firm was not affiliated to any international organisation; (c) UK firm in 1975 was Thomson McLintock; (d) International firm in 1975 was McLintock Main LaFrentz; (e) UK firm in 1975 was Whinney Murray & Co; (f) UK firm in 1975 was Thornton Baker;

(g) In 1975 Thornton Baker were internationally associated with Hurdman and Cranstoun; (h) International firm in 1975 was Lasser, Robson Rhodes and Dunwoody International; (i) International firm in 1975 was Binder Hamlyn Singleton, Fabian.
Sources: Institute of Chartered Accountants (1975; 1985); various firms' publications

However of those that did operate on a multinational basis, five firms – Coopers & Lybrand, Deloitte Haskins & Sells, Touche Ross, Price Waterhouse and Peat Marwick Mitchell – operated international networks of more than 200 offices each (see Table 4.5). As many as ten firms operated networks consisting of more than 200 offices and six of these had in excess of 300 offices world-wide. The increase in the number of offices has been accompanied by an intensification of the multinational character of the firms. By 1985, all the leading twenty firms had acquired an enhanced international capability as measured by the number of countries in which they were active (see Table 4.6).

Table 4.6: Level of multinationalisation of accounting firms: countries operated in 1975–85

Firm	Countries		Increase 1975–85	
	1975	1985	no.	%
Coopers & Lybrand	73	97	24	33
Price Waterhouse	76	93	17	22
Arthur Young	42	83	41	98
Touche Ross	48	82	34	71
Peat Marwick Mitchell	68	73	5	7
Deloitte Haskins & Sells	60	67	7	12
Ernst & Whinney	32	65	33	103
Grant Thornton	4	58	54	1,350
KMG Thomson McLintock	28	55	27	96
Robson Rhodes	25	51	26	104
Arthur Andersen	32	45	13	41
Deardon Farrow	1	39	38	3,800
Stoy Hayward	1	38	37	3,700
Clark Whitehill	5	20	15	300
Binder Hamlyn	15	17	2	13
Hodgson Impey	1	17	16	1,600
Spicer & Pegler	9	15	6	67
Pannell Kerr Forster	29	59	30	103
Moore Stephens	7	11	4	57
Neville Russell	4	5	1	25

Sources: Institute of Chartered Accountants (1975; 1985); various firms' publications

Between 1975 and 1985 there has been more consolidation and continuation of the large scale international presence of the larger of the international accounting groups. Those firms that demonstrated an extensive multinational character in 1975 have pushed further into new countries and substantially extended their total networks. Nevertheless, by 1985 the international capability of the established international firms was starting to be matched by a new generation of multinational accounting firms. For example, the nine firms that could boast an international office network of more than 100 offices in 1975, between them operated some 88 per cent of all the non-UK offices run by the twenty firms in that year. However, in 1985 these same firms were responsible for only 71 per cent of total offices. This reduction in the share of total world-wide offices has occurred despite the larger of the twenty firms themselves experiencing steady growth in their international operations.

The internationalisation of the smaller accounting firms since 1975 has been enhanced by a series of multi-firm mergers between leading national partnerships. These firms previously possessed only limited international office networks and formed international partnerships with other foreign national firms to enable them to compete at the international level with the established large practices. These mergers have been essentially defensive in character. They resemble the international mergers between Anglo-American practices in the 1980s although the more recent formations have been distinctly more European in orientation than the traditional Anglo-American formations.

Stoy Hayward's merger with the London practice of Hesketh Handel Hirschheed in 1975 provided the firm with admission to the multinational firm of Horwarth and Horwarth (Accountancy 1975). Hodgson Harris' (later Impey) first steps in the construction of an overseas office network occurred in 1978 when it jointly formed the international accounting group Berger Hoffman and Harris (Accountant 1978), although it subsequently realigned itself with Landau (a US firm) in 1980 when the UK firm Mann Judd withdrew from the international firm of Mann Judd Landau following its merger with Touche Ross in 1979 (Accountancy 1980).

By forming associations with established international firms and with several similarly placed national practices, the smaller of the accounting groups have been able to construct international networks of offices in a relatively short period of time.

The formation of these new international groupings compared with the continued growth of the older international firms has ensured that the influence of the large accounting firms is now felt in virtually every country world-wide. Some examples of the changes in the number of offices, by country and continent, for each international practice are illustrated in Figure 4.2.

4.4 GEOGRAPHICAL IMPACTS: BUSINESS AND EMPLOYMENT BY REGION

Despite the relative decline in the number of offices operated in North America by comparison with the rest of the world, the region is still by far the most important in terms of the numbers of people employed and fee income earned. Between 1981 and 1985 North America accounted for more than half of the total world-wide chargeable hours worked by Peat Marwick Mitchell (see Table 4.7) and a similar analysis for Arthur Andersen in 1983 and 1984 indicates that some two-thirds of chargeable hours are worked in North America (see Table 4.8).

Table 4.7: Peat Marwick Mitchell: chargeable hours by region 1981–5

	Asia–Pacific		Africa–Middle East		Europe		South America		North America		Total	
	Mill	(%)	Mill	(%)	Mill	(%)	Mill	(%)	Mill	(%)	Mill	(%)
1981	3.4	(12.9)	0.7	(2.7)	5.9	(22.3)	1.3	(4.9)	15.1	(57.2)	26.4	(100.0)
1982	3.9	(13.6)	1.5	(5.2)	6.1	(21.3)	1.5	(5.2)	15.7	(54.7)	28.7	(100.0)
1983	4.1	(13.9)	1.5	(5.1)	6.2	(20.9)	1.5	(5.1)	16.3	(55.1)	29.6	(100.0)
1984	4.3	(13.9)	1.6	(5.2)	6.7	(21.6)	1.7	(5.5)	16.7	(53.9)	31.0	(100.0)
1985	4.5	(13.7)	1.9	(5.8)	7.0	(21.3)	1.8	(5.5)	17.6	(53.7)	32.8	(100.0)

Source: Peat Marwick (1985)

Table 4.8: Arthur Andersen: chargeable hours by region, 1983–4

	Asia–Pacific		Africa–Middle East		Europe		South America		North America		Total	
	Mill	(%)	Mill	(%)	Mill	(%)	Mill	(%)	Mill	(%)	Mill	(%)
1983	1.2	(4.7)	0.5	(1.9)	5.0	(19.5)	1.7	(6.6)	17.3	(67.3)	25.7	(100.0)
1984	1.4	(5.0)	0.5	(1.8)	5.9	(21.0)	1.8	(6.4)	18.5	(65.8)	28.1	(100.0)

Source: International Accounting Bulletin (1986)

Figure 4.2: Changes in the world-wide distribution of offices of the 20 largest accountancy practices in the UK, 1973 and 1985.

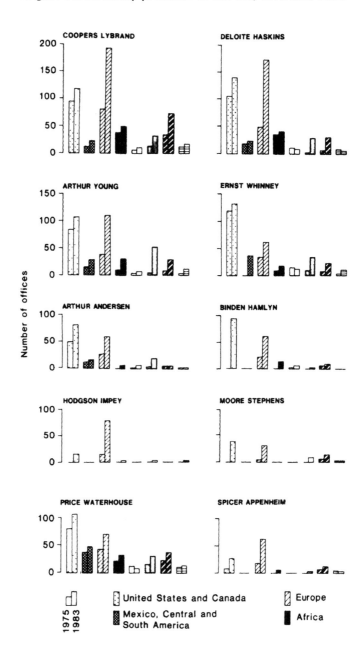

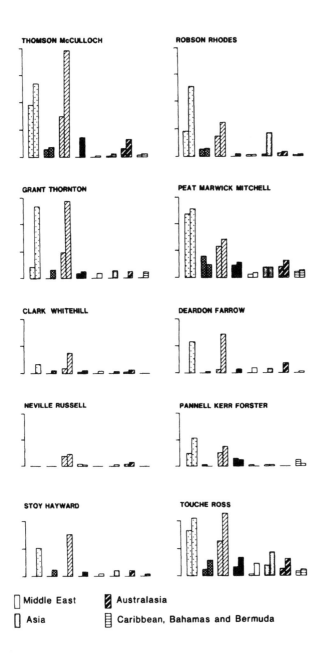

THOMSON McCULLOCH

ROBSON RHODES

GRANT THORNTON

PEAT MARWICK MITCHELL

CLARK WHITEHILL

DEARDON FARROW

NEVILLE RUSSELL

PANNELL KERR FORSTER

STOY HAYWARD

TOUCHE ROSS

☐ Middle East   ▨ Australasia

☐ Asia   ☰ Caribbean, Bahamas and Bermuda

99

However, the dominance of the region is even greater when viewed in terms of the income earned. For example, the proportion of Arthur Andersen's world-wide net fees earned in the US alone in 1985 accounted for some 75 per cent of total earnings. Indeed, the proportion of fees earned in the US increased from 69 per cent in 1981 (see Table 4.9).

Table 4.9: Arthur Andersen: fee income earned in the United States and the rest of the world, 1981–5

	United States		Rest of the world		Total
	no.	%	no.	%	
1981	671.3	69	302.8	31	974.1
1982	808.3	72	315.3	28	1,123.6
1983	909.3	73	328.6	27	1,237.9
1984	1,027.9	74	360.0	26	1,387.9
1985	1,182.0	75	391.9	25	1,573.9

Source: International Accounting Bulletin (1986)

The North American arm of the international partnerships also typically have more employees than any other region. For example, in 1984 some 46 per cent of Price Waterhouse employees were located in North America as compared to some 23 per cent located in Europe (11.7 per cent in the UK; see Table 4.10).

Table 4.10: Price Waterhouse: world firm staff by region, 1984

Region	Total staff (thousands)	%
UK	3.1	11.7
North America	12.1	45.7
Pacific and Far East	4.1	15.5
Europe	2.7	10.2
South America	2.2	8.3
Africa, Middle East and Asia	2.3	8.7
Total	26.5	100

Source: Price Waterhouse (1984)

Similarly, some 59 per cent of all Arthur Andersen world-wide employment was located in North America, of which some 97 per cent was within the United States (see Table 4.11).

Table 4.11: Arthur Andersen: world firm staff by region, 1985

Region	Total staff (thousands)	%
UK	2.1	4.9
North America	19.7	45.6
(United States)	(19.0)	(44.0)
Pacific	4.5	10.4
Europe	4.4	10.2
South America	2.1	4.9
Africa, Middle East	6.7	15.5
Asia	3.7	8.6
Total	43.2	100.0

Source: Arthur Andersen (1985)

It is also possible to map the international distribution of partners and/or employees of major accountancy conglomerates (see Figures 4.3, 4.4 and 4.5). It is important to stress that these maps show the distribution of offices by country; in practice the majority of the partners and supporting staff operate from capital cities or major financial centres such as Frankfurt or Sydney. The location-specific effects of the kinds of international expansion noted in this paper have hardly been analysed but clearly merit further examination of the extent to which they are fostering disequilibrium in labour markets or of access to the highest quality accounting services.

4.5 CONCLUSION

The main purpose of this chapter has been to identify the causes and the broad spatial outcomes of the recent emergence of large, and increasingly multinational, accountancy conglomerates. Organisational requirements have been particularly significant together with the effects of competition and active attempts to create new markets by colonising locations not previously served. As the empirical evidence has been assembled additional research requirements have emerged and at this interim stage there are at least four themes. Firstly, much more has yet to be done on the division of labour within large accountancy firms,

Figure 4.3: Distribution of Arthur Andersen's partners and staff by office, 1985

DISTRIBUTION OF ARTHUR ANDERSEN'S
PARTNERS AND STAFF BY OFFICE, 1985

Figure 4.4: Deloitte, Haskins and Sells International: world distribution of offices and number of partners, 1986

DELOITTE, HASKINS AND SELLS INTERNATIONAL
WORLD DISTRIBUTION OF OFFICES AND NUMBER OF PARTNERS, 1986

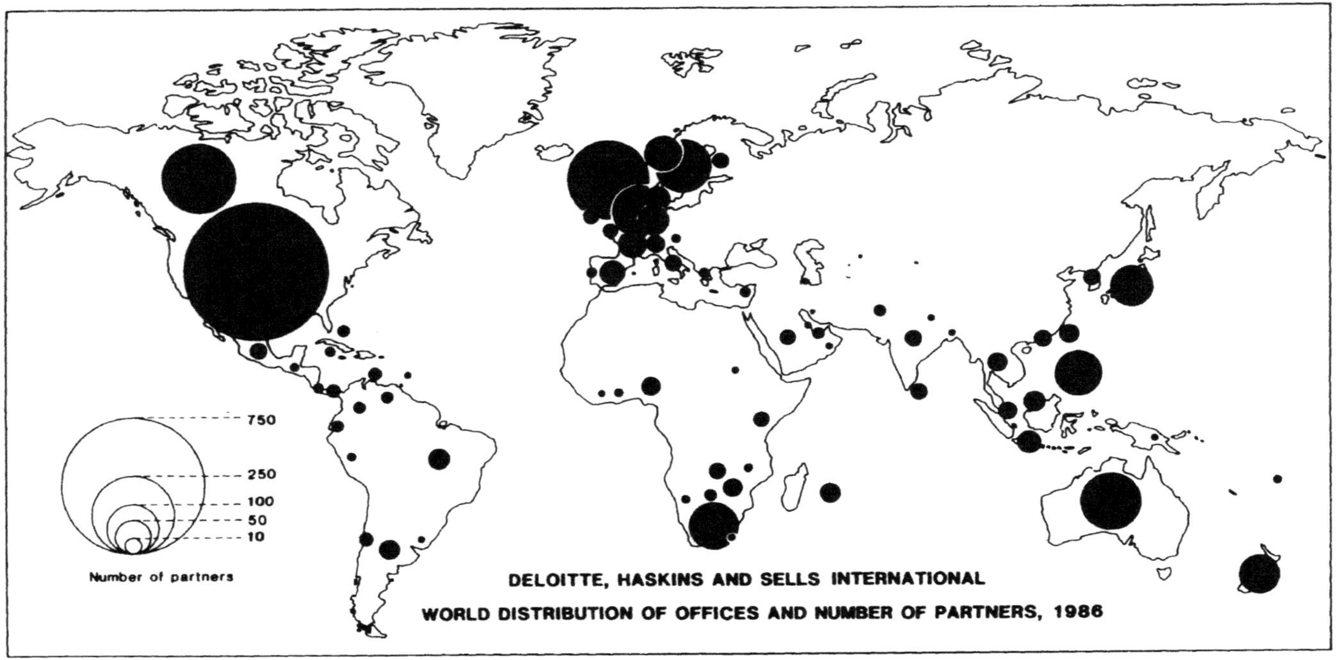

Figure 4.5: Price Waterhouse: world distribution of offices and number of partners, 1985

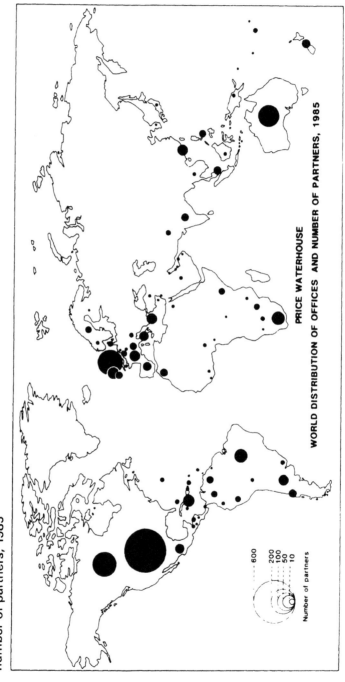

PRICE WATERHOUSE

WORLD DISTRIBUTION OF OFFICES AND NUMBER OF PARTNERS, 1985

600
200
100
50
10

Number of partners

both nationally and internationally. Topics needing to be addressed include: the gender division of labour; the skill division of labour (paying particular attention to the effects of changing technology on the ratio of professional to clerical staff); and so on. Secondly, more research is needed on the importance of individual offices, nationally and internationally. Through the number of staff, referral of work, partner status, degree of specialisation and other indicators it should be possible to assemble an absolute picture of the importance of a particular office within the organisational hierarchy for the spatial division of labour within the service industries. It is hoped to pursue this theme further. Thirdly, more consideration needs to be given to the links between accountancy firms, their different offices and particular segments of British and international industry (see for example Table 4.12).

Table 4.12: Audit appointments by industry 1983, leading 20 UK accounting firms 1985

Firm	Industrial sector[a]										
	0	1	2	3	4	5	6	7	8	9	Total
Peat Marwick Mitchell	1	10	14	14	33	9	20	0	62	20	183
Deloitte Haskins & Sells	0	6	10	23	23	6	16	3	80	29	196
Price Waterhouse	0	8	15	18	30	4	12	3	58	28	176
Ernst & Whinney	0	7	11	17	24	2	9	3	38	14	125
Arthur Young	0	5	7	8	15	3	10	3	53	7	111
Coopers & Lybrand	0	0	9	21	15	1	5	4	31	24	110
Thomson McLintock	0	9	4	7	8	3	10	2	35	11	89
Touche Ross	0	2	5	15	11	4	11	4	29	7	88
Binder Hamlyn	0	0	6	10	10	0	5	1	24	5	61
Spicer & Pegler	0	1	2	8	12	6	4	0	21	1	55
Thornton Baker	0	1	9	5	14	0	9	2	10	4	54
Arthur Andersen	0	3	3	14	3	3	4	1	6	6	43
Pannell Kerr Forster	0	1	5	5	8	2	2	0	9	0	32
Deardon Farrow	0	4	4	2	7	1	1	1	8	1	29
Stoy Hayward	0	0	0	0	7	0	2	0	6	3	18
Clark Whitehill	0	1	2	3	1	2	1	0	3	1	14
Hodgson (Harris) Impey	0	0	1	4	3	1	2	0	0	0	11
Neville Russell	–	–	–	–	–	–	–	–	–	4	4
Robson Rhodes	0	0	2	6	3	2	1	0	2	1	17
Moore Stephens	0	0	0	2	0	1	1	1	3	0	8

Notes: (a) Key to industrial sector: (0) agriculture, forestry and fishing; (1) energy and water supplies; (2) extraction of mineral ores (non-fuel)/ metal and chemical manufacture; (3) metal goods, engineering and vehicles industries; (4) other manufacturing industries; (5) construction;

(6) distribution, hotels and catering, repairs; (7) transport and
communications; (8) banking, finance and other business services; (9)
other services; N.B. includes an unspecified number of audits of national
industries that are also included in the appropriate industry column.
Source: Bohdanowicz (1984)

Finally, more attention needs to be given to the local socio-
economic effects of big accounting firms. These may have quite
important local employment multiplier effects, for example (1)
through their ability to generate local business (e.g. demand for
supplies, for printing, for equipment servicing; (2) through their
own direct local employment; and (3) through the salaries of
operators and staff spent in particular locations (which provide
retail buying power, including effects on the housing market).
In addition, the partners of these firms tend to be 'joiners' in
local communities, partly as a means of securing business, so
they have social effects disproportionate to their numbers. The
growth of the 'service class' is linked with the growth of
organisations like large accounting firms.

NOTES

1. The research reported in this chapter has been made possible by
a grant from the Economic and Social Research Council (grant no.
D0023 2194).
2. Klynveld Main Goerdler has now merged with Peat Marwick
Mitchell, and become part of the Big Eight.

5

Multinational News Agencies[1]

Oliver Boyd-Barrett

5.1 INTRODUCTION

The primary function of news agencies or 'wire services' is to report 'the news'. In this they are similar to other news media. But the news agencies traditionally are 'wholesale media' in the sense that typically they do not supply news reports directly to the public, but to press, broadcast and cable media which then 'package' agency news for 'retail' purposes. The nature of the 'packaging' will vary according to the news values, priorities, and the alternative news sources available to the different 'retail' media. The news agencies therefore tend not to figure so prominently in the public eye as do the 'retail' media which to varying degrees feed off the agencies. A new category of 'retail' client is the commercial data-base, several of which now carry news-agency files, although some agencies may require that such files should be at least 24 hours old in order to protect their usefulness to 'retail' news media. In many countries, the services of the major transnational news agencies are distributed indirectly to 'retail' media by national news agencies. The agencies also serve non-media clients, of which the most significant are the banks, brokerage houses and other financial institutions who subscribe to general, economic, financial and commodity news services. Such non-media clients account for over 90 per cent of the revenue accruing to Reuters each year, but for substantially less in the case of the other major agencies.

5.2 THE IMPORTANCE OF NEWS AGENCIES

At the time of writing the major agencies of the world are

commonly considered to be Agence France Presse (AFP), Associated Press (AP), Reuters, Telegrafnoye Agentstvo Sovietskovo (TASS) and United Press International (UPI). This chapter primarily concerns the 'Big Four' western agencies: AFP, AP, Reuters and UPI. But it also relates to important issues concerning national and regional agencies. At the time of writing UPI was continuing to fight a severe financial crisis. Of the four major agencies, Reuters is the largest with an annual income in 1984 of £313 million and profits of £74 million. AP's gross income in 1984 was $200 million (approximately £166 million). The revenue base of the other two agencies was considerably smaller: AFP's 1984 turnover was 630 million francs (approx £60 million), UPI's 1983 income was $93 million (approximately £58 million).

AFP is a publically-owned French agency. AP is a cooperative, registered in New York and owned (in 1983) by approximately 80 per cent of all US daily newspapers. Reuters is a limited liability company quoted on the Stock Exchange (since June 1984), but a majority of whose voting shares are controlled by member newspapers of the Newspaper Publishers' Association and the Press Association of Great Britain and Ireland. Up until June 1982, UPI was owned privately by the North American newspaper group, E.W. Scripps Co. In that month it was sold for a nominal fee to two Tennessee media entrepreneurs who attempted unsuccessfully to reverse the company's long economic decline, until March 1985 when the agency's creditors pressed for a reorganisation of the company which gave majority power to the agency's management, employees and creditors. AP and UPI derive most of their income from news-media members or clients, Reuters earns most of its income from non-media financial institutions, while AFP is dependent on the French government for 60 per cent of subscription revenue. Geographically the single most important source of revenue for AP and UPI is the United States, for Reuters it is Western Europe and for API it is France. Revenue from Third World countries represents a very small percentage of income in all cases.

For many decades these agencies have been by far the most significant gatherers and suppliers of 'wholesale' international news around the world, both in terms of the scope of their news gathering and distribution and in terms of the resources they deploy for these undertakings. This statement may puzzle readers based in countries where the 'retail' visibility of the major agencies is low (e.g. where there are relatively few attributions of stories to agency sources) and who may think that international sales of leading newspapers would constitute an equivalent source of news. In 1983, for instance, the Associated Press report reached news media in 115 nations, and AP maintained 81 bureaux in 65 countries outside the US, and 132 bureaux within the US. In that year Reuters media news services were distributed in 158 countries, its news and information services for business subscribers went to 112 countries, and the agency maintained reporting bureaux in 93 cities (rising to 103 by 1985), including 10 in the US. In 1985 Reuters employed 658 full-time journalists, of whom I estimate a total of 420–70 were based outside of the UK. In 1983 AP employed 1,101 domestic US news and photo staffers and 430 foreign news staff.

These figures may not seem very great when set against the magnitude of the task of world news coverage, but they are considerably greater than the foreign reporting staffs fielded by other news media. The BBC team of news correspondents in 1983, for example, amounted to only 24, together with a team of monitors working from Caversham who monitor international radio broadcasts as well as the transmissions of some foreign news agencies. Of the national newspaper press in the UK, the *Financial Times* maintains the largest team of foreign news correspondents, but in 1985 the *FT* fielded only eight journalists in North America against Reuters' 78. Some of the 'supplemental' news agencies in the US, run by leading newspapers or newspaper groups to help defray the costs of their own newsgathering have increased in size over recent years. One of the largest of these is the *Los Angeles Times–Washington Post* (LAT-WP) news service. In 1983, this service drew on a total number of 21 foreign bureaux (many of them one-man operations) maintained by its member newspapers — high, but a long way short of AP's 81. LAT-WP services that year reached 600 clients in 56 countries (transmitted via the global communications network of the West German national news agency, Deutsche Presse Agentiv (DPA)), again high, but a fair way short of AP's (1982) 10,000 non-US 'outlets' in 115 countries, 1,325 daily newspaper members and 5,700 broadcast members in the US. (However an extension of LAT-WP distribution through DPA's communication network in 1985 took this service to a total of 110 countries, signifying potential future growth of the leading supplemental services on world markets.) AP's annual report

109

for 1983 claims that AP's news report reached an average of 55 per cent of the print and broadcast media in 43 major countries around the world, and AP photos reached 54 per cent.

The elite news media of many developed countries do field teams of foreign correspondents, therefore, but none of these are equivalent in the size of their operations to the major agencies. Furthermore, the correspondents of 'retail' media tend to be concentrated in the major capitals of the western world and the major geo-political regional centres of the Third World (Boyd-Barrett, 1976, pp. 627–37; 1977, pp. 21–3). The overall pattern of the agencies' resource distribution is similarly weighted in favour of the developed world, but the agencies are much more likely to have full-time representation in countries where elite 'retail' media have only stringer representation, and to have regular stringers (or news-exchange agreements with national news agencies) in countries where 'retail' media have no representation at all. 'Retail' news media typically do not see themselves as being in competition with the major agencies. Rather they look to the major agencies to provide a basic news report of any given country and then to concentrate their efforts on more analytical, in-depth and interpretive coverage. Whereas the staff of any one 'retail' medium work only to the deadlines of their employing newspaper or broadcast station, the major agencies attempt to meet the deadlines of morning and evening newspapers and broadcasters in all the time zones of the world. The staff of a particular newspaper or broadcaster are writing only for, and will transmit only to that organisation. Their choice of stories will reflect its editorial policies and the perceived interests of its local audience. The major agencies on the other hand are writing for clients across the world, and transmitting simultaneously and at high speed to thousands of clients.

Various studies of the content of press, broadcast, and national news-agency media around the world have shown that the multinational agencies account for a substantial proportion of all 'international' news items (i.e. items of news originating outside the country of any given news medium). Figures in the range of 50–90 per cent are not uncommon (Boyd-Barrett, 1980a, pp. 15–19; 1985, pp. 36–40). But even where the proportion appears to be substantially less there is often reason to think that reports are simply not being attributed to the agencies, perhaps because stories from two or more agencies customarily are fused into composite rewrites prepared by a medium's own correspondents.

These comments apply to the role of the major agencies as suppliers of 'international' news. But AP and UPI are extremely important inside the US as reporters and suppliers of US national, state, and local city news for US news media. The US media market is still their major source of revenue. Agence France Presse is the major national news agency in France, and earns the bulk of its revenue from French state and media clients. Reuters is not a national news agency, but the Press Association, which is the national news agency of the UK, holds a substantial block of voting shares in Reuters, and the two organisations share premises on Fleet Street. In certain countries outside their own 'home' markets, the agencies also act as 'national' news agencies: for example, in France and Germany, AP and Reuters cover national news for French and German media; Reuters covers major US news for US media. However, where the agencies cover national news outside their own home markets, for sale within the country in which that news has been reported, they are generally not regarded as primary news sources for national news.

The major agencies do not produce only print news. Other services in which they are engaged include news photos, audio reports for broadcast and television subscribers, text and graphics reports for cable television networks. Through its part-ownership of Visnews, the world's largest television news agency, Reuters is also involved in television news-film. The sale of agency services to the business community, to government departments of state, overseas embassies, defence and intelligence establishments is a testament to their importance as factors in economic and political decision-making. Although these clients will have other sources of information, few alternative sources are as comprehensive or as fast. Moreover the public character of agency services can itself be a benefit: even among allied countries, for example, the passage of intelligence reports from one country to another is subject to delays while necessary clearance is sought through bureaucratic and diplomatic channels. Sometimes the agencies have themselves altered the character of decision-making procedures, as happened with the Reuters money market monitor service, which provided a form of 'clearing house' which previously did not exist. Other ventures in which the agencies are involved include the development and sale of communications hardware and software related to the distribution and handling of information services, the leasing out of their own extensive communications facilities to media and non-media clients, and consultancy and training services for new national news agencies.

5.3 THE GLOBAL NEWS 'SYSTEM'

Important as the multinational agencies undoubtedly are, they are big fish in a large pool, swimming with a great many other smaller fish. Reference has already been made to the national news agencies. Most countries today have a national news agency. The majority of these have no foreign correspondents of their own, some have a small number of correspondents in neighbouring countries and/or in one or two major capitals, and a few have a relatively substantial network of correspondents. In the majority of cases, however, the foreign coverage of such agencies is oriented to news of direct relevance to their national interests. One or two of the largest national news agencies, such as DPA of West Germany and Kyodo of Japan do provide some-what broader services for international clientele. DPA, for example, has been described as the fifth largest wire service by the general manager of the *Los Angeles Times/Washington Post* news service, which distributes DPA to its clients in North America (IPTC News, (1985)). Other suppliers of news for international consumption include various cooperatives of different clusters of national news agencies (e.g. PANA), the major broadcast monitoring services (e.g. the BBC), specialist news and feature services (e.g. Depth News, Gemini), 'supple-mental' news agencies (e.g. LAT-WP, *New York Times* news service (NYTNS)), international editions of prominent national news media (e.g. *Wall Street Journal*, *Financial Times*, *Time* and *Newsweek*).

The activities of these different organisations are interlinked in various patterns of collaboration and competition. Over many years, for example, it has been customary for national news agencies to establish exchange relations with certain other national agencies so that each receives a version of the news service which the other has to offer, with appropriate arrange-ments for covering the necessary communications cost. The principle of news exchange is itself very well established in the news agency business. Up until the inter-war years, the major European agencies and Associated Press operated a news cartel involving the mutual exchange of news, together with agreements that allocated to each agency exclusive rights of service distribution in particular countries. This arrangement controlled the costs of news-gathering, and guaranteed assured sources of revenue. The principle of exchange still informs the relations between major agencies and national agencies, where each subscribes to the service of the other, although the national agencies must still pay substantial additional cash sums. A national agency typically will subscribe to more than one of the major agencies and will have exchange agreements with many other national agencies. In many countries the major agencies are required by law to distribute their news through the national agencies rather than directly to 'retail' news media. The multinationals generally no longer take one another's services; however AFP subscribes to AP's domestic US service, for cash payment plus the provision of AFP's domestic service to AP.

The principle of news exchange also underlies the development over the past ten years of a generation of regional or continental agencies, involving the systematic exchange, collation and distribution of services from many different national agencies of a geo-political region: e.g. the Non-Aligned News Agencies Pool, the Pan-African News Agency, the Asian News Exchange (ANEX), Action by National Information Systems (ASIN, a Latin American and Caribbean news exchange pool). The purpose of these, in the medium term at least, is to supplement the services of the major agencies, but there is sometimes the hope that some day the Third World countries might mount a credible substitute for the major agencies. In the meantime, member agencies of these cooperatives continue to subscribe to the major agencies and in some cases benefit from communications and consultancy services which these have to offer.

5.4 KEY FEATURES OF THE MULTINATIONAL WESTERN NEWS AGENCIES

The earliest systems of international news gathering and distribution were rooted either in the courts of nobility (e.g. the courts of various princelings in Central Europe) or in the chambers of commerce and banking (e.g. House of Fugger, Lloyds of London, and Rothschilds in Frankfurt) or both. In this respect therefore they had important affinities with many of those news agencies of today which depend primarily on one or both of these two sources – government and business – for patronage and revenue. The earliest agencies also operated the principle of news exchange between different centres of news, a vigorous principle which as we have seen still informs a great deal of today's international news activity, both because it is economical and because politically it is inevitable wherever independent access to certain news centres is restricted or prohibited. The growing development of newspapers, themselves very often the off-shoots of government or business interests, provided a third important element in the foundation of a system of international news provision.

The development of the largest western news agencies may be summarised by reference to the following salient features.

5.4.1 Longevity

Each of the existing multinational agencies can claim long heritage. AFP is direct successor to Havas, which was founded in 1835. The birth of Associated Press can be established as 1848, and that of Reuters as 1851. UPI started life as United Press Associations in 1907, and had indirect links with an older organisation known as United Press, which was instituted in 1882.

5.4.2 Developed-world orientation

From their early days the headquarters of the major European agencies were based in the capital cities of the greatest imperial powers, centres which afforded them relatively cheap and convenient access to communications, news-sources and clients. All the major agencies developed within the world's most industrially-advanced nations and they formed an essential part of the structure of industrial capitalism. Regulation of news-gathering and distribution in these countries was relatively liberal, and the development of news media for mass markets was pronounced. More recently, this profound affiliation with the Western developed countries has rendered the multinationals vulnerable to criticisms from developing countries that their interests are not adequately represented in the agencies services. The extent to which such criticism is justified is still a matter for debate. But it is evident that many developing countries do depend very largely on essentially foreign organisations to handle news of their affairs for foreign consumption and to provide news of the world for domestic consumption. The close affiliation with the wealthier countries does mean, in effect, that the cost of Third World news reporting and distribution is in large measure 'subsidised' by income from Western markets. Because income from the Third World represents a small fraction of the agencies total income, developing countries may feel they have relatively little bargaining power with which to exert pressure for changes in editorial policy.

5.4.3 Large domestic markets

The domestic markets of the major agencies have always represented considerable wealth in media terms and have remained by far the most important sources of income for the American and French agencies, accounting for 75 per cent or more of total revenues in each case over many years. This dominance of the domestic market reflects in part the status of each of these organisations as national agencies in their respective countries. In the case of Reuters (which does not operate as a national agency for the UK), with its huge non-media market for economic news services, overseas income has grown to over 80 per cent of its total revenue. 50 per cent of this income in 1983 came from Western Europe (of which 32 per' cent derived from the UK), 26 per cent from Asia, Australia and New Zealand, and 17 per cent from Reuters North America. The two single most important national sources of revenue for Reuters are the UK and the US each accounting for about 16 per cent of total revenue.

There are ties other than those based on revenue which underwrite the importance of domestic markets for the multi-national agencies. Domestic clients or members generally enjoy a special relationship with their respective agencies. Full membership of the AP, for example, is restricted to US daily newspapers, and US newspaper and broadcast members enjoy a more active role in the direction and management of the agency than do foreign clients. At the time of writing UPI was still as it had always been: an American-owned agency. AFP is a public French body. Up to June 1984, over 80 per cent of the shares in Reuters were owned by the national and provincial daily newspaper press of Great Britain and Ireland. Since the 1984 flotation there are two classes of shares in Reuters. 'A' shares, representing 25 per cent of the equity, continue to be held by the pre-1984 owners. These shares entitle their holders to four votes per share on most matters, giving them an overall 58 per cent control of the votes, whereas 'B' shares have only one vote per share. The sale of 'A' shares is restricted. Both the NPA and PA vote their 'A' shares *en bloc* as decided by a majority of each. While Reuters is a good deal more international than it was, UK newspaper interests continue to enjoy a strong ownership position.

Each of the agencies has been characterised by this curious role of domestic 'owner-clients', i.e. owners who were also important sources of subscription revenue. In the case of AP in the US the cooperative non-profit structure has helped to ensure continuing willingness on the part of members over the years to meet higher subventions as required in order to sustain the service at a time of escalating capital investment. The same is true, by and large, of government and media clients of AFP in France. From its foundation in 1907 to 1982, UPI was owned by E.W. Scripps Co., one of the largest US newspaper groups. Under E.W. Scripps the UPI management also developed an advisory structure to represent the interest of US newspaper and broadcast clients (later extended to additional advisory bodies for overseas areas).

In the US and in France, the 'owner-clients' expected the agencies to be domestic first and international second. This helped secure the domestic markets as the most important sources of revenue for the agencies. The involvement of 'owner-clients' in the control and pricing structure also served to reduce the domestic price of services compared with what they might have been had the agencies sought to maximise profits. This also helped deter would-be competitors based in other parts of the world from encroaching on to the domestic markets of the major agencies. Such competitors would have found it extremely difficult in any case to compete with the major agencies on these agencies' home ground, in the task not only of securing favoured relations with news clients, but also with news sources.

In the more competitive conditions operating outside their

domestic markets, revenue was less secure, and it proved difficult to charge truly economic rates to overseas clients. The US agencies tended to regard overseas sales as a way of reducing the costs of foreign news-gathering rather than as a way of making profits. UPI's interest in developing an international news service was motivated originally by AP's membership of the 'news cartel' up to 1934 whereby AP received much of its foreign news from Reuters, Havas of France and Continental of Germany. It was more important for UPI than for AP to establish a network of independent correspondents and to help cover the expense by expanding overseas sales. But the primary driving force was to compete with AP on the domestic market (where UPI was always in second place) by proclaiming as a virtue its independence of other major news agencies in securing foreign news. AP fought back by increasing its own foreign staff, abandoning the news cartel and competing directly with UPI. Even so, neither American agency did much before the Second World War to penetrate those parts of the world which had come to be regarded as Reuters or AFP territory, as in the colonies of Great Britain and France in Africa and Asia. Even today, for example, the European agencies are stronger in Africa than the Americans, while the US agencies are strongest in Latin America. For AFP the sustaining of an operation of foreign news-gathering and news-distribution owed as much to the interest of government clients in promoting the international image of France, as it did to the French daily news media, some of whom would have been content with just a national news agency and stable subscription rates. The owners of Reuters were antithetical to the idea of direct government involvement in Reuters, but without a domestic revenue base as large as that of AP or UPI, the agency's resources were greatly strained for the early post-war period, during which time Reuters depended on other news suppliers for such important regions of the world as the Middle East and South-east Asia.

5.4.4 Non-government character

All four major agencies originated as non-government organisations and to varying degrees they have maintained this character to the present day. In the inter-war years of the present century, Reuters cultivated a relatively close relationship with

British imperial and colonial governments although it is disputed whether the benefits which Reuters enjoyed from these ties amounted to a 'subsidy', hidden or otherwise. There were government subsidies during the two World Wars, and for some years after the Second World War Reuters contracted to distribute its news services in the Middle East through the Arab News Agency (ANA), an organisation which was a beneficiary of British government funds and which also provided a Middle-Eastern news service to Reuters. The payment to Reuters by ANA may have been crucial to the financial stability of the agency in the period preceding the maturation of the financial news services (Lawrenson and Barber 1985, pp. 99–101).

From early in its history, AFP's predecessor, Havas, received a government subvention to help meet the cost of overseas news-gathering. In the late 1930s the French Foreign Office exercised substantial influence in its affairs. The successor, AFP, is heavily dependent on government assistance, in the form of service subscriptions by central and local government departments, which account for 60 per cent of annual revenue. AFP also benefits from government loans and endowments to meet deficits and pay for capital improvements. The tariffs for state clients are fixed in line with press rates, but the number of state clients is determined by an annual agreement between agency and government. The government also has a general power to block price increases. The agency is managed by a *Conseil d'Administration*, on which representatives of press media clients and journalists enjoy numerical superiority over representatives from French departments of state and broadcast media.

In the case of the American agencies there is no available evidence to suggest that at any time there has been quite the same degree of close cooperation between government and agencies as has been found for certain periods in the case of the European agencies, although, from time to time, particular circumstances have provoked questions as to whether the agencies were or were not compliant with government pressures and interests. US agency coverage during the two World Wars and the Korean war seems to have been more compliant in this respect than it was during, say, the Vietnam war. (See Boyd-Barrett 1976, pp. 833–55; 1985 pp. 145–60.) Overall, the relative independence of the 'Big Four' agencies compares very favourably with the majority of national news agencies around the world.

5.4.5 Contractual relationships

In their relationships with clients, the multinational agencies almost universally operate on a contractual basis, involving the exchange of their services for money, possibly supplemented (as in the case of relations with many national news agencies) by access to the news services of client organisations for the purpose of redistributing a selection of their news. The cash relationship places the multinationals in a different category from government-backed or other agencies which supply news services free of charge: it encourages clients to take a more serious interest in the quality of the service which they are paying to receive, and requires the major agencies to have regard for the criticisms of their clients – not the same thing, of course, as having to accept those criticisms as well-founded, or as criticisms they are in a position to respond to.

5.4.6 Client media participation

Scope for clients to participate in the formulation of policy and to comment on the adequacy of agency services comes about most visibly through the media-based character of the ownership and management structure of each of the agencies: client or member interests are represented at the top-most levels of the agencies' organisational structures. Formal consultative machineries are most well developed in the case of the American agencies: in particular through AP's Associated Press Managing Editors' Association which has both national and state-wide committees and at whose annual conference a number of committees report back on aspects of AP performance during the course of the year. Until recently this formal consultative structure was confined to the US, but recent initiatives have been taken to establish nation-wide consultative machineries in some European countries. UPI holds an annual conference for its client editors, and has also established a national advisory board for the US, and advisory boards in Europe and Latin America. But there was some division of opinion in the agency about the usefulness of these boards, and the vice-president for the Asian region resisted the introduction of an Asian advisory board. The current financial difficulties of the agency do not augur well for the further development of consultative structures outside the US. In general it is arguable whether the scope for client consultation and participation in the operation and news coverage of the major agencies has been explored as fully as it might have been in non-domestic media markets, especially in the developing world. This does not mean that client needs in developing countries are not taken account of. For example it is a notable feature of all major agency wires that approximately half the number of stories on any given wire (and each agency has different wires for different parts of the world) are about or may be said to have particular relevance to the region of the world to which that wire is directed (Boyd-Barrett 1980a pp. 60–7).

5.4.7 Product similarity

The agencies focus, above all, on 'spot news', the latest developments. This is still by far the most important emphasis for Reuters, although the scope for data manipulation on Reuters Monitor services greatly enhances the client's own analysis capability. The US and French agencies have increased their attention over recent years to feature articles, analysis, 'enterprise' reporting, 'trend' reporting (involving collation and review of reports from many different centres), and various original ideas for the 'packaging' and display of news to take account of the growing feature orientation of many newspapers, itself a reaction to the competition of broadcast media and a response to growing public interest in social, economic and political 'trends'. Although the number of specialist reporters in agency circles has grown for such news coverage as economics, sports, politics and consumer affairs, it would be unusual for more than 20 per cent of the effort or output of a given bureau to be devoted to anything other than spot-news reporting.

Each of the four Western-based news agencies is committed formally to the provision of a news service which is accurate, objective, impartial and world-wide. For example, aims of this kind form part of the constitutional status of both AFP and AP, and at Reuters they are underwritten by a special trust. General studies of agency news content tend to exonerate the agencies from deliberate bias. Stevenson and Cole (1980) for example analysed wires from each of the agencies for their 'tone': that is, whether each specific country mentioned was presented favourably, negatively, or in a neutral or mixed (balanced) manner. Ninety per cent or more of the news of each wire service was neutral or mixed. This would seem to have to do with the question of explicit bias. But a different sort of bias may come about as a result of news values: that is, agencies may tend to provide an unfavourable image of certain countries because, given the application of western news values, some countries seem to offer more stories of an 'unfavourable' character than others. This is confirmed by Rimmer (1981) who reports that Third World regions have a consistently 'unfavourable' balance of stories, i.e. of stories which focus on conflict, disorganisation, instability, weakness, etc. Similar observations have been made in other studies. Stevenson and Cole (1980) observe that where such stories occur in the developed world they also get reported, the implication being that certain kinds of story simply occur less often in the developing than in the developed world.

Claims to impartiality or objectivity cannot override objections that the agencies are necessarily selective in what they report. There is clear evidence that the agencies tend to concentrate on certain categories of news in preference to others (Boyd-Barrett 1980a pp. 103–11). Half to three-quarters of the news content in most studies of the agencies' general news wires are accounted for by stories of government affairs, international relations, defence, war and economics. News of such issues as technology, education, culture, race, religion, and labour relations typically ranks low as a percentage of total volume. Coverage of so-called 'development' news from the Third World also ranks low. The geography of world news on any given wire tends to give priority to news originating from the region to which that wire is directed, followed by news of the US and Western Europe. News of Third World regions (other than the Third World region to which a given wire is directed) tends to rank fairly low, with the exception of crisis spots which have implications for the relations between the super-powers. News of the Soviet bloc tends to be proportionately slight. Selectivity is also implied in the distribution of the agencies' human resources, with the largest numbers of correspondents clustered in the US and Western Europe and in major regional centres of the other world regions such as Hong Kong or Buenos Aires. Within news reports themselves the predominant news sources are official government and other authoritative sources, and the origins of news are more likely to be urban than rural.

5.4.8 Competitive relationships

Up to the 1930s, three of the 'Big Four' agencies, in alliance with Wolff's agency, Continental, in Germany and various other national agencies operated a 'news cartel'. This involved the exchange of news between members of the cartel on an exclusive basis and agreements not to compete in each other's domestic and reserved markets. Since the break-up of the cartel the general climate of agency operations has become progressively more competitive. This is not to say that competition is equally intense in all areas. Up to the early 1980s, for example, AP and UPI were much stronger sources of general news for media clients than Reuters or AFP in Latin American markets while AFP and Reuters were much stronger in the Middle East, Africa and parts of Asia. The intensity of competition has further sharpened in the past ten years or so: the major agencies compete more fiercely among themselves; they find themselves increasingly in competition with other media and non-media organisations in the developed world; and in the Third World there has emerged a range of new kinds of agency service based largely on existing national news agencies.

Competition between the major agencies was intensified in the early 1970s when Reuters decided against renewing its exchange arrangements with Associated Press and with Dow Jones, and from then set about covering the US with its own correspondents, carrying its own US news on its North American wires and establishing the sale of commodity and financial news services to US financial institutions. In retaliation, AP and Dow Jones joined together to sell economic and financial news services outside the US in competition with Reuters. More recently they have joined up with other US suppliers of stock and finance news, Telerate and Quotron. There are plans for a new financial-information service to be launched by Telerate, IBM and Merrill Lynch. But at the time of writing, Reuters was still the leading supplier of economic, financial and commodity news outside of the US. One of its main advantages has been its ability to offer the full world-wide range of such services in combination together with sophisticated purpose-designed hardware and software. Reuters' success in the sale of economic news to financial institutions has provided a wealth of funds for the further strengthening of its reporting resources for both economic and general news. This has had implications for the viability of other major agencies.

In 1983 Reuters purchased the overseas news-photo service of the ailing UPI and set itself up for the first time as a news-photo agency. It had already laid a very sophisticated global communications network for the economic services, more than paid for by the revenue which these generated. On the back of surplus communications capacity it was able then to launch new ventures which otherwise would not have been profitable. The acquisition of UPI's non-US photo network (and Reuters also has an exchange arrangement with UPI which entitles it to the international distribution of UPI's US photos) places Reuters in a stronger position to compete with AP for media clients both within the US and world-wide. UPI's sale of photos in Latin America, for example, was thought to be one reason why UPI's sales of general news were also strong in that part of the world, and the venture was operationally profitable even though UPI would have had difficulty in raising the necessary capital for modernisation. During 1984 and 1985 there were indications that Reuters was becoming more interested in establishing itself as a major supplier to the US media market when it entered negotiations with UPI in the spring of 1985 with a view to possible purchase of that agency. If Reuters was to penetrate even the market of small to medium circulation newspapers in the US, the Reuters name would become much more familiar across the continent as a credible source of world-wide news, and news sources (financial and others) would be more inclined to supply to Reuters than to any US media organisation. A firm basis would have been laid for further penetration of the more lucrative financial news markets.

The involvement of companies like Telerate, Quotron, and Merrill Lynch in the competition between the multinational agencies also indicates the extent to which these major agencies increasingly find themselves in competition with non-media as well as media organisations. In the market for general news the multinationals have found they have had to contend with competition from the news services of supplementary agencies like those of the *Los Angeles Times-Washington Post* and *New York Times*. The rising sales of these services has been a major factor in the decline of UPI, related to the rapid decline in the number of US cities with more than one morning or afternoon paper. When there had been at least two competing papers in each city, generally one paper would subscribe to AP and the other to UPI. Sometimes both papers would take both services. But today's monopoly newspapers, outside the largest metropolitan centres, are more inclined to subscribe to the leading US agency, AP, and then to one or more supplemental agencies, rather than to two similar major news agencies. AP provides the basic routine coverage of the world, while the supplemental agency gives in-depth reporting of the key news issues. UPI became more dependent on the less lucrative broadcast media market.

Reference has been made to the growth in the Third World of new regional agencies on the basis of exchange agreements between national agencies, many of which are themselves only recent creations. This generation of new agencies, some supported by Unesco, has been stunted from birth by a combination of difficulties. There is a general shortage of financial and suitable trained human resources. Resources have been insufficient in some cases even to mount a regional alternative to the regional news provision of the 'Big Four' services. Regional cooperatives of agencies that are mostly government-controlled cannot overcome easily the deep hostilities or suspicions that often exist between nations in any given region. Government-controlled agencies invariably are very sensitive about the kinds of news they will release for international consumption. The news that is released is very often poorly selected and edited from the point of view of its likely interest and intelligibility for international consumption. There is a tendency to emphasise 'protocol' news, e.g. news of the arrival and departure of foreign dignitaries, etc., which have little real substance for international clientele. Telecommunications are sometimes poor and usually expensive, and together with the shortage of trained staff help account for the inability of many of these newer agencies to compete in speed with the major agencies, or even to follow up their spot news with suitable analysis and backgrounding. The 'new world information order' rhetoric which has inspired the formation of some of these initiatives is less evident in practice than might have been anticipated. Dare's (1983) study of the Nigerian News Agency found that NNA relied on AP, Reuters and AFP for the bulk of its foreign news. Its gatekeeping was limited to selecting a number of foreign stories from the files of these agencies for inclusion in its bulletins. Not much attention appeared to be given to the type of story selected or its content. There was no bias in favour of stories about development. News stories from Third World countries were more numerous than those from developed countries, but large areas of the world such as China, the Soviet Union, Latin America and Eastern Europe largely went unreported.

5.4.9 Technological innovation

The major agencies have each developed extensive and complex systems of communication for news-gathering and news-dissemination appropriate to their world-wide activities and large numbers of clients. They have been innovators in adapting existing communications technologies to their own task requirements. Increasingly they have become innovators in the design, production and sale of new communications technology. Their large size affords them economies of scale enjoyed by few other news organisations. The agencies were among the first news organisations to use computerised message-switching centres, video-display units, satellite news distribution and electronic picture-editing. Reuters, which in 1984 spent £12 million on research, has developed much of its own hardware and software, and produces its own terminals. This kind of communications expertise can be of great value to clients, who may be offered access to agency communication facilities and consultancy services. Technological developments allow the agencies to transmit, process and distribute news at faster speeds, in greater volume, and with higher reliability than in previous periods. Staff are deployed more cost-effectively, and as organisations the agencies have grown much more capital-intensive than they were. But the cost of establishing and then periodically updating and replacing highly sophisticated computer systems is of a scale unknown in earlier periods, and requires the agencies to find new ways of raising money. This is one factor behind the public flotation of Reuters, whose owners argued that Reuters would no longer be able to find the necessary sums from its own record profit levels, but would have to offer equity. Of course, the interest of 'owner-clients' in directing some of the agency's new found wealth into their own organisations' pockets was the main driving force. But Associated Press has also experienced similar cost pressures, so that in 1983 it was obliged to add a permanent new element to the annual subvention to cover the cost of capital investment. AP's services to domestic media in the US, while they represent its largest source of revenue are now run at a loss, and the leading American agency is looking increasingly to the overseas sale of general and economic news services, the leasing of space on its communications networks and other ventures, to maintain its future viability. In France, the era of high capitalisation means that AFP has had to look to the government for increasingly sizeable loans and endowments, and has spurred AFP management to investigate new revenue devices, including specialist news services. The financial weakness of UPI, however, has meant that rather than spend the necessary sums on further capitalisation of the company, the owners had to sell off some of its more promising ventures – the UNICOM commodity news service for overseas clients was sold (for £1 million) in 1983, likewise UPI's share of the news-film agency United Press International Television News (UPITN), and its overseas photo operation.

5.4.10 Diversification

The sale of general news to news media rarely has been regarded as much more than a break-even business, at best. The privileged position of owner-clients in moderating the rate of subscriptions on domestic markets, and price competition on the more open non-domestic markets has helped to maintain that position. On the other hand, competition has also been a stimulus to diversification, which has taken the form both of new services for media clients and the sale of existing or new services for non-media clients. The development of photo, broadcast and audio services or the involvement of the agencies in news-film supply are examples of the former, while the rapid growth of economic, financial and commodity services for banks, brokers and commodity dealers, etc. exemplify the latter. It is mainly through such strategies for diversification that surplus revenues in the agency business are generated, if at all, and diversification will very likely be the dominant theme for the foreseeable future.

Diversification in recent decades has confined itself mainly to the information business, whether media or non-media: information is regarded as a suitably 'neutral' activity that does not embarrass the agencies' claims to impartiality and objectivity. It remains to be seen whether there will ever be anything to compare with Baron de Reuter's involvement in the development of Persia, or his son Herbert's establishment of the ill-fated Reuters bank before the First World War.

5.5 NEWS DEPENDENCE AND THE DEVELOPING WORLD

The section 5.4 described how many developing countries, in attempting to counter the influence of western news organisations, have participated in the setting up of regional news agencies, and that the development of these as credible supplements or even alternatives to the established international news diet has been hindered by various factors. It might be argued with justification that after only a few years in operation it is still too early to pass firm judgement as to whether these ventures have been useful, let alone to compare them against the major news agencies.

Despite their apparent weaknesses the new regional agencies may already have delivered certain benefits. For example, they have improved the communications infrastructure for multilateral news exchange; they have increased the overall volume of news that is exchanged; they have added to the number of organisations around the world who can bring pressure to bear on national PTTs for lower communications rates, and in some countries rates have been reduced to ease the burden on the national news agencies; they have helped raise awareness generally of the problems involved in ensuring an adequate supply of regional news; they have helped generate a much more sophisticated dialogue between agencies and end-users about the philosophy and principles of news-gathering for developing countries; the setting up of such agencies has prompted governments to further consideration of the need for better resourcing and training for agency work.

Despite the positive benefits which may be attributed to the Third World regional news cooperatives, it has been argued that there is little room for optimism about the success of these or any other such ventures. Somarajiwa (1984) believes that under existing market conditions it is impossible for new agencies to establish themselves given the advantages enjoyed by the multinational agencies particularly with regard to first-copy costs, vertical integration, and diversification.

First-copy costs represent a very high proportion of total costs.

A new entrant to the field of international news supply needs to find very high capital costs and very high recurrent costs just to make the first copy. It is no use competing with just part of the existing multinationals coverage, because it is the world-wide comprehensiveness of their files that make their services so attractive. Even if they can draw on other sources, many client editors prefer to handle only one or two comprehensive world files for most of the time rather than deal with a scattering of specialised agencies which they then have to piece together. Because the global agencies are already in place, with most of their first-copy costs paid for by domestic subscribers among the world's most affluent media markets (affluent because of the high availability of advertising) they can sell their services to additional clients at very low prices. Incumbent agencies have a great deal of flexibility in deciding what to charge their non-domestic subscribers, and they can easily shut out new competition by selling at low prices where necessary. New Third World news agencies do not enjoy such flexibility. Their domestic clients cannot afford to pay very much, because advertising revenue is in short supply and there are relatively fewer 'retail' media in any case. Nor can they hope to secure positions in North America, Britain or France in any way comparable with the positions there of AP, UPI, Reuters or AFP, because these agencies' strength on their domestic markets is based not only on economics but also on a substantial cultural rapport established with clients over many decades and with which foreign entrants could not compete. The multinationals are also vertically integrated with their home-buyers. It is not in the interests of domestic members or clients to give too much support to external competition. Prices charged to domestic clients are lower than they would be were it not for vertical integration. A new entrant could not establish a position in such a market by charging fully economic rates.

The existence of specialised news services such as those of Reuters also helps subsidise the general news services and improves the major agencies' competitive edge against new competition. The major agencies are better able to offer packages of both general and specialised news, delivered by means of sophisticated electronic storage and retrieval systems. Most newcomers would find it difficult to mount the necessary investment in hardware, software development, telecommunications networks, etc., and would be unlikely to negotiate equivalent access to the major money, stocks and commodities markets in the developed countries for the necessary information with which to furnish a news service.

In the face of these entry barriers Somarajiwa suggests that state intervention is necessary to restructure market conditions. He wants news access to be used as a bargaining counter against the Western agencies. A major news agency wishing to maintain a news bureau in a Third World country would have to enter into an agreement to bear the expenses of a Third World news-agency bureau in a designated Western capital. Such a reciprocity agreement, he argues, would result in a freer two-way flow of news. He also suggests that in some parts of the world there should be a floor price below which the transnational agencies would not be allowed to sell their services. He further suggests that some Third World agencies should have exclusive rights to the provision of certain commodity and financial information that originates from within their own territories (Somarajiwa 1984).

The problems with this analysis lie in Somarajiwa's concentration on the difficulties faced by Third World agencies and not enough on the difficulties of the major agencies. These problems are real enough, as the condition of UPI had demonstrated for some time. To impose further heavy costs on the major agencies might threaten to reduce their number still further, thus weakening the already limited diversity of news organisations in the developed world. More likely, the agencies simply would not negotiate access, and instead would develop alternative means of covering the countries in question – providing possibly a less satisfactory news service for all countries of the world. Furthermore, Somarajiwa's proposal could do little to guarantee the quality of access to news sources within a given country, almost as important as access to the country itself. The developed Western countries currently operate a reciprocity arrangement to secure the representation of Western news media in Moscow, but this has done little or nothing to bring about more openness of political sources in the USSR.

5.6 CONCLUSION

We have seen that news agencies are important suppliers of 'spot news' of political, economic and other developments round the world. Among the many different kinds of news agency that go to make up the actual global system of news traffic, the Western-based multinational agencies have been pre-eminent in terms of their market position, the scale of their global distribution and the news-gathering resources which they deploy. These agencies depend primarily on their domestic or developed world markets for revenue, and even in these markets media clientele do not provide a guaranteed, secure base for the viability of four major news organisations. These features have implications for the extent to which the major agencies can commit resources to coverage of the information requirements of the Third World.

Taken as a group, the multinational agencies may be characterised by a cluster of descriptive variables, the combination of which accounts for their historical pre-eminence. These are: longevity; developed world orientation; high revenue dependence on and special relationships with domestic market 'owner-clients'; non-government character of operation; client media participation in their organisation and control; 'spot-news' product emphasis together with commitment to goals of accuracy, impartiality, etc.; increasingly competitive business environment; technological innovativeness; and increasing diversification of activity.

There is a good case for arguing that features to do with first-copy costs, vertical integration, and diversification at present constitute insurmountable barriers to successful new entrants to 'Big Four' class. However remedies that have been proposed which depend on the imposition of constraints on the existing operation of the news market seem to offer insufficient protection either to Third World or developed world interests in the provision of an adequate system of news traffic. On the other hand it has been demonstrated that the market can support the development of specialist news agencies which service to complement or supplement the services of the major agencies in particular ways. In both the major agencies and others there is likely to be a continuing strong interest in diversification across media and non-media markets.

NOTES

1. Except where otherwise indicated the major sources for this

chapter are Boyd-Barrett (1976; 1980a; 1985) and Boyd-Barrett and Palmer (1981). In addition, the author is grateful to the Open University for a travel grant in support of a research visit to New York and Washington, November 1984, for the purpose of interviewing news-agency personnel. Where not otherwise attributed, recent company financial data are derived from annual reports or trade publications – in particular, *Editor and Publisher* (*E+P*), and *UK Press Gazette* (*UKPG*).

6

Multinational Contracting

Peter Enderwick

6.1 INTRODUCTION

The overseas operations of contracting firms has a long history. In the colonial era British companies played an important overseas role in the provision of infrastructure such as road, rail and port facilities. US construction companies were establishing foreign operations in a number of countries by the 1920s (Wilkins 1974). The intervening period has witnessed an enormous growth in the size and sophistication of overseas contracting. In addition, international contractors are now to be found in a wide range of developed, and increasingly, developing nations.

This chapter explores the area of international contracting. It sets out the characteristics of the contracting industry and the extent and pattern of overseas operations. This is followed by an application of current theoretical perspectives on the multinational enterprise (MNE) to international contracting. Data drawing on a number of sources are offered. To obtain further insight into the operational forms and problems of overseas contractors data was obtained from a number of the largest UK-based firms. The top 20 largest contractors were approached. Ten firms indicated a willingness to complete a postal questionnaire. Four companies were either not operating overseas (two had recently withdrawn from overseas markets) or were such that overseas work constituted only a very tiny proportion of total activity. In the event nine usable replies were received. While more comprehensive coverage would have been preferred these firms are likely to represent a significant proportion of all UK-based international contracting. Thus in 1981–2 the top 20 firms obtained 91 per cent of all new contracts with the top five firms accounting for 70 per cent. Clearly, a small number of contractors account for a very large proportion of all overseas work done. While the problems of international contracting (dealings in multiple fluctuating currencies, unfamiliarity with local business practices, conditions etc.) are similar to those experienced by manufacturing multinationals, an understanding of the characteristics of the construction industry helps to illustrate the motives for international operations.

6.2 THE NATURE OF THE CONTRACTING INDUSTRY

The characteristics of the construction industry most relevant to a discussion of international contracting are its fragmentary industrial structure and vulnerability to cyclical fluctuations in output and employment.

The British construction industry had an average firm size of 13 employees in 1977 (Fleming 1980). More than three-quarters of all firms employed less than eight persons. At the other end of the spectrum firms employing 80 or more accounted for only 2 per cent of all firms but over 50 per cent of employment. Construction is one industry which has remained immune to the general trend of increasing concentration evident in much of British industry. Thus, the industrial structure of the 1960s was virtually identical to that of 1851 (Price 1980). In recent years the number of largest firms has declined. The number of firms employing 1,200 or more fell by a half from 80 to 39 between 1973 and 1981 (Hillebrandt 1984). This tendency was also observed in the Italian construction sector (Villa 1981).

A number of economic factors explain this industrial structure. The pattern of demand with a large number of small-value orders, the extensive division of labour and specialisation of skills, ease of entry, particularly into the specialist trades, minimal vertical integration and limited opportunities for the achievement of absolute cost advantages through large-scale activity are all compatible with industrial fragmentation. An interesting question is what separates the largest, and multi-national, contractors from the majority of firms. A partial explanation is to be found in the economic advantages offered by multi-locational firms of infinite duration. The fact that construction firms have an expected existence which exceeds the duration of individual projects and operate at multiple locations suggests that firms possess knowledge that is both general and durable and which is enhanced by application (Casson 1985). Since much of this knowledge resides in individuals there are incentives for the maintenance of team membership. Where output is subject to cyclical fluctuations, diversification with regard to the sources of work bestows considerable advantages.

The cyclical nature of construction results from its constituting a derived demand and the possibilities for postponing capital expenditures. Fluctuations in output are mirrored in the instability of employment. In the British construction industry output stagnated between 1975 and 1979 after marked falls in the recession of the early 1970s. A further downturn occurred after 1979. The post-1979 recessionary impact has dramatically reduced direct employment within the largest contractors. Employment figures for the top 20 UK contractors between 1977 and 1981 are shown in Table 6.1.

Table 6.1: Employment[1] of the top British contractors

	1977	1978	1979	1980	1981
Top 10 companies	128,025	125,926	126,109	121,134	108,082
Second 10 companies	48,896	44,905	49,803	48,438	41,754
Top 20 companies	176,921	170,831	175,912	169,572	149,836

Notes: 1. Average weekly number of employees.
Source: *Construction News*, 8 July 1982

Table 6.1 shows that the greatest shakeout occurred after 1980 when the top ten contractors shed 15 per cent of their workforce. Employment losses of nearly 14 per cent were experienced by the second ten largest firms. Superimposed upon this cyclical trend is a sizeable seasonal component. Thus, in the US construction industry employment can fluctuate by more than one million over a twelve-month period (Tschetter and Lukasiewicz 1983). The results of such instability show up in the forms of high unemployment rates (typically rates in construction run at double those for all industries combined), high inter-industry labour mobility, high levels of self-employment and the growth of labour-only subcontracting.

If there are incentives to the maintenance and enhancement

of team-specific knowledge we should observe management strategies designed to reduce their vulnerability to cyclical fluctuations. Three principal strategies are discernible. The first is reliance on short-term contracting whereby inputs such as labour and plant are hired on a basis offering considerable flexibility. The second is product diversification where contractors move into related products and activities. There is little in the way of backward integration into materials production by contracting firms. The wide range of material inputs required and extensive economies of scale available in their manufacture mean that it is generally uneconomic for a contractor to produce his own material inputs. There is some evidence of diversification into related processes such as energy products, quality inspection and management services. Such diversification offers only limited protection against industry cycles. There is very little in the way of diversification into non-related areas although one large UK contractor has moved into energy extraction. In view of the limited opportunities for product diversification the appeal of international operations (geographical diversification) is obvious.

6.3 THE INTERNATIONAL CONTRACTING MARKET

Table 6.2 shows the breakdown of overseas awards obtained by the top 250 international contractors in developing regions in 1982.

Table 6.2: Foreign awards taken by the top 250 international contractors in developing regions 1982 $bn

Source Nation	Middle East	Asia	Area of Work Africa	Latin America	Total
USA	18.5	9.4	2.8	3.9	34.6
South Korea	10.7	2.4	0.6	–	13.7
France	3.7	1.3	4.4	0.9	10.3
Germany	2.4	1.8	1.3	0.6	6.1
Japan	2.5	5.6	0.8	0.1	9.0
Italy	2.8	0.2	1.5	3.1	7.6
Britain	3.0	1.1	0.9	0.4	5.4
Turkey	1.9	–	0.8	–	2.7
Others	5.7	1.7	4.6	1.3	13.3
Total	51.2	23.5	17.7	10.3	102.7

Source: *Engineering News Record*, 1983

The market is dominated by contractors based in the developed nations although the second most important source nation is South Korea. US-based companies accounted for more than one-third of all overseas awards. Their particular competitive strengths relate to the large-scale technologically sophisticated projects including process plant design and installation. This point is brought out in Table 6.3 which shows net receipts from overseas operations for US contractors in 1980.

Table 6.3: Net receipts from contract operations of US construction, engineering and other technical services firms 1980 ($m) and per cent

	$m	%
Total	1,563	100.0
By type of service:		
Engineering and design	1,105	70.7
General construction	112	7.2
Technical assistance	225	14.4
Consulting	91	5.8
Other[a]	30	1.9

Notes: (a) Includes diverse services such as dredging, some drilling services and underwater diving services.
Source: Dilullo (1981)

Over 85 per cent of US contractors' receipts came from engineering, design and technical services, general construction contributing only 7.2 per cent. The less developed countries constitute the major market for overseas contracting; some 80 per cent of US contractors' receipts originated in these areas in 1980, with OPEC member countries accounting for almost 50 per cent. South Korean contractors, in contrast, concentrate on the less sophisticated, labour-intensive projects where they are best able to exploit their readily available supplies of relatively low-cost skilled and semi-skilled labour. As Table 6.2 makes clear, this cost advantage has allowed them to achieve a very high degree of market penetration particularly in the Middle East region where suitable labour is often scarce. With the exception of Turkey, developed market economies provide the major sources of competition in overseas contracting.

The importance of the developing nations in generating contracts has already been mentioned. The Middle East region provides the single most important geographical segment, being particularly crucial for South Korean, British and Turkish contractors. The importance of particular regions for particular source nations follow predictable lines. Thus, colonial links and proximity explain the strong French presence in Africa, Japanese success in Asia and US and Italian contracts in Latin America.

Tables 6.4 and 6.5 present more detailed information on overseas work undertaken by British contractors in the period 1973–84.

Table 6.4: Value of overseas work undertaken by British contractors 1973–84 (current prices)

Year	Value of overseas work done (£m.)	Value of all work done (GB + abroad) (£m.)	Overseas work as % of all work
1973–4	363	9,182	4.0
1974–5	458	10,264	4.5
1975–6	859	11,573	7.4
1976–7	1,253	12,920	9.7
1977–8	1,597	15,445	10.3
1978–9	1,678	18,435	9.1
1979–80	1,384	20,921	6.6
1980–1	1,287	20,146	6.4
1981–2	1,478	21,214	7.0
1982–3	2,314	23,655	9.8
1983–4	2,381	25,619	9.3

Source: Department of Environment (1985) Tables 1.7 and 1.11

Table 6.4 shows the value of overseas work undertaken by British contractors in the period 1973–84. One problem with these figures is that they are based on current prices. Ideally, they should be corrected for inflation to show real trends. The non-availability of an index for correction where work and inputs are obtained in many different nations means that deductions must be tentative.

There is some evidence of an acceleration in overseas work between 1974 and 1978. This period was one of rapid growth in expenditure by Middle Eastern nations following the first oil crisis. British contractors appear to have lost competitiveness after 1978 with the relative importance of overseas work declining. This may be partly attributable to rapid UK inflation (pushing up the value of indigenous work) but coincides with a

Table 6.5: Geographic spread of new contracts, work done and work outstanding of British contractors 1973–84 (%)

Region	Year										
	1973–4	1974–5	1975–6	1976–7	1977–8	1978–9	1979–80	1980–1	1981–2	1982–3	1983–4
European Community	1.9	1.2	0.8	0.4	0.7	1.9	2.0	2.4	1.4	0.7	0.5
Rest of Europe	10.3	10.9	6.4	5.2	7.5	6.9	7.4	7.6	0.9	2.3	2.1
Middle East in Asia	31.3	45.0	41.5	50.1	47.5	45.7	41.0	30.2	31.9	26.5	27.2
Middle East in Africa	0.2	0.2	1.3	1.8	3.4	3.8	6.9	5.7	2.3	2.0	3.6
Rest of Asia	3.3	2.8	2.7	3.1	1.9	8.9	7.6	9.5	12.9	12.7	10.5
Rest of Africa	26.3	24.0	32.7	24.8	24.3	19.4	14.4	20.8	20.7	27.3	21.8
America	9.9	6.5	6.0	7.0	7.8	6.4	14.5	15.7	21.3	20.0	27.2
Oceania	16.8	9.4	8.6	7.6	6.9	7.0	6.2	8.1	8.5	8.5	7.1
All countries	100.0	100.0	100.0	100.0	100.0	100.0	100.0	100.0	100.0	100.0	100.0

Source: Department of Trade and Industry (various years) *British business*, HMSO, London

high exchange rate and real growth in the domestic market. The rising importance of overseas work after 1981 occurs as the domestic market continues to experience difficult trading conditions.

Table 6.5 gives a regional breakdown of overseas work by British contractors. The most important markets are the Middle East, Africa and America. In the period since 1973 rapid growth has occurred in the American and Asian regions with a marked growth in the importance of the Middle East market between 1973 and 1979. The declining significance of this region since 1979 is notable. British contractors do comparatively little work in the other member states of the European Community where competition from indigenous contractors is well developed. The success of British firms in the African and Oceanic regions may be attributed to historical trading and other links with these areas. The growth in significance of British contracting in America since 1979 may be partly the result of the rapid increase in foreign direct investment in this area by British-based MNEs. This investment in plant and other facilities has provided opportunities for source nation contractors.

Returns from the major UK contractors provide more information on the geographical spread of overseas work. All respondents confirm the continuing, but declining, importance of the Middle East market and there is widespread agreement on the growing potential of the Asian region. The largest firms provide confirmation of the low degree of penetration achieved in the European region with this area typically accounting for less than 3 per cent of all overseas work.

6.4 MULTINATIONAL CONTRACTING AND THE THEORY OF THE MNE

6.4.1 The modern theory of the MNE

Theoretical analysis of the MNE is dominated by the eclectic approach associated, in particular, with the work of Dunning (1981). (See also Buckley and Casson 1976, 1985.) This approach models the overseas market servicing decision in terms of three sets of related factors: ownership, internalisation and locational advantages.

Ownership advantages are required by the investing firm to

compensate for the inherent disadvantage of operating in an unfamiliar overseas environment. The strength of such an advantage clearly depends on the relative competitiveness of indigenous enterprises. Ownership advantages derive from three sources; they may be firm-specific, industry-specific or country-specific. Since all viable firms are likely to possess industry-specific advantages the main sources of competitive edge are attributable to firm- and country-specific factors. Firm-specific advantages provide a basis for product differentiation, the most significant relating to proprietary technologies, marketing skills and favoured access to key markets or inputs. Differences in factor endowments, particularly those embodying human capital, suggest that there will be observable differences in competitive strategies of contractors from different source nations.

The second conditional factor is that foreign direct investment (FDI) requires that the most profitable overseas commercialisation of these advantages occurs within the organisation; that is they are exploited internally. Since it is easily demonstrated that a system of complete and perfect markets provides the most efficient mode of exchange, a preference for internalisation suggests imperfections or the absence of markets. In this case external exchange in the form of licensing may be costly or impossible to achieve. Clearly, the relative benefits of internalisation depend on the nature of the assets being transacted. Internalisation is likely to be an economically superior mode when the asset in question is a complex embodiment of the firms' output, reputation and image (Seymour, Flanagan and Norman 1985). For such an intangible advantage there may be problems of ensuring the licensees performance and quality maintenance since it may be impossible for the consumer to separate the inputs and contribution of both licensor and licensee. Where underperformance could generate external costs for the licensor there are considerable incentives for internalisation.

Where these two conditions are met FDI will only emerge when there exist locational factors encouraging an overseas presence. In the case of contracting the nature of the product requires local production in most cases. The immobility of the finished output (with the exception of offshore oil production platforms for example) suggests that it is the production process and not the finished good that will be exported. In such a case an overseas presence, albeit of a temporary nature, is a necessity.

6.4.2 Firm-specific advantages and multinational contracting

As suggested in Chapter 1 the firm-specific advantages (FSAs) of international contractors are likely to differ from those normally associated with the success of manufacturing MNEs. The derived demand for much contracting activity limits the extent to which firms can influence the level of demand for their services. In lowering the return to marketing skills the incentive to invest in such assets is reduced. Similarly, the general nature of and rapid diffusion of much construction technology suggests that with the exception of process plant contractors, few firms will base their competitive edge on the acquisition of such technology.

In the case of contracting, FSAs are more likely to reflect the higher returns on general managerial and coordinating skills. Contracting differs from a large proportion of industry in demanding management by continuous intervention rather than exception (Casson 1985). Similarly, firms are likely to display considerable specialisation. This follows from the intangible nature of advantages which tend to embody the firm's name, reputation and experience. Specialisation facilitates the diffusion and evaluation of distinct corporate profiles in a world of imperfect markets in information. In addition, specialisation reduces the probability of international contractors facing indigenous competition. Where such competition is under-developed FSAs are primarily a form of product differentiation amongst contractors based in the major source nations. There is considerable support for these assertions from the survey returns of large UK-based contractors. Even where firms were widely engaged in general contracting most claimed particular specialist expertise in, for example, mining contracting or process plant industries. There is evidence of a strong relationship between degree of specialisation and source of competition. In the case of general contracting indigenous firms and contractors based in the developing nations are the major sources of competition. Where a large proportion of overseas work is specialised the major competitive threat is provided by contractors based in other advanced nations. The role of output differentiation is reflected in the low rating given by respondents

141

to the competitive threat posed by other UK-based companies. Differentiation appears to occur between the major contractors within each source nation.

A similar relationship appears to exist between degree of specialisation and type of competitive advantage. For contractors displaying a high degree of specialisation the most significant sources of advantage were access to particular technologies and prior experience in particular types of construction. Those firms engaged in more general work stressed the importance of world-wide corporate reputation and the extent of home government support in the forms of risk assurance, finance etc. For such firms the difficulty of generating distinct competitive assets and intensely competitive environment they face suggests that source government support provides an important means of risk reduction when operating overseas. There was unanimous agreement that skills in coordinating construction projects formed the major competitive advantage available to contractors. Interestingly, a UK base was not regarded as an important source of competitive strength.

There is also interesting evidence from respondent's replies on the relationship between competitive advantages and multi-nationality. While the eclectic model recognises that multi-nationality can augment FSAs it assumes that multinational status is achieved on the basis of pre-existing compensating advantages. The survey results offered a variety of evidence that the effects of multinationality provided a major impetus to competitiveness. First, there was widespread agreement that UK contractors were disadvantaged in overseas markets in comparison with indigenous firms who had considerably superior knowledge of the local market and in earlier identification of project opportunities. This sort of disadvantage can be attenuated by a permanent foreign presence and presumably decreases over time with the accumulation of experience. Second, company sources provided the major conduit for information on projects. There are likely to be synergistic benefits from an increasingly multinational network. Third, prequalification processes are operative for almost all competitive tenders. Such processes, which attempt to establish the capability of tendering firms, focus on previous experience in work of a similar type or in similar conditions. There are likely to be fewer obstacles to prequalification for large international contractors with accumulated overseas experience.

Fourth, returns on the reasons for operating overseas suggest that compensating advantages may not be a prerequisite for all overseas projects. The most important factor rated was an approach by a previously satisfied client. This suggests that the firm may have enjoyed preferential status in the eyes of the commissioning organisation. Fifth, competitive disadvantages can be partially or wholly offset by the judicious use of joint ventures. Such ventures were widely reported, particularly in the Middle East and Africa. Joint ventures with indigenous contractors offer opportunities for diversifying risk in politically unstable areas, hedging against possible discrimination by host governments and in meeting local government requirements as well as a low cost means of market introduction. Firms also participate in joint ventures with other multinational contractors. A casual survey of 'Who owns whom?' for 1983 reveals that the top 20 UK contractors were active in over 42 overseas consortia. These were most prevalent in the Middle East and EC regions. Where projects are extremely large such as within the Middle East, joint ventures allow combination to achieve capability. Such ventures bring other benefits. They allow firms to complement their technical, managerial and productive resources, to diversify risk in politically unstable areas and to enhance their reputation when bidding.

The form of FSAs is significantly influenced by country-specific factors. US-based contractors have extensive technological expertise, particularly in the area of process plant construction. This expertise was founded upon the growth of the US petroleum industry (Barna 1983). Japanese contractors and exporters have expertise in industrial plant which derives from the post-World War II restructuring of Japanese industry with its emphasis on chemical and other heavy industry. In addition, the global networks of Japanese general trading companies provide valuable information on project opportunities (Kojimi and Ozawa 1984). British-based contractors may benefit from the spinoffs provided by its internationally-competitive related professions such as engineering consultancy, surveying etc. Italian contractors have acknowledged expertise in dam construction based on experience gathered in the source nation as well as extensive oil-related construction technology. The existence of communist-controlled cooperative enterprises has opened up opportunities in nations of a similar ideological orientation, particularly in Africa. Both Japanese and Italian contractors benefit from the existence of a well-developed domestic capability in the production of steel and construction plant (Economist 1978).

A similar capability is enjoyed by Brazilian contractors who are able to transfer expertise in large scale infrastructure development under extremely harsh conditions. In addition, their experience in training construction labour translates into a valuable externality for clients based in the developing world. More generally, LDC-based contractors are able to formulate a competitive edge through their experience in meeting developing country standards, more appropriate factor mixes and in the management of developing nation labour forces (Wells 1983). Furthermore, contractors from India and South Korea enjoy cost advantages because they have a plentiful supply of well-trained labour at relatively low cost. This factor would explain the phenomenal success of these countries in the high cost, labour scarce Middle East market (Agarwal and Weekly 1982).

6.4.3 Internalisation and multinational contracting

The diversity of international contracting activity suggests that a wide variety of methods of market servicing are likely to be observed. There is very little vertical integration in the domestic construction (Fleming 1980) or process plant (Barna 1983) industries of the UK. The cyclical fluctuations characteristic of much construction work means that firms will tend to favour short-term contracts and the supply of inputs on an arm's-length basis. If this is the case contractors are likely to have limited experience in the management of hierarchically administered internal markets. The volatility of contracting, and in particular the tendering process, encourage multiple modes of market servicing (Seymour *et al.* 1985). The most widely used combination is likely to involve simultaneous FDI and the exporting of personnel to meet demand peaks.

The survey results reveal that the major determinant of the mode of market servicing is the type of project. Licensing is widely used for process plant projects where proprietary technologies exist. Licensing, as expected, is most prevalent in the developed regions of Europe, America and Oceania. Management contracts and turnkey arrangements are used by firms engaged in industrial plant and heavy civil work particularly in the developing areas of the Middle East, Asia and Africa. Again, this is in line with expectations: many of these nations lack suitably qualified management. UK contractors maintain a permanent presence generally in the form of majority – or wholly-owned subsidiaries – in the largest market regions, typically North America, Oceania and the Far East. Regional offices or agent representation are retained in the more geographically remote areas such as the Middle East and Africa. In these regions local knowledge and involvement are often a prerequisite to business success. Indeed, there is some evidence of a relationship between a regional office or agent and the contractors' use of joint ventures, presumably with indigenous firms. As suggested above multiple modes of market servicing, particularly simultaneous exporting and direct investment, are widely used in the very large and volatile Middle East and North American markets.

Respondents rated the existence of a large market and the need for a permanent presence for competitive reasons as the primary motives in a direct investment decision. Little weight was given to the desire to integrate overseas operations within a global strategy or the difficulties of managing licensing or other contractual relationships. The implication of this is that UK-based contractors operate more as international companies than truly multinational enterprises with globally integrated market and product strategies.

This conclusion is supported by respondent's returns on parent–affiliate relations. Affiliate bidding was in all but one case under the instruction or acknowledgement of the parent organisation. In the one exceptional case affiliate independence only applied to projects under a certain value. Where this was exceeded, local bidding was on parental instruction. Employment relations also suggest active parent participation with nucleus staff being employed by the affiliate, and additional personnel supplied from the parent or other source when required. There is some evidence of global sourcing in the purchase of materials. All respondents reported greatest reliance being placed on sourcing from the lowest cost world market, when other factors e.g. import restrictions, project terms etc. allow. Perhaps the major factors encouraging internalisation (and market servicing through direct investment) are the imperfections which exist in markets for managerial know-how. International contracting involves the overseas transfer of the production base rather than the final output. The production process is embodied in the know-how of skilled labour and managerial staff. Internally administered hierarchies offer a number of advantages over the arm's-length exchange of managerial know-how. Managerial labour is notoriously heterogeneous and the a priori evaluation of ability extremely difficult. The incomplete nature of contracts for management and importance of managerial discretion result in very high information costs. Furthermore, the costs of erroneous judgement in managerial selection tend to favour internal markets for monitoring managerial manpower.

Internal transfer offers a number of advantages. The ability to assess incumbent managements past performance significantly reduces screening costs. Firm-specific training can be productively employed where overseas assignments occur within the same organisation. Finally, internal transfer of management is encouraged by the restrictive immigration controls and underdeveloped labour markets of many developing nations. Such restrictions and thin employment markets inhibit managerial mobility. To a large extent these constraints can be bypassed by internal transfer.

6.4.4 Location factors and multinational contracting

As suggested above the spatial nature of contracting projects and markets implies a major role in international operations for location-specific factors. For many projects the degree of locational substitutability is extremely low, often zero. The physical embodiment of value added must occur at the point of consumption. In such a case internationally mobile inputs (labour, materials etc.) will be combined with location-specific factors (the immediate project environment).

More general locational influences on international contracting include the size, riskiness and degree of development of a market. Survey returns indicated that the probability of a permanent corporate presence was positively related to the existence of a large market. Similarly, contractors had withdrawn from areas where the volume of work could no longer sustain the overheads of a permanent presence. The riskiness of international contracting was reflected in the existence of a number of countries and areas where firms would not consider operating. These included politically unstable regions and those where insurance against non-payment was unavailable. Specialist contractors often maintain a presence in the most technologically advanced markets, particularly the United States. For European process plant contractors entry by acquisition to the US market has allowed them access to the most sophisticated technologies which are often developed by client industries such as steel, chemicals and oil (Barna 1983).

There are two important qualifications to our discussion. First, the success of Japanese plant exporters indicates that for some types of contracting market penetration can be achieved through exporting. Japanese producers tend to concentrate on the less technologically-advanced processes and have competitive strengths in steel and fertiliser plant based upon their access to a highly cost competitive indigenous steel industry. Their integration, often within the very large general trading companies, yields economies in information and financing. Plant exporters display considerable flexibility with respect to changing market conditions. They have drawn upon the experience of trading companies in the field of leasing to offer attractive financing alternatives to the debt ridden, developing nations (Kojimi and Ozawa 1984). Furthermore, recognising their competitive strengths in basic process plant they have cultivated a number of joint ventures with Third World-based contractors to offer appropriate packages to some of the least developed nations (Agarwal and Weekly 1982).

Second, advances in the field of information technology have dramatically increased the possibilities for locational substitutability within international contracting. Advances in microelectronics and communications technology have reduced storage, processing and transfer costs of information. This has opened up new possibilities for producing contracting services in one location and utilising them in another. World-wide differentiation of time zones even allows the production of services at one location and point in time, subsequent transfer and the utilisation of that service at another place and time. One example of this type of management is provided by the large US contractor Bechtel (Feketekuty and Hauser 1985). Such advances encourage the centralisation of key management and coordinatory functions while simultaneously lowering the operating costs of internal markets where communication systems are networked.

6.5 POLICY IMPLICATIONS

The preceding analysis highlights a number of important implications for both corporate and government policy. First, there is widespread evidence of multiple modes of market servicing. Particularly popular is simultaneous exporting and direct investment. This may represent a rational response to fluctuating market demand but it also raises the possibility of gradualism in overseas operations. It may be feasible for a contractor seeking overseas work in a new area to compete successfully without initially establishing a permanent local presence. Alternatively, local agent representation provides a low-cost and low-risk entry strategy for markets where a local presence is a prerequisite, either for market intelligence reasons or to comply with government requirements. This suggests that in the case of contracting at least, a process of gradual internationalisation may be a feasible strategy.

Second, there is evidence from questionnaire replies that some large British contractors are not fully exploiting their competitive strengths. Thus, there is widespread agreement on those geographical areas likely to provide expanding opportunities for overseas contracting in the future. Similarly, British contractors emphasise their competitive strengths based on skills in project coordination, their corporate reputation and home-government support. This degree of similarity in replies would not be expected where contractors claim a degree of product differentiation which means that their main sources of competition are to be found in other advanced nations. General contractors indicate the growing competitive threat from Third World-based firms. In the increasingly competitive environment of the late 1980s and with the declining importance of very large-scale projects there is a strong case for increased differentiation and specialisation by contractors. The dangers of relying on past successes and traditional competitive elements have been pointed out recently by Mansfield (1986) in discussing the strategies of British consulting engineers.

The ability of contractors to adapt to changing market conditions should not be overestimated. The importance of pre-qualification processes and imperfect markets in information imply that great significance will be attached by both contractors and clients to corporate reputation and accumulated expertise. One valuable strategy to achieve change would be selective involvement in joint ventures. With the declining importance of very large project consortia a competitive edge could be achieved by the use of integrated service packages offering combined consulting, contracting and maintenance services. Consortia of this type have recently received official backing (Withers 1985).

Third, despite the limited opportunities for influencing demand there is a case for increased expenditure on the marketing function. Marketing offers an important means of market intelligence gathering and monitoring. As respondent replies indicated the principal sources of information on new projects were internal, notably related operations. More effective international marketing offers the possibility of information collection and dissemination as the contractor increases client awareness of his capability. A potentially useful angle for a marketing campaign might be to stress the beneficial externalities which can accrue to the client nation particularly in the form of training spinoffs and upgrading of infrastructure. This strategy appears to have contributed to the success of Third World-based contractors operating in other developing nations.

Fourth, at a number of points the relationship between multi-nationality and advantages has been highlighted. As suggested above, the selective development of competitive advantages has enabled new source-nation contractors to make significant inroads into the markets of a number of developing countries. Furthermore, the dynamic feedback effects of multinationality upon competitiveness suggest that these contractors will become an even more effective force in the future. As the degree to which they can exploit appropriate technologies and low-cost labour as OSAs declines, they may be expected to move into more complex construction technologies. This is reinforced by the rapid industrialisation occurring within source nations such as South Korea. Japanese contractors have perceived the mutual benefits of joint ventures with Third World contractors and have been able to overcome some of the barriers to market entry. The established contractors of the advanced nations will be increasingly forced to invest in lower cost methods of project management (computer-based design and management, satellite communication networks, etc.) to remain competitive. An important source of strength for them are the barriers to entry in contracting arising from problems of quality and capability assurance which face potential entrants and which are reinforced by the widespread use of prequalification processes.

Fifth, our survey returns reveal the importance of government policies with respect to international contracting. All respondents felt that the major problem facing them was matching the financing and credit insurance arrangements available to contractors in competing nations. Particular criticisms were made of UK aid policy and the Export Credits Guarantee Department (ECGD).

Aid policy in the UK has placed particular emphasis on supporting projects with a high probability of generating secondary orders, usually for manufacturing industry. This policy focus is becoming increasingly inappropriate as the number of very large projects decreases. Similarly, a more bilateral orientation to aid would ensure the flow of work to enterprises in the donor country. Some respondents expressed a preference for increasing emphasis on international loan facilities, possibly at the expense of aid monies. Many of the Far Eastern nations have indicated a preference for soft loans as opposed to aid funds. Japanese contractors have exploited this feeling with soft loans offering payback periods of up to 30 years. The recent government announcement (12 November 1985) of a soft-loans scheme to help gain overseas contracts of some £500 million a year in developing countries should go some way towards appeasing UK contractors' concern. The proposed scheme allows banks to offer soft long-term loans for development projects agreed intergovernmentally. The cost of softening loans will be met by the Overseas Development Administration. In addition, there is to be a doubling of Aid and Trade Provision funds to British companies. In recognising the competitive disadvantage currently suffered by British companies the government is to continue to push for multilateral controls over the practice of soft loans which is widespread amongst OECD nations. Two features of this scheme are of particular significance to contractors. First the scheme is fundamentally bilateral with funds being lent on intergovernmentally approved projects. This should ensure the maximum spillover of related work to the lending nation. Second, the loan scheme will be particularly attractive to Far Eastern nations, a market region of growing importance to UK contractors.

Criticism of the ECGD has resulted in a review of its activities (Matthews 1984). This review coincided with the ECGD's first experience of a trading deficit which amounted to £107.9 million for the year ending March 1984. The ECGD covers almost 30 per cent of UK visible non-oil exports and its services encompass more than 10,000 firms each year. The report's conclusions echo the concerns of UK contractors about the flexibility and responsiveness of a civil service administered department. It recommends that the department should become a commercially viable government-owned corporation managed by a board of directors.

There are other areas where UK contractors feel disadvantaged *vis-à-vis* their competitors. A significant amount of evidence (ITI 1983) confirms that there are financial advantages enjoyed by foreign service organisations in their international operations which are not currently available to UK-based firms. This position is not unique to contracting and raises important issues with regard to policy assistance to all service-sector MNEs.

Part Three

7

Soviet and Eastern European Service Multinationals[1]

Malcolm R. Hill

7.1 INTRODUCTION

Investment by Soviet and East European commercial organisations in Western countries, through the medium of wholly- or partly-owned companies is a topic worthy of study for several reasons. First of all, it is important to estimate the range and size of these activities in both individual countries and in global terms, in view of the generally accredited importance of multinational activities in national and international policies. Secondly, it is possible to consider the time scale of development of these activities to compare them with the time scale of multinational operations by Western companies. Thirdly, it is interesting to view the success of these Western subsidiaries of Soviet and East European multinationals according to Western criteria, bearing in mind that the executives of these companies are operating in different political and economic conditions from those encountered in their domestic environment.

The research reported in this chapter was part of a pilot study on Soviet and East European multinationals, initiated by the Institute for Research and Information on Multinationals (IRM), Geneva. The particular direction of that study was built upon the pioneering works of Professor Carl McMillan (1979a; 1979b) on the global scale and structure of investment by the socialist states in the West and developing countries, but supplementing this research by paying closer attention to activities in individual Western European countries. The research carried out by the present author and reported in this chapter has been concerned with Soviet and East European activities in two countries only, namely the United Kingdom and Sweden, in view of the stringent, and similar, company reporting requirements in those two countries compared with elsewhere. Other researchers (Professors P. Knirsch and E. Zaleski) participating in the IRM project studied Soviet and East European multinational activities in Austria, West Germany and France, and an initial survey was also carried out on these activities in individual developing countries. It was decided to delay publication of the results contained in this present chapter until the other surveys were complete, in order that comparisons with other West European and developing countries could be made.

The chapter is divided into six main sections. The first of these is a short account of the activities of foreign trade organisations in the socialist countries, and is followed by an introductory survey of the degree to which specific foreign trade organisations engage in investment activity in Western countries in general. The third section includes a survey of the dates of establishment and the range of activities of British and Swedish subsidiaries of socialist multinationals. This is followed by a section which summarises the information available from a series of case studies of a sample of British subsidiaries of socialist multinationals during two adjacent sample years at the end of the 1970s and the beginning of the 1980s, and comments on their financial performance. This section is followed by a similar appraisal of socialist-owned banks in the United Kingdom. This chapter is concluded by general comments on the information gained from the research, and suggestions for further research.

7.2 SOVIET AND EASTERN EUROPEAN FOREIGN TRADE ORGANISATIONS AND WESTERN COMPANY OWNERSHIP

7.2.1 Socialist foreign trade organisations

In all of the socialist countries of Eastern Europe, the export and import of products and associated services are the responsibility of organisations accredited to carry out these tasks by the relevant country's Ministry of Foreign Trade. These may be 'foreign trade organisations' (FTOs) or 'foreign trade enterprises' (FTEs) directly responsible to the country's Ministry of Foreign Trade; or organisations (including 'foreign trade organisations') responsible to an industrial ministry, manufacturing enterprise or state committee which have received Ministry of Foreign Trade accreditation. For the sake of simplicity, however, the term 'foreign trade organisation' is used throughout this chapter to denote any organisation within the socialist countries having the right to engage in foreign trade activity. There are currently about 350 of these organisations spread across the socialist countries of Eastern Europe, as shown in Table 7.1.

Table 7.1: Summary of foreign trade organisations investment activity in Western-based companies

Country	Total number of foreign trade organisations	Number of foreign trade organisations engaged in investment in Western-based companies	Number of Western companies in which investment has been made
Bulgaria	41	11	20
Czechoslovakia	52	9	19
GDR	34	7	16
Hungary	72	19	42
Poland	50	26	101
Romania	45	19	28
USSR	54	30	105

In general, an individual foreign trade organisation is restricted to exports and imports of a particular product line, and duplication between the activities of foreign trade organisa-tions is discouraged although apparently not forbidden (Franklin 1982). It is probably easier to understand the functions of these foreign trade organisations by viewing them as export and import agents for a defined range of manufacturers. In some cases, they may be administratively separate from their customers as is the case in the USSR, or they may be controlled directly by a manu-facturing enterprise as is frequently the case in most of the other socialist countries. Foreign trade organisations are also usually supported in their activities by a number of other socialist organisations providing various banking, insurance and other financial services; although these latter organisations may be also independently engaged in foreign economic activities in Western markets. It is difficult to be specific about the sales

157

turnover of foreign trade organisations, in view of the absence of any detailed published data. Estimates can be made, however, by comparing published data on the total export sales of a socialist country with the quantity of its foreign trade organisations. From such estimates, it appears that the annual average sales turnover of a Soviet foreign trade organisation in the late 1970s was of the order of $1 billion per year, and varied from the $180 million to $400 million level for the remaining socialist countries. The exception to this was Hungary, whose average export sales turnover per foreign trade organisation was less than $100 million, but this was partly due to Hungary's policy of decentralisation of foreign trade activities into a large number of organisations.[2]

The majority of the socialist countries carry out most of their foreign trade activities with each other through the Council for Mutual Economic Assistance (CMEA or COMECON). Consequently, the majority of the expertise resident in these foreign trade organisations relates to trade with countries having similar political and economic systems to themselves. Nevertheless, the expertise of these organisations in their dealings with the West is quite considerable, with about 20 per cent to 35 per cent of each country's (except Bulgaria) export sales turnover being delivered to Western markets, rising to approximately 45 per cent in the case of Hungary.[3]

7.2.2 'Socialist multinationals'

In addition to their usual foreign trading activities through imports and exports, several foreign trade organisations have engaged in investment and ownership-related activities in Western-based, or Western-registered companies. Consequently, such organisations are sometimes referred to as 'socialist multinationals' (McMillan 1979a; Goldman 1980) or even 'Red multinationals' (Hill 1977; Meyer 1977). The less pejorative term has been used throughout this chapter, although the use of the term 'multinational' in this context may be questioned until more evidence is produced of coordinated strategies of overseas manufacturing, servicing, and transfer pricing by these organisations. Furthermore, there is evidence from Zurawicki (1979) and Sobell (1984) to show that the socialist countries are experimenting with the development of socialist multinational activity within the borders of the socialist countries themselves. This chapter, however, is concerned with the activities of socialist multinationals in Western countries only.

Foreign trade organisations carry out their export activities in a number of ways including direct sales, agency selling, and distribution through wholly-owned and partly-owned foreign-based companies. Since this pilot study is concerned with the latter type of commercial organisation, it was initially decided to obtain the quantity of foreign trade organisations engaged in investment activities in Western countries and the quantity of their subsidiary Western companies. These organisations were listed in Morgan (1979), the most recent edition of the 'Carleton Directory' which was available when this research was commenced. These quantities are summarised in Table 7.1 (p. 157) together with data also available for 1979 from the London Chamber of Commerce and Industry (1980) on the total quantity of foreign trade organisations listed for each socialist country.

From these figures, it appears that the Eastern European socialist countries have operated different policies from the viewpoint of ownership presence in Western countries. In the first place, it appears that in global terms Poland and the USSR, and to a lesser extent, Hungary, have been far more active in the ownership of Western-based companies than Bulgaria, Czechoslovakia and the GDR. For example, 26 Polish and 30 Soviet foreign trade organisations had invested in 101 and 105 Western-based companies respectively; compared with only 11, 9 and 7 Bulgarian, Czechoslovakian and GDR foreign trade organisations respectively, which had investment in some 55 Western-based companies in total. Hungary and Rumania appear to fall into a middle range of ownership activity, with some 19 foreign trade organisations from each country engaged in ownership activity in Western-based companies, with Hungarian organisations having investment in some 42 such companies.

It is also apparent that further information can be obtained from some of the data shown in Table 7.1 (p. 157), and this is presented in Table 7.2. From this data, it seems that an individual Soviet, Polish or Rumanian foreign trade organisation has been more likely to engage in Western ownership activity, than its counterpart in either Bulgaria, Hungary, GDR, or particularly Czechoslovakia, where only 13 per cent of foreign trade

Table 7.2: Comparative ownership activity of foreign trade organisations

Country	% of foreign trade organisations with investments in Western-based companies (from columns 2 & 3, Table 7.1)	Ratio of Western-based companies containing Eastern investment, to number of FTOs engaged in Western investment activity (from columns 3 & 4, Table 7.1)
Bulgaria	27	1.8
Czechoslovakia	17	2.1
GDR	21	2.3
Hungary	26	2.2
Poland	52	3.9
Romania	42	1.5
USSR	56	3.5

organisations have investment in Western companies compared with 55 per cent in the case of the Soviet Union. In addition, it also appears that those Soviet and Polish organisations which had ownership in Western companies, were more active in terms of the numbers of such companies, compared with their counterparts in the other socialist countries (see Table 7.2, col. 3).

These average figures clearly need to be treated with caution, however, since they include some foreign trade organisations that had investments in one Western company only, and some others that had investment in more than twenty. Those foreign trade organisations with the most frequently recorded cases of Western ownership activity in the 1979 'Carleton Directory', are listed in Table 7.3.

It is apparent, therefore, that those 25 foreign trade organisations with investment in 5 or more Western-based companies, which represented almost 25 per cent of the 107 foreign trade organisations with investment in Western companies, had investments in more than 55 per cent of the named Western-based companies. The activities of these organisations are worthy of further study in their own right, but were thought to present too many difficulties in research procedure at the stage of the study described in this chapter. For reasons of economy in research effort, therefore, it was decided by the present author to focus on the activities of

160

Table 7.3: Foreign trade organisations having a high frequency of investment in Western-based companies

Foreign trade organisation	Number of Western companies containing investment
Dal (Poland)	21
Sovinflot (USSR)	12
Balkancarimpex (Bulgaria)	9
Ciech (Poland)	n/a
Metalexport (Poland)	n/a
Paged (Poland)	n/a
Traktorexport (USSR)	n/a
Carl Zeiss Jena (GDR)	8
Sovfracht (USSR)	n/a
Soyuzneftexport (USSR)	n/a
Stankoimport (USSR)	n/a
Hungarotex (Hungary)	7
Animex (Poland)	n/a
Tungsram (Hungary)	6
Avtoexport (USSR)	n/a
Motokov (Czechoslovakia)	5
Medimpex (Hungary)	n/a
Agros (Poland)	n/a
Polimex-Cekop (Poland)	n/a
Chimimportexport (Romania)	n/a
Energomashexport (USSR)	n/a
Exportles (USSR)	n/a
Soyuzchimexport (USSR)	n/a
Techmashexport (USSR)	n/a

Source: Compiled from data provided in the index of Morgan (1979)

'socialist multinationals' in the UK, in view of the available information submitted by British limited companies under UK company law. This was supplemented by research on the activities of socialist multinationals in Sweden, when it was found that Swedish regulations for the disclosure of information by limited liability companies were similar to those operating in the UK. The focus of the study presented here, therefore, was more concerned with micro-level studies of the activities and size of socialist multinationals, to supplement the macro-level information presented by McMillan (1978).

Table 7.4: British subsidiaries of Soviet and East European multinationals

Year established	Main business activity	Name of company	Ownership Shareholders (East European)	% East European ownership
		Bulgarian investment and ownership		
1966	Travel agents	Balkan Holidays Limited	Balkantourist	50%
1966	Transport services	Balkan and Black Sea Shipping Company Limited	Vodentransport	100%
1967	Reinsurance brokers	European Reinsurance Brokers Limited	Bulstrad, Bulgarian Foreign Insurance and Reinsurance Co.	49%
		Czechoslovakian investment and ownership		
1926	Glass marketing (technical)	Vitrea Merchants Limited	Transakta	100%
1928	Marketing food and agricultural products	Pilsner Urquell Co. Limited	Prague Nominees Limited	100%
1941	Marketing textile and knitting machines	Omnipol Trading and Shipping Company Limited	Transakta	80%
1946	Travel agents	Cedok Limited	Cedok-Naradrie	100%
1946	Marketing metallurgical products	Exico Limited	Transakta	83%
1946	Transport services	Intrasped Limited	Cechofracht, Czechoslovak Ocean Shipping	100%
1947	Crystal glass marketing	Henry Marchant Limited	Glassexport	100%
1965	Marketing and servicing cars	Skoda (GB) Limited	Motokov	100%
1969	Marketing matches	Samaco Limited	Ligna	100%

GDR investment and ownership

Year	Activity	Company	Partner	Ownership
1955	Marketing scientific instruments	CZ Scientific Instruments Limited	Carl Zeiss Jena Ltd	50%
1960	Travel agents	Berolina Travel Limited	Reiseburo DDR	100%
1963	Transport services	Deutrans (London) Limited	VEB Deutschfracht, Seereederei Rostock	100%
1964	Trade marks	Carl Zeiss Jena Limited	Carl Zeiss Jena Ltd, Stiftang	100%
1968	Marketing consumer goods	Gebrinex Supplies Limited	CZ Scientific Instruments, (Carl Zeiss Jena)	100%
1969	Marketing textiles and packaging	Unitechna (Services) Limited	Unitechna	100%
1975	Marketing office machinery	Robotron Export-Import Limited	Buromaschinen Export-Import	100%
1978	Marketing domestic electrical appliances	Heim Electric (UK)	Heimelectrik Import-Export	100%

Hungarian investment and ownership

Year	Activity	Company	Partner	Ownership
1958	Marketing chemical products	London Chemical Co. Limited	Chemolimpex	80%
1968	Marketing leather fashion wear	Richmond Distributors Ltd	Tannimpex	50%
1969	Marketing textiles	T H Faulkner (Europe) Limited	Hungarotex	50%
1976	Marketing fruit and vegetables	Central European Fruit Limited	Hungarofrucht	1% (previously 50%)

Romanian investment and ownership

Year	Activity	Company	Partner	Ownership
1967	Marketing foodstuffs	Inter-Atalata Limited	Prodexport	50%
1968	Marketing chemical	Arcode Trading Co. Limited	Chimimportexport	50%
1974	Transport services	Navlomar Limited	Navlomar, Romtrans	100%
1976	Marketing nuclear energy components	GEC Romanian Nuclear Limited	Romanian Inst. of Atomic Physics	50%

Table 7.4: British subsidiaries of Soviet and East European multinationals (contd.)

Year established	Main business activity	Name of company	Ownership Shareholders (East European)	% East European ownership
		Polish investment and ownership		
1939	Marketing foodstuffs and household goods	Anglo-Dal Limited	Dal	100%
1940	Shipping and forwarding	PSA Transport Limited	C A Hartwig S.A.	100%
1941	Transport services	Gdynia America Shipping Lines (London) Limited	Polish Ocean Lines, Polish Steamship Co., Polfracht, Central Fisheries Board, Ciech	100%
1959	Marketing chemicals	Daltrade Limited	Dal, Stalexport, Ciech	85%
1969	Book publishers	Earlscourt Publications Limited	Interpress Polintra (London) Limited	5%
1974	Marketing metals and electrical products	FLT & Metals Co. Limited	Anglo-Dal Limited, Impexmetal, Dal Limited	100%
1975	Marketing chemical equipment	Polibur Engineering Limited	Polimex-Cekop	50%
1976	Marketing shoes and leather goods	Skorimpex-Rind Limited	Skorimpex	100%
1976	Marketing	Polintra (London) Limited	ARS Polona, Agpol	50%
1976	Marketing wood and wood products	Polish Timber Products Limited	Paged	49%
1976	Marketing of meat products	Ridpath-Pek Limited	Anglo-Dal Limited, Animex	50%

Year	Activity	Company	Soviet partner	Ownership
1977	Travel agents	Polorbis Travel Limited	Orbis	100%
1978	Marketing tools and machine tools	Toolmex Corporation (UK) Limited	Metalexport, Pezetel	100%

Soviet investment and ownership

Year	Activity	Company	Soviet partner	Ownership
1923	Marketing woods and wood products	Russian Wood Agency Limited	Exportles	50%
1923	Transport services	Anglo-Soviet Shipping Limited	Sovinflot	100%
1925	Financial services	Black Sea & Baltic General Insurance Co. Limited	Ingosstrakh	100%
1959	Marketing oil and oil products	Nafta (GB) Limited	Soyuzneftexport Russian Oil Prods Limited Arcos Limited, Anglo-Soviet Shipping Limited	100%
1962	Marketing and servicing of instruments	Technical and Optical Equipment (London) Limited	Technointorg, Mashpriboringtorg, Moscow Narodny Bank	100%
1969	Marketing and servicing construction and transport equipment	Umo Plant Limited	Traktorexport, Avtoexport, Mashinoexport, Techmashimport, Energomashexport, Sudoimport	100%
1969	Marketing consumer goods	Razno & Co. Limited	Raznoexport	100%
1974	Transport services	Sovfracht (London) Limited	Sovfracht	100%

Notes: (1) The names of most of the companies listed in this table were extracted from the pre-publication issue of Institute of Soviet and East European Studies (1983). This pre-publication issue was provided by the Institute of Soviet and East European Studies, Carleton University, Ottawa. The exceptions to this general rule are as follows: Cedok, Unitechna (Service) Limited, Robotron Export-Import Limited, Heim Electric (UK), Transport Machinery (UK) Limited, Wemex Limited and Hoglatex (UK). The first company was discovered by chance, and the names of the remainder were provided by the UK Department of Trade.

(2) In addition to the companies listed in Table 7.4 BKC Impex Limited had been set up by the Bulgarian Balkancarimpex foreign trade organisation in 1979, with 80 per cent Bulgarian ownership. To date, there have been no financial returns for 1979.

(3) In addition to the companies listed in Table 7.4 above, there was no financial information available on the following companies which had listed returns in 1979: Transport Machinery (UK) Limited, Wemex Limited, Hoglatex (UK) Limited, James Griffiths Limited. The first three companies are 100% GDR-owned, established in 1970, 1966 and 1978 respectively. The latter company is 50 per cent Hungarian-owned and was established in 1972. Furthermore, the following companies were established in 1980, but no financial information was available for that year:

Bulgarian Vintners Co. Limited (100 per cent Vinimpex ownership);
United Sterling Corporation Limited (50 per cent Ibernia (GDR) ownership);
Fortschnitt Machinery UK Limited (100 per cent GDR ownership);
Raznoimport (UK) Limited (100 per cent Soviet ownership, Raznoimport and Promsyroimport).

A further company, Hibtrade, 100 per cent owned by the Hungarian International Bank was established in 1981.

(4) The 1983 'Carleton Directory' also listed the following companies for which the present author could not find information on ownership by a socialist foreign trade organisation: Polonez, Elco Clocks and Watches Limited; Global Watches, Fanuc Machinex Limited; Pol Anglia Limited; CET Plant Limited.

Furthermore, no financial information could be located on the following companies which were also listed in the 1979 'Directory': Mutual Trade Limited; Photographic Instruments (Elstree) Limited; East-West Leasing Company Limited; Black Sea and Baltic (UK Provincial) Limited; and Chemie Export-Import, a GDR owned company listed by the Department of Trade.

(5) A Czechoslovakian-owned company, Sigma Engineering Limited, was established by Intersignia in 1967 to market and service pumps. This company is probably now 100 per cent British-owned.

7.3 INTRODUCTORY SURVEY OF BRITISH AND SWEDISH SUBSIDIARIES OF SOCIALIST MULTINATIONALS

7.3.1 Introduction

This section contains a list of the companies located in Britain and Sweden containing investments from, and consequent ownership rights resting with, socialist foreign trade organisations. The British companies were initially identified from the 1979 'Carleton Directory' (Morgan 1979), although updated information for their 1983 'Directory' was also provided to the author by the Institute of Soviet and East European Studies at Carleton. Although it is clearly possible that this list may not be fully comprehensive, McMillan suggests in another publication (McMillan 1978), that Morgan's (1979) survey included approximately 90 per cent of all Western companies containing East European investment. In addition, the name of one further company was obtained from the London Chamber of Commerce and Industry, and the names of a further six from the UK Department of Trade. The names of more than 60 companies were traced from all of these sources, but detailed information on company operation was only available for 51 for the reasons given in the notes to Table 7.4

The Swedish companies were originally compiled from a pre-publication issue of the 1983 'Carleton Directory', and supplemented by information from correspondence with the Exchange Control Department of the Sveriges Riksbank in Stockholm. These companies numbered 26 in total, but complete information was available for only 16 of them for reasons given in the notes to Table 7.5.

For the purposes of this initial part of the study, it was decided to extract the following data included in company annual statements as part of the minimum disclosure requirements laid down by British and Swedish law:

name of company
main business activity
ownership of company
date in which the company was established as a subsidiary of a socialist foreign trade organisation

Table 7.5: Swedish subsidiaries of Soviet and East European multinationals

Year established	Main business activity	Name of company	Ownership Shareholders (East European)	% East European ownership
Bulgarian investment and ownership				
1969	Import/export machine parts for trucks	Nordcar Truck AB[c]	Balkancarimpex	n/a
Czechoslovakian investment and ownership				
1952	Marketing and servicing	Zetor Sweden AB[c]	Motokov	100%
1968	Marketing and servicing hydraulic pumps	Scansigma AB[a]	Intersigma	n/a
1968	Marketing and servicing machine tools	Tjecho-Svea AB[a]	Strojimport	75%
1970	Marketing chemicals and pharmaceuticals	Chemapol Svenska AB[a]	Chemapol	50%
GDR investment and ownership				
1957	Marketing chemicals and metals	Gunnar B. Janson AB[c]	Some East German interest	n/a
1959	Marketing heavy machinery	Svenska Wemex AB[c]	Some East German interest	n/a
Hungarian investment and ownership				
1928	Marketing and manufacturing lamps	Tungsram AB[a]	Tungsram	100%
1969	Marketing and manufacturing construction equipment	Bygging-Ungern 31 AB[a]	State Building Enterprise No. 31	50%

Polish investment and ownership

Year	Description	Company	Trade organisation	Ownership
1947	Transport services	Polbaltica Svensk-Polska Befraktnings AB[a]	Polfracht	n/a
1966	Marketing, import and export of metal products	Nilstal Nils Ake Nilsson AB[a]	Stalexport	n/a
1969	Marketing wood products	Nordiska Unipol AB[a]	Ciech, Dal, Paged	n/a
1974	Travel agents	Norbis Travel AB[a]	Orbis	100%

Soviet investment and ownership

Year	Description	Company	Trade organisation	Ownership
1957	Marketing and servicing vehicles	Matreco Handels AB[a]	Avtoexport, Konela	100%
1959	Transport services	Scansov Transport[a]	Sovfracht	60%
1979	Servicing fishing fleet	Scarus Marine Nutrition[a]	Sovrybflot	n/a

Notes: (1) The names provided by the Sveriges Riksbank were those of companies that had applied for a permit to receive Soviet or East European investment. This permit may not have been actually used, however, since no East European investment could be found in the accounts of Expert Falkenberg.[c] Furthermore, no evidence of the existence of VEB Deutrans Internationale Spedition AB,[c] Bulmak Sverige AB,[c] or BarCol-Air AB[c] could be found in information provided by the Swedish company registry.
(2) In order to provide a consistent base for comparison with the British companies shown in Table 7.4, the years 1979 and 1980 were cited for examination. A further six companies were thereby removed from the sample, since no accounts for 1979 or 1980 were available for AK Optik Instrument AB,[b] Junemaskiner Mats Hultgren AB[c] (last accounts in 1977), Pol-Line AB[c] (last accounts in 1977) and Rederiaktiebolaget Nike[a] (last accounts also in 1978). Furthermore, Soentronic AB[c] went into liquidation during 1977, and Terminal-Syd AB[c] does not appear to have actively traded in the years specified. The elimination described above resulted in a final sample of 16 Swedish registered companies with socialist foreign trade organisation ownership.
Sources: (a) from both Carleton Directory (1983) and Sveriges Riksbank (1982); (b) from Carleton Directory (1983) only; (c) from Sveriges Riksbank (1982) only.

The information obtained for these companies is presented in Tables 7.4 and 7.5. This data relates to 1980, which was the latest year for which complete company accounts could be obtained for the UK and Sweden at the time of carrying out the research.

7.3.2 Ownership preferences

The information contained in Tables 7.4 and 7.5 provides some useful guidelines with regard to ownership preferences amongst the various socialist countries. In the first place, it can be seen that Soviet, GDR and Czechoslovakian foreign trade organisations appear to prefer to maintain complete ownership in their British-based companies, whilst Hungarian and Rumanian foreign trade organisations appear to prefer to operate on a partly-owned basis (usually 50/50). Polish foreign trade organisations in their turn appear to be equally willing to operate on either a partly-owned (usually 50/50) or 100 per cent ownership basis. Section 7.5 also investigates the volume of sales turnover of these various companies, and it is interesting to note that two out of three of those countries of origin whose companies were found to have a fairly high turnover in the UK (i.e. Czechoslovakia and USSR) appear to prefer to operate with 100 per cent company ownership (see Tables 7.6 and 7.8). A final point of interest arising from this survey is that Czechoslovakian ownership activity in the UK appears to be fairly high compared with other Western countries (see Tables 7.3 and 7.6).

Table 7.6: Ownership patterns of British affiliates of socialist multinationals (1980)

Country of ownership	Number of companies in UK having less than 100% ownership	Number of companies in UK having 100% ownership	Totals
Bulgaria	3	2	5
Czechoslovakia	2	7	9
GDR	2	11	13
Hungary	5	1	6
Poland	6	7	13
Romania	3	1	4
USSR	1	8	9

Source: Compiled from data shown in Table 7.4

In the case of the Swedish companies, it can be seen that four of the companies listed in Table 7.5 were 100 per cent owned by Soviet or East European foreign trade organisations, and four had between 50 and 100 per cent of such ownership. The percentages of socialist shareholding in the remaining eight companies were not stated. Under Swedish company law, therefore, it does not appear to be compulsory, to state the extent of the owners' commitment in the articles of association or financial accounts. Consequently, unlike British companies, the percentage of ownership for which East European foreign trade organisations are responsible, is often unknown in Swedish organisations.

7.3.3 Dates of company establishment

It can be seen from Table 7.4 that multinational operation is not necessarily a recent activity for the socialist countries, since three Soviet-owned companies had been set up in the UK in the 1920s. Some Polish and Czech companies had also been established prior to the Second World War, and the activities of these companies were then continued by the relevant foreign trade organisations following the establishment of a socialist government and the nationalisation of foreign trade activities. It is clear, however, that the major growth in the establishment of affiliates of multinationals occurred in the 1960s and 1970s with approximately 70 per cent of the 59 companies being established during those decades, whilst the activity is still continuing into the 1980s (see Table 7.7).

Table 7.7: Dates of establishment of British affiliates of socialist multinationals

Country of ownership	1920s	1930s	1940s	Decade 1950s	1960s	1970s	1980s
Bulgaria	–	–	–	–	3	1	1
Czechoslovakia	2	–	5	–	2	–	–
GDR	–	–	–	1	6	4	2
Hungary	–	–	–	1	2	2	1
Poland	–	1	2	1	1	8	–
Romania	–	–	–	–	2	2	–
USSR	3	–	–	1	3	1	1
Totals	5	1	7	4	19	18	5

Source: Compiled from data shown in Table 7.4

All of the Swedish companies, with the exception of Tungsram AB and Polbatica Svensk-Polska Befraktrings AB, were established between the beginning of the 1950s and the end of the 1970s; with the majority of the companies established in the 1950s and 1960s, and only a further 3 of the 16 companies established in the 1970s (see Table 7.5). These figures suggest, therefore, that the continued establishment of new affiliates of socialist multinationals in the late 1970s and early 1980s is less evident in Sweden than in the UK.

7.3.4 Company activities

All of the British and Swedish companies appeared to be engaged in the provision of services related to import and export activities, with no evidence of any British company and only two Swedish companies (Tungsram AB and Bygging-Ungern 31) being engaged in manufacture. Subsequent research found a manufacturing subsidiary of Tungsram to be operating in the Republic of Ireland, (*Financial Times*, 2 December 1982) but this factory was subsequently closed in 1984 because of falling demand in the UK (*Financial Times*, 2 February 1984).

Soviet and East European multinational activity, therefore, in Britain and Sweden, appears to be predominantly concerned with the provision of service activities, and not of manufacture. This is not entirely unexpected, however, in view of higher labour costs in Western Europe than in the socialist countries of Eastern Europe, and the apparent lack of many market niches for Soviet and East European manufacturing technology to provide a comparative advantage (Hill 1983a). Furthermore, a low level of activity in manufacture is also to be expected from the profile of ownership of the parent foreign trade organisations, few of which are directly engaged in production in the socialist countries themselves.

Most of these service activities appear to be directly related to the provision of marketing and related support activities of a defined product range. In addition, some companies are engaged in the specific service activities of transport and insurance, although these activities in their turn are clearly related to international trade. The next section, therefore, consists of conclusions drawn from case studies of a sample of five British subsidiaries of socialist multinationals, to provide an indication of their range of activities.

7.4 CASE STUDIES OF BRITISH SUBSIDIARIES OF SOCIALIST MULTINATIONALS

7.4.1 Introduction

This section is a summary of the activities and management policies and practices of five British companies, which are either partly owned or wholly owned by foreign trade organisations from the socialist countries of Eastern Europe. A sample of companies was originally selected from those larger affiliates of socialist multinationals listed in Table 7.4 using information available on sales turnover and assets as discussed in section 7.5 below. The selected companies were as follows:

Skoda Cars Limited
CZ Scientific Instruments Limited
London Chemical Company Limited
FLT and Metals Limited
Skorimpex-Rind Limited
Nafta (GB) Limited
Technical and Optical Equipment Limited
Anglo-Soviet Shipping Limited

An introductory letter was written to either the chairman or managing director of each company, briefly explaining the objectives of the research project, and requesting their cooperation by a willingness to grant an interview to the author. London Chemical Company Limited, FLT and Metals Limited, and Skorimpex-Rind Limited agreed to cooperate in the project; but negative responses were received from Skoda Cars Limited, Technical and Optical Equipment Limited, and Anglo-Soviet Shipping Limited. Although negative responses were not received from CZ Scientific Instruments Limited, or Nafta (GB) Limited, it proved impossible to arrange an interview with the managing director of either of these companies within the time constraints of the project. A short account of the development of the latter company, however, was published by Goldman (1980).

In view of the extreme smallness of the sample of companies agreeing to be interviewed, it was decided to contact another company located relatively near to the researcher's university (Toolmex Polmach Limited), and a further company reputed to be engaged in manufacturing activities (Ridpath-Pek Limited).

These companies readily agreed to be interviewed, giving the sample which was interviewed in the order listed below:

London Chemical Company Limited
Toolmex Polmach Limited
Skorimpex-Rind Limited
FLT and Metals Limited
Ridpath-Pek Limited

All of these companies are owned by either Polish or Hungarian foreign trade organisations, but the willingness of these companies to be interviewed was considered to outweigh the possible disadvantages of any bias in national patterns of ownership within the sample.

During either late 1982 or early 1983, a visit was made to each of the above companies for interviews with senior executives covering the following broad topics: (i) company activities; (ii) advantages and disadvantages of British company ownership, compared with other methods for export marketing to the UK. An explanatory sheet and checklist of questions was used for this part of the survey, in order to provide a structured format for the interview. The information obtained from these interviews was then written in case-study format, as presented in Hill (1983b). The conclusions from these case studies are outlined below.

7.4.2 Company activities

(a) The main activities of the majority of companies interviewed in this sample consisted of the import into the UK of products made in the country of origin of the socialist owners. The one exception to this general rule was FLT and Metals, which was primarily engaged in general world-wide export trading activities related to Polish products, using London as a location for reasons of access to the Metal Exchange.

(b) In addition, the majority of the companies were also engaged in export activities back to that socialist country in which the parent foreign trade organisation was domiciled. The companies consequently played important roles in the sourcing of relevant imports for the socialist owners, and they also assisted

Western companies in their export activities.

(c) Each of these import and export activities referred to above were sometimes supplemented by exporting and importing from and to other locations beside the socialist country of ownership and the UK. As mentioned previously, this was a major activity of FLT and Metals anyway; but other companies found it necessary to sometimes source from third countries to broaden their product range, and useful to use the UK company as a base for re-export to other markets.

(d) All of the companies engaged in the sale of manufactured products also provided a complete after-sales service function.

(e) No company carried out product and process licensing activities within the UK, although one company (Toolmex Polmach) was engaged in the setting up of industrial cooperation agreements between Polish organisations and British companies.

(f) None of the sample of companies were engaged in manufacturing activities, with the exception of some meat slicing and packaging carried out by Ridpath-Pek Limited. This is hardly surprising in view of the lower direct costs of production in Eastern Europe compared with the UK, and the ownership profile of the parent foreign trade organisations.

(g) The only insurance, freight, shipping and financial activities carried out by the samples of companies were the normal tasks related to their import and export activities.

7.4.3 Advantages and disadvantages of company ownership

(a) The sample of companies were divided in their views concerning whether company ownership led to higher sales, income, and profits, compared with operating from Eastern Europe through a British agency. All of the companies agreed that costs were certainly higher, in view of the costs necessary to set up a company, acquire premises, and employ permanent staff. In the most recent cases of company establishment, it was expected that improved marketing would provide sales income in excess of those costs; but economic problems in the West in general, and in the UK in particular, had prevented the generation of high sales incomes.

(b) In spite of these problems, none of the companies stated that income and profits were lower than operating through other modes of selling and distribution; and consequently it appears that these companies are:

(i) providing their owners with much-needed foreign currency;

(ii) covering their costs of operation, and also generating some profits as a basis for future investment;

(iii) looking towards improved trading conditions to create the environment for better business performance.

(c) All of the companies were strongly of the opinion that their presence in the West enabled them to market their socialist-manufactured products far better than sale through agents. The reasons for this improved marketing were as follows:

(i) a close physical location to the market with associated improved access to sources of market information;

(ii) the possibility of pricing products much nearer to the relevant 'market price', together with the possibility of achieving unified pricing (e.g. unified meat product pricing by Ridpath-Pek Limited);

(iii) the possibility of arriving at a product range much closer to the requirements of the market, as a result of better market information;

(iv) the possibility of focusing promotional material much more closely to the requirements of the market;

(v) faster decision-making in view of close proximity to the market;

(vi) finally, and of major importance for manufactured products and capital equipment, opportunity to provide a far better after-sales service.

(d) Most of the companies found access to British expertise to be important in the establishment and the day-to-day running of the company. This expertise provided by their British employees was usually joined in a beneficial fashion to detailed product knowledge provided by the socialist owners.

7.5 FINANCIAL CHARACTERISTICS OF BRITISH AND SWEDISH AFFILIATES OF SOCIALIST MULTINATIONALS

7.5.1 Introduction

For the purposes of the study described here, it was decided to extract the following data on British subsidiaries to provide a financial perspective to the operations of the companies listed in Table 7.4:

turnover
profits before tax
fixed assets
current assets
current liabilities

This information is included in company annual statements of accounts as a part of the minimum disclosure requirements laid down by British law.

The information obtained for these 58 companies for the two most recent years when full financial data was available at the time of carrying out the research (1979 and 1980) is presented in full detail in Hill (1983b). From this information it is possible to advance certain tentative hypotheses with regard to the size of subsidiaries of socialist multinationals operating in the UK, and their financial performance.

Throughout the research, attempts were made to standardise the categorisation of the financial data presented in the company accounts. Since each company has its own style of presentation of financial data, however, there may have been some differences between a specific company's own definition of the size of the relevant financial parameter, and the value presented in Hill (1983b) as a result of recategorisation by the author. Such differences have been generally very small, however.

It was originally intended, in this research project, to analyse the Swedish companies in a similar fashion to those studied in Britain. Since Swedish accounting practices differ from their British counterparts (Svenska Handelsbank 1980; Nordic Bank 1981) certain assumptions had to be made with both sets of published accounts to achieve comparable figures. Some of these differences have their roots in the differences in national company tax systems between the two countries, and are as follows:

(a) Profit before tax is a slightly misleading figure for comparison since Swedish companies' transfers to an 'anti-cyclical investment fund' are made prior to the declaration of this figure. This is a means of avoiding tax on profits which is

177

heavily utilised by Swedish companies, despite the requirement to deposit an additional amount equal to 50 per cent of the transfer in a non interest-bearing account with the Sveriges Riksbank (i.e. the equivalent of the sum saved in tax). There are also other tax deductible allocations including the inventory reserve and the statutory legal reserve. Consequently, profit before tax and before profit allocations has been used in the present analysis although there might, in certain cases, have been some justification for taking some account of certain interest/commission movements. This figure was also preferred to 'profit after tax' as a basis for comparison, since that value of corporation tax averages 57 per cent in Sweden, and is payable in the year that it is incurred. Therefore, the profit-after-tax figure cannot be used to compare the performance of British and Swedish companies as the UK percentage equals a maximum of 52 per cent.

(b) Fixed assets are also accounted for differently in the two countries. In Sweden depreciation on buildings varies between 2 per cent and 5 per cent per annum depending on their expected economic life, and depreciation on machinery is based on 30 per cent (plus acquisitions and minus sales) to be completely written off in the fifth year. As UK law allowed 100 per cent depreciation on machinery in the first year and 79 per cent on buildings in the first year with 4 per cent per annum thereafter, some differences will inevitably occur in the figures (Pratten 1976).

(c) Another difference on the assets side of the Swedish company balance sheet is that small companies in particular tend to report the unutilised portion of their overdraft-checking account facilities as cash due from the bank on their current assets, and to book the entire amount of the overdraft facility on the liabilities side under long-term debt. There is also some indication that a number of companies may include the compulsory deposit at the Sveriges Riksbank in their figure for current assets, thereby further changing the values of this financial parameter from those presented by their British counterparts.

Taking due note of these points, figures have been extracted from the published accounts of the Swedish affiliates of the socialist multinationals, and these are presented in Hill (1983c).

7.5.2 Turnover

Table 7.8 is a summary of the turnover of the 34 of the 50 British companies in 1980, which provided that data.

Table 7.8: Total turnover of British subsidiaries of socialist multinationals

Country of ownership	Total turnover of 'multi-nationals' in UK (1979)[a]	Total turnover of 'multi-nationals' in UK (1980)[a]	Volume of British imports (1980)[b]	Total turnover of 'multi-nationals' as % of British imports (1980)
Bulgaria	1,021,666	1,004,174	14,425,000	7
Czechoslovakia	43,757,295	36,227,784	87,812,000	41
GDR	15,359,176	16,088,945	88,127,000	18
Hungary	9,381,481	8,628,591	43,327,000	20
Poland	115,687,170	147,012,883	194,523,000	76
Romania	7,418,091	14,991,479	64,975,000	23
USSR	955,801,361	906,534,426	786,176,000	115
Totals	1,148,426,240	1,130,488,282	1,279,365,000	88

Sources: (a) calculated from data presented in Hill (1983b), (b) source for British imports: Department of Trade and Industry (1980)

From this table, it can be seen that the total annual turnover from these companies was at least £1.13 billion, and probably slightly larger than that figure, since some companies had not returned turnover information. The total turnover figure for 1979 was found to be some £1.15 billion for approximately the same number of companies (37) suggesting that there was little growth in the turnover for these companies from 1979 to 1980. Consequently, the average turnover per company was in the region of £28 million per year during those years.

During both 1979 and 1980, Soviet-owned companies alone accounted for some 80 per cent of this total turnover; with Soviet-owned and Polish-owned companies together accounting for some 90 per cent. This is not surprising however, since the Soviet Union and Poland were also the source of some 75 per cent of British imports from the socialist countries during 1980 (see Table 7.8).

Study of the figures for each country in Table 7.8 also reveals that the aggregate turnover figure is influenced to a great extent by the large Soviet figure, which in its turn is influenced by the high value of £720 million for Nafta (GB). If this turnover figure

179

is discounted, the average turnover for the remaining companies reduces to approximately £11 million per year. Furthermore, the subsidiaries of Soviet, Polish and Czech multinationals based in the UK, appear to turn over an appreciable proportion of their respective countries exports to the UK (greater than 100 per cent, 76 per cent and 41 per cent respectively), whilst in the cases of Bulgaria, GDR, Hungary and Rumania the proportion is far less (7 to 20 per cent). Finally, since for one country at least (the USSR) the total turnover of its wholly-owned British subsidiary is higher than total British imports from the respective socialist country, it can be tentatively concluded that these subsidiaries are engaged in other business activities besides the straightforward import of products into the UK. As outlined in the previous 'case study' section of this chapter, these activities include the export of products from the UK (in some cases this is explicitly stated), or engaging in overseas international trading activities operating from the British base.

The total turnover figures for Swedish subsidiaries of socialist multinationals is provided in Table 7.9.

Table 7.9: Turnover of Swedish subsidiaries of socialist multinationals (1979 and 1980)

Country of ownership	1979 turnover (Swedish Krona)	1980 turnover (Swedish Krona)
Bulgaria	n.a.	3,085,000
Czechoslovakia	78,122,800	81,926,060
GDR	77,106,794	92,190,265
Hungary	30,822,769	34,293,168
Poland	22,036,320	27,487,745
USSR	174,520,634	284,563,122
Total	382,609,317	523,545,360

Note: Exchange rates between the Swedish Krona and the US Dollar were 4.28 and 4.23 in 1979 and 1980 respectively, and exchange rates between the US Dollar and the £ sterling were 2.12669 and 2.32577 respectively. Consequently, the rate of exchange between the Krona and Pound was some 9.1 in 1979 and 9.80 in 1980.
Source: The above table is compiled from Hill (1983c), pp. 6–13.

From this table it can be seen that the total turnover of these companies was some Sw. Kr 380 million in 1979 and some Sw. Kr 520 million in 1980. Consequently, turnover appeared to increase by some 36 per cent for those companies from 1979 to 1980, with increases in aggregated turnover for each of the companies, but especially those owned by the Soviet Union (Scarus Marine and Scansov Transport AB).

If it is assumed that £1 was approximately equal to Sw.Kr 10 during those years (see note to Table 7.9) it would appear that the total turnover for these companies was more than £35 million in 1979 and £50 million in 1980. This total turnover is far lower than that for the British subsidiaries of socialist multinationals during those same years even when the large turnover figure for Nafta (GB) is discounted. The average turnover for a Swedish affiliate was found to be some £2.5 million to £3 million per annum during the years studied, whereas the average turnover for the British affiliates, even when the turnover for Nafta (GB) was discounted, was more than £10 million per annum for the years studied.

Using turnover as a criterion, the socialist country which is best represented in ownership of Swedish affiliates is the USSR, followed by GDR and Czechoslovakia, and then Hungary. Poland is less well established, especially when compared with the turnover of Polish companies within the UK, whilst Bulgarian activity is very small, and Rumanian activity is non-existent.

7.5.3 Size of investments

The size of the investments of the socialist foreign trade organisations in the UK is summarised in Table 7.10, for 1979 and 1980.

Table 7.10: Fixed assets and net assets for British affiliates of socialist multinationals (1979 and 1980)

Country of ownership	Fixed assets of British affiliates (£)		Net assets of British affiliates (£)	
	1979	**1980**	**1979**	**1980**
Bulgaria	740,396	705,264	666,142	711,181
Czechoslovakia	2,604,018	4,106,680	4,656,689	5,630,066
GDR	1,060,552	967,946	1,827,324	1,630,457
Hungary	21,557	48,205	314,732	186,971
Poland	2,339,494	2,236,329	2,124,110	2,446,274
Romania	20,162	40,972	502,243	567,942
USSR	15,180,883	15,415,603	13,305,223	15,455,944
Total	21,967,062	23,520,999	23,396,463	26,628,835
No. of companies	46	43	54	47

Source: Compiled from data shown in Hill (1983b), pp. 18–28.

From this summary, it appears that the fixed assets of socialist foreign trade organisations in British companies accounted for some £22 million in 1979, and £23.5 million in 1980. The total assets for these companies accounted for some £218 million in 1979 and £196 million in 1980, demonstrating that the majority of the investments in these companies was in the form of current assets, although this is a typical asset structure for trading and marketing organisations. The net assets for these British affiliates during these years were some £23 million and £26.5 million respectively, which accounted for approximately 0.2 per cent of the total net assets of overseas companies in the UK private sector, and approximately 0.1 per cent of the total overseas investment in the UK private sector.[4] By these measures, therefore, it is apparent that the investment activities of socialist multinationals in the UK is currently very small, compared with the investment activities of their counterparts from other countries.

Furthermore, it is also apparent that some 90 per cent of the fixed assets and some 85 per cent of the net assets owned by the British affiliates of the socialist 'multinationals' in the UK, were held by companies containing investment from either the USSR, Poland or Czechoslovakia during 1979 and 1980. Soviet-owned companies alone accounted for 70 per cent of the fixed investment of the socialist multinationals in the UK, and 50 per cent of the net assets, illustrating the proportionately high investment activity of Soviet foreign trade organisations, particularly in fixed assets, compared with their counterparts from other socialist countries.

The data obtained for the assets and liabilities of Swedish subsidiaries of socialist multinationals show that the majority of the companies' assets are accounted for by current assets, which are almost balanced by current and long-term liabilities. This is partly to be expected from the nature of the business in which these companies are engaged and the special features of Swedish accounting practices referred to in the previous section.

Data for total fixed assets and net assets of Swedish affiliates of socialist multinationals are summarised in Table 7.11. From this data, it can be seen that the total fixed assets for the Swedish affiliates increased from Sw.Kr57 million in 1979 to Sw.Kr88 million in 1980, whilst the total net assets remained at Sw.Kr24 million for both years, although this latter figure includes a negative value of Sw.Kr3 million for the net assets of Bulgarian-

Table 7.11: Total fixed assets and total net assets of Swedish affiliates of socialist multinationals (1979 and 1980) (Swedish Krona)

Country of ownership	Fixed assets		Net assets	
	1979	**1980**	**1979**	**1980**
Bulgaria				(3,344,600)
Czechoslovakia	10,354,594	9,145,175	3,210,410	(6,344,600)
GDR	2,085,404	3,059,781	3,207,185	(3,054,759)
Hungary	1,552,000	2,034,000	3,932,000	(4,400,562)
Poland	492,690	777,596	707,952	950,582
USSR	43,763,441	88,708,707	24,606,705	24,659,284

Note: the use of brackets in the table denotes a negative value.
Source: compiled from data shown in Hill (1983c), pp. 6–14.

owned Swedish affiliates. The assets of Soviet-owned companies account for a large proportion of these total figures: more than 75 per cent of the fixed assets, and 55 per cent of the net assets. The majority of this Soviet investment, in its turn, is accounted for by the assets of one company alone, namely Matreco Handels AB, a company engaged in the marketing and servicing of vehicles, which increased its fixed assets from Sw.Kr40 million in 1979 to Sw.Kr70 million in 1980.

As a final point, it is useful to compare the investment figures for these Swedish companies with those of their British counterparts. The total fixed assets for over 40 British companies in 1979 and 1980 was almost £30 million, giving an average of almost £750,000 per company, whereas for the 16 listed Swedish companies, the total fixed assets were some £6 million, and net assets some £2.5 million. Thus, the average fixed assets for the Swedish affiliates work out at approximately £375,000, and the net assets at approximately £160,000. Consequently, the average level of investment of socialist multinationals appears to be lower in Swedish affiliates than in their British counterparts, by a factor of two.

7.5.4 Profitability

Introduction

The final stage of this discussion on the financial aspects of the

183

Table 7.12: Profitability of British affiliates of socialist multinationals

Country of ownership	Company	Indicator (%)					
		Profit/turnover		Profit/total assets		Profit/net assets	
		1979	1980	1979	1980	1979	1980
Bulgaria	Balkan & Black Sea Shipping Company	10.7	17.4	2.6	4.7	16.2	24.5
	European Reinsurance Brokers	2.5	(1.2)	0.1	–	7.7	(2.4)
	Vitra Merchants Limited	26.4	17.9	16.7	10.3	40.5	15.3
	Cedok	–	–	(6.4)	4.7	(8.8)	12.6
	Henry Marchant Limited	4.2	3.9	4.6	1.7	39.8	4.1
Czechoslovakia	Samaco Limited	0.1	1.3	0.3	3.1	4.9	38.6
	Pilsner Urquell Company	1.0	0.9	4.7	0.5	60.3	2.9
	Omnipol Trading & Shipping	15.4	23.9	12.1	16.0	26.4	38.8
	Exico	0.9	(0.8)	2.7	(2.8)	17.9	(15.6)
	Skoda (GB)	1.9	(1.3)	3.1	(1.7)	17.5	(9.8)
	Intrasped	–	–	8.3	11.5	95.6	97.3
GDR	Berolina	–	–	(6.2)	(5.8)	10.7	48.2
	CZ Scientific Instruments	1.8	0.9	2.6	0.1	14.9	0.9
	Gebrinex Suppliers Limited	(1.2)	2.6	(1.8)	6.3	(145.4)	96.4
	Carl Zeiss Jena Limited	0.5	0.2	48.3	14.6	(0.9)	(14.2)
Hungary	Central European Fruit	–	–	(4.0)	21.8	(60.3)	81.4
	T.H. Faulkner (Europe) Limited	–	–	4.8	1.3	15.0	3.7
	James Griffiths Limited	(8.0)	–	5.0	–	(424.6)	–
	London Chemical Company	0.6	0.4	4.2	4.1	35.6	22.2
	Richmond Distributors	0.2	0.8	0.7	0.9	13.9	(19.1)

Country	Company						
Poland	Toolmex Corporation (UK)	(0.4)	(2.5)	(0.2)	(1.4)	(3.9)	91.8
	Anglo-Dal	0.2	(0.2)	0.9	(0.7)	5.7	(3.1)
	TI Polmach	2.9	n/a	2.6	n/a	241.7	n/a
	Polintra London	n/a	n/a	15.3	(28.2)	23.5	(40.5)
	Polish Timber Products	4.6	6.3	8.2	13.5	(28.2)	104,580
	Polibur Engineering	6.1	0.2	6.9	0.7	30.7	3.2
	Daltrade	15.0	4.7	15.9	7.5	47.2	19.1
	Gydnia American Shipping	n/a	n/a	0.7	(01.8)	6.8	(8.8)
	Ridpath-Pek	0.3	0.5	2.3	3.5	20.9	19.3
	Earlscourt Publications	2.3	(2.8)	4.5	(8.4)	(97.0)	62.2
	Polorbis Travel	n/a	n/a	4.5	13.0	36.2	60.5
	PSA Transport	0.4	(0.5)	2.2	3.1	29.7	59.3
	FLT and Metals Company Limited	0.1	0.2	1.5	3.9	16.5	21.7
	Skorimpex-Rind	0.3	0.2	0.6	1.0	(16.9)	(15.7)
Romania	Arcode Trading	0.2	0.7	0.5	0.2	4.2	1.1
	Navlomar	n/a	n/a	49.2	6.6	84.4	15.3
	GEC Romanian Nuclear	n/a	n/a	7.2	10.7	7.5	11.9
	Inter Atalata	3.2	1.5	21.1	13.3	77.5	74.6
USSR	Sovfracht (London) Limited	37.5	47.0	42.4	35.4	116.2	178.9
	Russian Wood Agency Limited	18.2	(5.5)	13.9	(5.0)	22.2	(7.6)
	Razno & Company Limited	0.7	0.4	1.9	1.4	11.4	6.1
	Nafta (GB) Limited	0.1	0.02	0.7	0.2	14.2	3.3
	Technical and Optical Equipment	2.0	(13.9)	1.5	6.9	5.8	(660.0)
	Umo Plant	(8.5)	(21.5)	(8.9)	(12.8)	(19.4)	(18.7)
	Anglo-Soviet Shipping	0.08	0.6	1.1	10.7	8.6	47.9
	Black Sea & Baltic General Insurance	12.9	1.8	1.3	0.3	(3.2)	(1.0)

Note: the use of brackets in the table denotes a negative value
Source: compiled from data shown in Hill (1983b), pp. 18–45.

subsidiaries of socialist multinationals is an analysis of the profitability of these companies based in the UK and Sweden, using the data compiled in the research study described above. From that data, calculations have been made of profit/turnover, profit/total assets, and profit/net assets for each company; and that information is presented in Table 7.12 for the British subsidiaries, and in Table 7.19 for their Swedish counterparts (pp. 191).

Profitability of British subsidiaries

It can be seen from this information that few of the companies have performed well in terms of profit as a percentage of turnover, since of the 34 companies reporting both profit and turnover figures in 1979 and 1980, 17 (or 50 per cent of the sample) yielded a profit/turnover percentage of 1 per cent or less in 1979 increasing to 22 companies in 1980. Only 7 of the companies reported a profit/turnover percentage of more than 5 per cent in 1979, this figure reducing to 5 in 1980; but it is interesting to note that 2 of the companies with the highest profit/turnover ratios (Balkan and Black Sea Shipping Company Limited, and Sovfracht (London) Limited) were in the business of selling services rather than products.

When the profit margins (i.e. profit/turnover) for the 34 companies are compared with those for UK business as a whole (see Table 7.13) it appears that socialist multinationals in the UK appear to operate at comparatively low levels of performance for that business indicator.

Table 7.13: Summary of (British) industry sector profit margins 1978/9 and 1979/80

Category	Lowest quartile	Median	Highest quartile
1978/1979			
Manufacturing industry sectors	−0.7%	7%	12.5%
Merchandising industry sectors	0.7%	5%	15.9%
Services industry sectors	−4.9%	8%	32.5%
1979/1980			
Manufacturing industry sectors	−2.2%	6.7%	12.3%
Merchandising industry sectors	0.8%	5.1%	12.1%
Services industry sectors	2.3%	4.5%	24.7%

Sources: Inter Company Comparisons (ICC) Limited (1981, p. xi) for 1978/9 data, (1982, p. xii) for 1979/80 data

Approximately 80 per cent of the Soviet and East European companies returned a lower profit margin than the median figure for that indicator for British merchandising companies during 1978/1979, and 1979/1980 (see Table 7.14), although the subsidiaries associated with insurance and transport services appeared to perform much better.

Table 7.14: Profit margins for British affiliates of socialist multinationals during 1979 and 1980

	1979			
Range of profit margins	Less than 0.7%	0.7–5%	5–15.9%	Greater than 15.9%
No. of companies within this range	17	11	5	3
	1980			
Range of profit margins	Less than 0.8%	0.8–5.1%	5.1–12.1%	Greater than 12.1%
No. of companies within this range	21	8	1	4

Source: compiled from data shown in Table 7.12

The Balkan and Black Sea Shipping Company Limited had a profit/turnover percentage which approximated to the median for the services industries, whilst the same performance indicator for Sovfracht (London) Limited was within the higher quartile.

Turning now to the indicator of profit/total assets, it is also apparent that those 46 and 44 companies which returned this financial information for 1979 and 1980 did not perform particularly well against this measure either, although they appeared to perform better against this indicator than against profit margins. Table 7.15 presents a summary of the data available for British industry as a whole between 1978 and 1980 from which it can be seen that the median figure of profit/total assets was of the order of 9 per cent.

Table 7.15: Summary of (British) industry sector profit/total assets 1978/9 and 1979/80

	Lowest quartile	Median	Highest quartile
1978/1979			
Manufacturing industry sectors	−0.9%	9.3%	18.9%
Merchandising industry sectors	3.0%	8.9%	20.6%
Services industry sectors	−3.2%	9.0%	25.6%
1979/1980			
Manufacturing industry sectors	−4.0%	8.6%	21.7%
Merchandising industry sectors	2.3%	10.3%	19.5%
Services industry sectors	2.2%	8.8%	23.1%

Sources: Inter Company Comparisons (ICC) Limited (1981, p. xiii) for 1978/9 data, (1982, p. xiv) for 1979/80 data

From the information presented in Table 7.12 (pp. 184), however, it appears that 80 per cent of the affiliates of the socialist multinationals located in the UK returned a profit/total assets figure of less than 9 per cent during 1978/80 (see Table 7.16).

Table 7.16: Profits/total assets for British affiliates of socialist multinationals during 1979 and 1980

	1979			
Range of profits/total assets	Less than 3%	3–8.9%	8.9–20.6%	Greater than 20.6%
No. of companies within this range	25	12	5	4
	1980			
Range of profits/total assets	Less than 2.3%	2.3–10.3%	10.3–19.5%	Greater than 19.5%
No. of companies within this range	22	12	8	4

Source: compiled from data shown in Table 7.12

The ratios of profit/net assets for the 32 companies presenting the requisite information appeared to be highly variable, but on average did not appear to compare unfavourably with British companies in general. The median profit/net assets figure for the merchandising sectors of British industry was some 17 per cent in 1978/79 (see Table 7.17) and some 20 per cent in 1979/80.

Table 7.17: Summary of (British) industry sector rates of capital employed (profit/net assets) 1978/9 and 1979/80

	Lowest quartile	Median	Highest quartile
1978/1979			
Manufacturing industry sectors	−1.5%	15.8%	34.0%
Merchandising industry sectors	7.7%	17.4%	48.7%
Services industry sectors	−4.1%	23.5%	64.1%
1979/1980			
Manufacturing industry sectors	−11.2%	15.1%	60.9%
Merchandising industry sectors	4.2%	19.9%	54.9%
Services industry sectors	7.6%	19.4%	56.8%

Source: Inter Company Comparisons (ICC) Limited (1981, p. xii) for 1978/9 data, (1982, p. xiii) for 1979/80 data

Nineteen of the 46 socialist multinational affiliates in Britain had a ratio equal to or greater than the relevant figure in 1979, and 17 out of 46 in 1980 (see Table 7.18).

It should be noted, however, that the relationship between current assets and current liabilities in some of these British-based socialist-owned companies, did not always appear to be of a magnitude that would be expected from purely commercial considerations. In many cases, current assets were approximately equalled by current liabilities, which frequently included substantial sums owing to the holding companies. The effect is that the net assets are of a smaller magnitude than would be usually anticipated, and hence the profit to net assets ratio is comparatively high. Furthermore, it appears that these companies engaged in the provision of services (e.g. Sovfracht, and Balkan and Black Sea Shipping) have performed better on most profitability indicators, than those companies engaged in the sale of products. These companies have also compared favourably with the median of profitability indicators for British service companies as a whole.

Table 7.18: Profits/net assets for British affiliates of socialist multinationals during 1979 and 1980

	1979			
Range of profits/net assets	Less than 7.7%	7.7–17.4%	17.4–48.7%	Greater than 48.7%
No. of companies within this range	17	10	13	6
	1980			
Range of profits/net assets	Less than 4.2%	4.2–19.9%	19.9–54.9%	Greater than 54.9%
No. of companies within this range	20	7	8	9

Source: compiled from data shown in Table 7.12

It is apparent, therefore, that a high rate of profitability does not appear to be one of the primary objectives of the subsidiaries of socialist multinationals in the UK, but clearly they attempt to obtain a return on their assets sufficient to enable them to continue in operation. It is also necessary, however, to view these figures against a backcloth of general difficulties for many companies operating in Britain as a consequence of the international recession in general, and British economic problems in particular. Nevertheless, it is probably safe to conclude that the socialist foreign trade organisations which own these companies do not necessarily view them primarily as a means of securing high profits, but as important channels for the receipt of foreign currency.

Some further analyses were also carried out on a selection of the larger affiliates of the socialist multinationals located in the UK namely Skoda Cars Limited, CZ Scientific Instruments Limited, London Chemical Company Limited, FLT and Metals Limited, Skorimpex-Rind Limited, Nafta (GB) Limited, Technical and Optical Equipment Limited, and Anglo-Soviet Shipping Limited. For each company, information was collected from the company accounts on sales, profit, fixed assets and equipment for each year over the 1975/80 time interval. The complete results from this research are presented in Hill (1983b), from which it could be seen that whilst profit/turnover margins

Table 7.19: Profitability of Swedish affiliates of socialist multinationals

Company	Profit before tax[a]/ turnover		Profit before tax[a]/ total assets		Profit before tax[a]/ net assets	
	1979	1980	1979	1980	1979	1980
Nordcar						
Truck AB	n/a	20.7	n/a	92.7	n/a	(19.1)
Scansigma AB	(0.1)	(0.6)	(0.08)	(0.4)	(10.3)	(36.4)
Chemapol						
Svenska AB	6.1	0.8	8.9	1.6	36.8	4.9
Tjecho-Svea						
AB	3.4	3.3	3.5	3.0	40.3	28.7
Zetor						
Sweden AB	0.06	0.06	0.04	0.06	0.4	0.4
Gunnar B						
Janson AB	1.8	3.9	5.2	8.7	40.8	108.3
Svenska						
Wemex AB	0.2	0.07	0.2	0.06	1.0	0.5
Tungsram AB	(0.5)	1.3	(0.7)	1.7	4.0	100.6
Bygging- Ungern 31						
AB	30.3	0.06	15.9	0.2	23.3	0.9
Nordiska						
Unipol AB	13.8	6.4	15.5	8.4	181.3	120.5
Nilstal Nils Ake Nilsson						
AB	0.09	1.4	0.2	2.3	7.1	50.8
Polbaltica Svensk-						
Polska AB	1.8	1.1	3.4	2.5	11.3	7.4
Norbis Travel						
AB	0.7	0.4	4.9	2.3	39.1	29.0
Matreco						
Handels AB	1.9	(13.7)	1.5	(6.8)	16.7	(142.8)
Scarus Marine						
Nutrition AB	5.1	1.5	6.7	5.4	14.9	101.0
Scansov Transport						
AB	1.9	1.8	5.6	10.2	75.8	61.1

Notes: (a) And before profit allocations.
The use of brackets in the table denotes a negative value.
Source: compiled from data in Hill (1983c), pp. 5–17

have remained stable at a low level, growth in turnover has been usually quite substantial. There is also evidence to show that the companies have increased their fixed assets, with some increase in equipment investment amongst some of the companies.

Swedish companies

An analysis of the profitability of Swedish affiliates of socialist multinationals is provided in Table 7.19. It is apparent from this analysis that there are wide fluctuations for these ratios between companies and also between the two consecutive years under consideration. The author was unable to discover a Swedish equivalent of the British publication of inter-company comparisons as a backcloth against which to analyse these financial ratios. Conclusions which may be drawn from this data must, of necessity, be tentative, but the similarities in the distribution for profitability indices between the British

Table 7.20: Ranges of profitability of Swedish affiliates of socialist multinationals

	Profit margin			
1979				
Spread	0.7%	0.7–5.0%	5.0–15.9%	15.9%
No. of companies	6	5	3	1
1980				
Spread	0.8%	0.8–5.1%	5.1–12.1%	12.1%
No. of companies	6	7	1	2
	Profit/total assets			
1979				
Spread	3.0%	3.0–8.9%	8.9–20.6%	20.6%
No. of companies	6	7	2	0
1980				
Spread	2.3%	2.3–10.3%	10.3–19.5%	19.5%
No. of companies	7	7	0	2
	Rate of capital employed			
1979				
Spread	7.7%	7.7–17.4%	17.4–48.7%	48.7%
No. of companies	4	3	4	4
1980				
Spread	4.2%	4.2–19.9%	19.9–54.9%	54.9%
No. of companies	6	2	3	5

and Swedish sample are striking. Approximately 80 per cent of UK affiliates fell below the median in profit margins analyses as they did in the profits/total assets when compared with a large sample of UK businesses (see Tables 7.13, 7.15 and 7.17, pp. 186, 188, 189). In the Swedish sample between 67 and 81 per cent of affiliates returned a profit margin less than the median of this index for British companies; and 86 per cent of the Swedish affiliates of socialist multinationals performed at a level lower than the median of British companies on the profits/total assets ratio (see Table 7.20).

This profits/turnover and profits/total assets figure suggests that, as in the case of their British counterparts, Swedish registered companies owned by Soviet and East European foreign trade organisations appear less profitable than wholly Western-owned companies. Consequently, it is likely that these companies are primarily viewed by their owners as avenues to secure Western currency, with sufficient profits being generated to remain in business, and to generate some expansion.

The profit/net assets ratios are not very reliable for assessing the business performance of these companies since liabilities do not consistently include loans from the parent companies, and the results are extremely varied – as also for the sample of British companies discussed in the previous section. High percentages of profit/net assets are attributed to small net assets as companies tend to match assets and liabilities, thereby producing a high margin on capital employed.

7.6 SOVIET- AND EASTERN EUROPEAN-OWNED BANKS IN THE UK

A similar structure of banking has been established in all of the socialist countries of Eastern Europe except Czechoslovakia and Poland, consisting of a national state bank, an investment bank, and a specially created foreign trade bank. The main function of these latter organisations is to provide the necessary finance for foreign trade by:

foreign exchange dealing;
securing of import and export credits and handling of the associated documentation;
making and collecting of payments.

193

In many ways, these activities are similar to the main business operations of the domestic overseas department of a British bank, and it is interesting to note that although there is no specific foreign trade bank in either Czechoslovakia or Poland, associated business functions are performed by two commercial banks, namely: Zivnostenka Banka National of Czechoslovakia and Bank Handlowy w Warszawie. Both of these banks maintain a presence in London; the Zivnostenka has a branch office and the Bank Handlowy also maintains a branch, both of which are licensed deposit-taking offices under the UK Banking Act of 1979. Furthermore, the Bulgarian Foreign Trade and the Deutsche Aussenhandelsbank maintain representative offices; whilst the Hungarian, Rumanian and Soviet Banks of Foreign Trade maintain correspondents, but conduct all of their business from the head offices in the respective home countries.

In addition, there are three other banks which merit further description: namely: the Hungarian International Bank Limited; the Anglo-Rumanian Bank Limited; and the Moscow Narodny Bank Limited. A brief description of the activities of each of these banks is given below, whilst their financial performance is summarised in Table 7.21.

Table 7.21: Comparative performances of Soviet- and East European-owned banks located in the UK (1979)

Indicator	Bank		
	Hungarian International Bank	Anglo-Romanian Bank	Moscow-Narodny Bank
Return on total assets	1.1%	1.1%	0.11%
Return on net assets	20.0%	25.6%	3.3%[a]
Volume of deposits (£)	114,114,727	115,087,959	1,522,247,000
Volume of loans	83,423,034 3,744,617[b]	99,787,147	1,189,801,000
Capital ratio %	5.5%[c]	4.0%	3.6%
Loans/deposits	76%	87%	78%
Advances/assets	69%	81%	75%

Notes: (a) profit after tax and transfers to reserves; (b) leased assets; (c) includes loan capital.
Source: compiled from *Bankers Almanac and Yearbook*, 1980–81 and the respective banks' financial returns.

(a) *Hungarian International Bank Limited.* A subsidiary of the National Bank of Hungary, established in 1973, and a recognised bank under the terms of the UK Banking Act of 1979. The activities carried out by this bank are as follows:

bill discounting and forfeiting;
inter-bank deposit dealing;
forex dealing;
short and medium term loans;
loan syndications;
documentary credits;
trading in CD's (Certificates of Deposit);
equipment leasing;
current and deposit accounts.

(b) *Anglo-Rumanian Bank Limited.* A consortium owned by the Rumanian Bank for Foreign Trade (50% shareholding), Barclays Bank International (30 per cent shareholding) and Manufacturers Hanover International Banking Corporation (20 per cent), established in 1973, and a recognised bank under the terms of the UK Banking Act of 1979. The main activities of the bank are currently documentary credits and short-term loans, although it is also intended to diversify into equipment leasing and ECGD export credits.

(c) *Moscow Narodny Bank.* This Soviet-owned bank was established in 1919, with its headquarters in London, and branches in Beirut and Singapore. The scale of operations of this bank is far greater than the Hungarian International and Anglo-Rumanian discussed above, and in terms of total assets is ranked about 250th in the world banking league.

The Moscow Narodny is engaged in all of the commercial activities listed for the Hungarian International Bank, in addition to the following:

sales of gold and bullion;
information and advice to the Soviet government;
training and education;
bond issues.

Both the Hungarian International and Anglo-Rumanian appear to have an adequate return on total assets and return on net assets. It is impossible to compute similar figures for the Moscow Narodny, since figures are issued after tax. The capital ratio for the Moscow Narodny appears to be at a fairly high level.

7.7 CONCLUSIONS

This preliminary research on British and Swedish subsidiaries of Soviet and East European multinationals has yielded much useful information on the scope and scale of the activities of these organisations. Furthermore, the information obtained from the other IRM-commissioned studies of the activities of these organisations in Austria and Germany (Knirsch 1983) in no way contradicts the results of the research presented here. It is not unreasonable to conclude therefore, that much of the information presented for Britain and Sweden is also true for Western Europe as a whole. The current study, compared with those for the other Western European countries has had the advantage, however, of being able to draw on detailed company-level information. From this research, it is possible to draw the following conclusions:

(a) The overwhelming majority of the subsidiaries of Soviet and East European multinationals were engaged in service activities. Of these, the great majority were engaged in marketing-related service activities to promote the sale in Western markets of products manufactured in the respective socialist country. In addition, many of these companies also acted as purchasing agents for a defined range of supplies required by their domestic industry.

(b) Several of the subsidiaries of Soviet and East European foreign trade organisations were found to be engaged in the service activities of transport, insurance and banking. Furthermore, many of these companies appeared to be performing quite well in terms of the normal Western criteria used to judge company performance.

It is probable that these activities may continue to grow in Western countries, and they should continue to be monitored in line with other studies of multinational service operations. It is unlikely that they will grow from a basis of technological advantage, however, although one subsidiary has recently been approved for calibration purposes by the British Calibration Service.[5]

(c) The majority of the subsidiaries of Soviet and Western European foreign trade organisations were established in the 1960s and 1970s when East–West trade was expanding rapidly. Although the number of these companies will probably continue to grow, it is unlikely that they will grow as rapidly as in those two decades, unless East–West trade grows at a much faster rate than at present.

(d) The number of these subsidiaries is comparatively small when compared with the quantity of Western multinationals, but the quantity of Soviet and East European organisations having the legal competence to invest overseas is also small.

It was found, on the other hand, that more than 50 per cent of foreign trade organisations in some of the socialist countries were engaged in multinational activities in Western countries. Consequently, the number of companies is probably restricted by the availability of scarce Western currency for investment, not the propensity to invest by foreign trade organisations.

(e) The scale of operation of Soviet and East European subsidiaries was found to be very small, in terms of total turnover and investment. To a very great extent, this is a reflection of the comparatively small volume of East–West trade, and the scarcity of Western currency referred to in the previous paragraph.

It can be concluded from this, therefore, that Western governments need not be over-concerned about the possible influence of these subsidiary companies on national economic activities in the host country. Any national policies directed towards these companies, therefore, will probably be a reflection of trade and foreign affairs policies towards the country of their parent organisations.

(f) It is considered that further useful work could be carried out on longitudinal studies of the development of these companies, updating much of the information presented in this present chapter. Furthermore, increased efforts could be made to secure interviews with a wider range of companies.

(g) Further work is also necessary on the activities of these subsidiaries in the developing world, since there is evidence to suggest that they may be more involved in manufacturing, extraction and related service activities than is the case in the developed West (Zaleski 1984).

(h) The parent Soviet and East European multinationals (or 'foreign trade organisations') themselves are worthy of further study, from the viewpoints of their international objectives and strategies related to investment in Western countries. Particular attention should also be paid to their activities in developing countries, where they may well have certain technological and pricing advantages, compared with host companies and Western multinational enterprises.

NOTES

1. The author has been provided with assistance during the preparation of this paper from a number of colleagues in the Department of Management Studies, Loughborough University of Technology, namely: Mr J.D. Blake, Mr N. Coulbeck, Dr D.W. Cowell, Dr M. King, Mr C.P. McEvoy and Mr J. Whittaker. In addition, much of the data of the most recent financial performance of British and Swedish subsidiaries of socialist multinationals was collected and analysed by Miss K.N. Stables, a final-year student in Management Sciences at Loughborough. Swedish company accounts and other financial information were obtained from the Swedish Royal Patents and Registration Establishment, Sundsvall by Mr M. Bodin of the Department of Industrial Economics and Organisation, Royal Institute of Technology, Stockholm and Mr P.A. Lawrence of Loughborough.

The author also wishes to acknowledge the continued provision of up-dated information on British affiliates of socialist multinationals from Professor C.H. McMillan, Mr P. Egyed and Mr F. Cadieux of the East–West Project at the Institute of Soviet and East European Studies, Carleton University, Ottawa. Further information was also provided by the UK Department of Trade and Industry, and the London Chamber of Commerce and Industry. Finally, the author wishes to record his thanks to those executives of British affiliates of socialist multinationals who were willing to be interviewed to provide information for the case-study section summarised in this chapter.

The financial support for the research described in this chapter was provided by the Institute for Research and Information on Multinationals, Geneva.

2. In 1978, Bulgaria exported $7.5bn through 41 foreign trade organisations, giving an average sales turnover per foreign trade organisation of $184m. The USSR, on the other hand exported $52bn through 54 foreign trade organisations, giving an average sales turnover per foreign trade organisation of almost $1bn. The remaining socialist countries lay between these two extremes, with the exception of Hungary which exported $6.4bn through 72 foreign trade organisations. (See foreign trade turnover data presented in London Chamber of Commerce and Industry (1980).)

3. The proportion of export sales delivered to the developed market economies in 1978 was as follows:

Bulgaria	11%
Czechoslovakia	21%
GDR	20%

198

Hungary 44%
Poland 33%
Rumania 35%
USSR 29%

(Calculated from data provided in London Chamber of Commerce and Industry (1980) and Council for Mutual Economic Assistance (1980).)

4. In Central Statistical Office (1983), Table 11.2, a figure of £13,855m. is given for the direct net assets of overseas companies in the UK private sector in 1979, and a total of £26,480m., including oil companies' investments and net borrowing from banks during that same year. For 1980, the respective figures are £16,315m. and £29,565m.

5. CZ Scientific Instruments Limited have received approval by the British Calibration Service for their laboratories to be used for calibration of measuring instruments and machines. (See British Calibration Service (1984), p. 25.)

8

Third World Multinationals in the Service Industries

Donald J. Lecraw

8.1 INTRODUCTION

Interest in multinational enterprises based in low- and middle-income countries, Third World Multinationals (TWMs), has increased rapidly over the last ten years since the first articles appeared in the mid-1970s. (See, for example Wells 1977, and Lecraw 1977.) This increasing body of research has recently culminated in three books (Wells 1983; Lall 1983; Kumar and McLeod 1981) which should stand as the definitive works on the subject until more systematic, broadly-based data is collected (an unlikely event). There are several reasons for this burgeoning literature: the relatively recent identifiability of the phenomena of TWMs; the interest of development economists in the effects of investment and technology transfer by TWMs on both the host and home countries; interest of international business researchers in the phenomenon of TWMs *per se* and in the effect of these firms on competition between multinational enterprises (MNEs) world-wide; and interest by policy-makers in host and home countries and in multinational organisations on the effects of TWMs and appropriate policy initiatives towards them.

What then is the contribution of this chapter? First, the area of TWMs in service industries has not been covered explicitly in previous work on TWMs. Yet, on an impressionistic basis, it would seem that a higher proportion of TWM activity is in the service sector than is the case for MNEs from high-income countries. Second, the basis for TWM activity in service industries is often different from that of their investment abroad in manufacturing. Third, this article gives me the chance to correct and modify some of my previous conclusions (Lecraw

1977, 1981, 1983) on TWMs based on more recent data and in light of current trends in the activities of TWMs.

The next section describes some of the problems of analysing TWMs in general and those in service industries in particular. Section 8.3 outlines a theoretical framework of analysis of TWMs and describes some of the conclusions of other studies on TWMs in the manufacturing sector. In section 8.4 this framework is used and extended to analyse TWMs in the service industries.

8.2 PROBLEMS IN RESEARCHING TWMs

The problems of data and methodology that often arise in research about international business are compounded for research on TWMs, especially those operating in the service industries. This complaint is a standard one among academic researchers, but, for several reasons, it is particularly severe for TWMs.[1]

Economic data in low- and middle-income countries is often incomplete, inaccurate, and biased (often in unknown directions). This problem is particularly true for statistics on inward foreign direct investment (FDI), but even worse for outward FDI. As examples, inward FDI data in Thailand is collected by the Board of Investment (BOI), but only for 'promoted' firms, which represent somewhere between a half and two-thirds of inward FDI. Outward FDI is not reported on a systematic basis at all. Even this BOI data, such that it is, does not adequately distinguish between the initial inflow of investment and changes from the initial position over time due to retained earnings, further inflows or outflows. The statistics for Indonesia record only 'approved' projects, but do not follow up on whether these projects were implemented and, if so, what the actual investment position is over time.

For MNEs based in the United States, Europe and Japan, researchers can often use the statistics of the home country for outward and inward FDI, but this is not possible for TWMs since they typically do not invest in these high income countries. The best data is found in Wells (1983), but even this is dated and its coverage often confined to specific areas of interest to Wells, his doctoral students and colleagues (Busjeet 1980; Balakrishnan 1976; Encarnation 1982; Lecraw 1976; and

Cordeiro 1978). In addition, many TWMs are privately held so that public information about their size, characteristics and international operations is spotty at best.[2]

There are also problems with the definition of TWMs. Wells (1978) describes the conceptual and data problems involved in measuring outward FDI from Hong Kong: the problem is to distinguish between British-owned and Chinese-owned firms. For Malaysia, the problem is somewhat different. In an attempt to decrease the extent of MNE activity in their economy and to increase ownership by *bumiputeras* (ethnic Malays), private businessmen, financial institutions, and state-owned enterprises have employed a variety of mechanisms to acquire the entire assets of several British multinational trading firms, often by purchasing their stock on the London Stock Exchange. In this way ownership of Sime Darby, Guthrie, Dunlop and other British trading companies was acquired by Malaysians (Panglaykim 1979). Sime Darby alone has manufacturing, plantation, trading, transportation and financial interests in Malaysia, Singapore, the United Kingdom, Australia, Hong Kong, Indonesia, Liberia, Thailand, India, Bangladesh, the Netherlands, the United States and Canada. Should Pernas (the major stockholder in Sime Darby and hence Guthrie) be classified as a TWM when it essentially became multinational by buying its international operations as it were, 'off the rack'?

Certainly Pernas is currently a major MNE, but the route by which it became a multinational does not fall within any of our theoretical frameworks of outward FDI by TWMs, and the inclusion of its operations in the analysis of TWMs will do much to advance our understanding of the general phenomenon.

For TWMs in service industries, there is another problem of analysis, one that is to some extent common in the analysis of MNEs in service industries based in all countries. The original research on MNEs focused on MNEs in the extractive and manufacturing industries. For firms in these industries, multinational activity required foreign direct investment of *capital* for plant and equipment in order to produce abroad and hence be classified as MNE: an MNE was a firm that made foreign *direct capital* investments.[3] Firms that solely engaged in exports, technology licensing, loans, or portfolio investment abroad, but whose assets (equity investment) were located solely in one country were not considered to be MNEs. Over time, as the forms of international activity of firms have become more complex, this distinction between MNEs (as foreign direct investors of capital) and firms with international activities (but with no direct foreign investment) has tended to blur. Yet the literature on MNEs has tended to focus on those firms with direct capital investments abroad.

For firms in many service industries, however, foreign direct investment abroad may not be necessary (or may represent a small, even token amount) to engage in direct activities in a host country. In service industries firm-specific advantage is often bound up in the human capital of the managers and staff sent abroad, not in plant and equipment. Hence substantial overseas activity can be undertaken without transferring substantial monetary capital. There may be substantial investment (transfer) of human capital, but this foreign direct investment does not show up on the accounting books of the firm or in statistics on foreign direct investment. This problem of book capital investment compared to people investment can be illustrated by the case of Korea. As reported by Kyung-II Ghymn (1980), in 1976 Korea reported *total* foreign direct investment (in all countries and in all industries) of only $64 million in 103 subsidiaries outside Korea. Yet in the same year Korean-owned construction firms just in the Middle East and just in the construction industry employed over 60,000 Korean nationals. The FDI of these Korean construction firms in the Middle East was quite small if financial capital only is counted. Yet their transfer of resources in the form of human capital was quite large. Traditionally, the wages earned by these overseas workers would be credited as an export of labour services. But this convention may not give a useful picture of the economic forces at work in this situation. This problem is of only minor consequence for MNEs in the manufacturing and resource sectors since their export of financial capital is large relative to their transfer of human capital. For firms in some service industries, however, the transfer of human capital can be the major avenue of transfer.

How then can we distinguish between a pure export of a service and multinational operations by an MNE in the service industry? Perhaps even this distinction is not a useful one any more, given the proliferation of the forms of international operations beyond the triumvirate of exporting, licensing, and foreign direct investment. Yet, to use an example, there would seem to be differences between: an advertising agency in New

York designing an ad campaign in New York for a British client for use in Britain; an ad agency in New York with an agent in the UK who directs work to the New York office; and an advertising agency with a full staff in the UK to service the British market.

Similar distinctions could be made in banking, insurance, shipping, construction, hotels, tourism, etc. These problems with delimiting boundaries between FDI and exports are particularly severe for TWMs in the service industries. Typically low- and middle-income countries are capital short and labour abundant. Moreover, the governments of these countries often impose restrictions on capital exports. Hence firms in these countries in the service industries are more apt to substitute their relatively inexpensive (but often human capital intensive) workers for capital, plant and equipment in their operations abroad. In many cases TWMs in service industries provide little or no capital for their operations abroad. Capital is accessed abroad or supplied by joint venture partners so that their only investment is in the form of human capital.

For these reasons, it would seem reasonable when analysing TWMs in the service industries to devote more attention to their transfer of human capital within the firm than to the transfer of money capital or physical plant and equipment. In fact, we can go one step further by *defining* TWMs in the service industries as those firms that transfer capital (human, money and physical) *within the boundaries of the firm*. The important characteristic is that resource transfers are made *within* the firm, not via the market. Using this definition on the example of Korean (or Filipino, Thai, Indian or Chinese) construction workers, an enterprise would be classified as an MNE if it operated abroad using its own workers to undertake construction projects on its own behalf. A Korean firm that merely contracted for workers to be employed by another unrelated firm abroad would be classified as an exporter of labour services. The questions to be answered in the next section on the theory of TWMs is how TWMs have generated the firm-specific advantages that enable them to operate abroad in competition with other MNEs and locally owned firms; why they choose to exploit them overseas; and why they internalise this transfer within the firm rather than via the market for services.

8.3 THEORY AND EVIDENCE ON TWMs

The theory of the MNE is well developed (Dunning 1981; Rugman 1981; and Buckley and Casson 1976). Dunning's eclectic theory of the MNE posits three conditions necessary for a firm to engage in multinational activity: firm-specific advantages which allow it to compete with firms in the host country; country-specific advantages which attract it to produce in the host country; and internalisation advantages which make servicing the foreign market through internal transfer of goods, services and factors of production more attractive than selling them via the external markets for goods, technology, capital and labour.

The eclectic model has been used to analyse the operations of TWMs in *manufacturing* industries by Wells (1983), Lall (1983), Lecraw (1977, 1981), and many others. (See the bibliography.) In summary, they found that the firm-specific advantages of these TWMs lay in three areas: (1) their proprietary process technology (small-scale, flexible, labour-intensive production technology suitable for producing a wide range of outputs using a wide range of inputs); (2) their product technology i.e. products appropriate for low income, labour-abundant countries (low-to-medium quality and price, low-to-medium technology, standardised, low advertising content, unbranded products); and (3) access to low-cost management and production personnel who could be sent abroad. TWMs were attracted abroad to protect their export markets when they were threatened by competitors in low- and middle-income host countries operating behind high tariff barriers and restrictive non-tariff barriers to trade; to circumvent quantitative restrictions in high income markets applied to their home country (for garments, textiles and footwear); to diversify the risk arising from operating in their potentially unstable home country; and to relieve domestic competitive pressures which arose from a small domestic market and a concentrated industry structure. These firms internalised their transfers of goods, services, and factors of production rather than selling them on external markets for several reasons. For firms motivated to go abroad to circumvent quotas and tariffs or to diversify their country risk, FDI was the only means by which they could accomplish their goals. For firms whose firm-specific advantage rested in their proprietary product and process technology, often the value of this technology was not readily apparent to a prospective buyer, not easily transferred via the market (e.g. no instruction manuals), and largely dependent on its operation by the firm's employees. Hence with exports impeded by high tariffs, increasing competition from domestic producers has forced these firms to undertake FDI.

TWMs in the manufacturing sector have typically invested in 'downstream' countries with lower wage and income levels and ones whose manufacturing sectors were at a lower stage of development and technological sophistication than the manufacturing sector in their home countries. Their proprietary process and product technology, ability to manage in low-income countries, and relatively low managerial salaries have enabled them to compete in some industries and in some market segments against locally-owned firms and MNEs based in high income countries. There has been some 'upstream' investment by TWMs in the manufacturing sector of three kinds: (1) to produce products to cater for nationals from their home country living in the host country; (2) as pure risk-diversifying measures to move capital abroad into more stable environments; and (3) to integrate backward to access essential inputs, or forward into final assembly operations from their base in the home country. This last group of TWMs is of particular interest since they may represent a strong competitive force in the future. They have discovered that the competitive advantage in their products lies in the intermediate assembly operations they perform in their home country and have integrated forward and/or backward in order to capture the profits available from the entire chain of production. This strategy is particularly feasible for TWMs based in countries with a broad manufacturing base (such as Korea, Taiwan, Brazil and Mexico), and less feasible for firms in countries in which pure export platform industry (especially if it is foreign owned) predominate (such as Singapore and Malaysia).

Turning to TWMs in the service industries there are both similarities and differences in their firm-specific advantages, location-specific advantages, and internalisation advantages. For TWMs in many service industries their prime FSA is their educated, skilled, trained, and relatively low-wage labour. Hence these firms are often found in such labour-intensive industries as construction and hotel management and are based in India, Pakistan, Bangladesh, the Philippines, Taiwan and Korea – countries that have traditionally exported labour. This relationship between the labour exports of these host countries and the existence of TWMs in the construction and hotel industries in these countries in some ways parallels the relationship found by Wells (1983) between goods exports and FDI by TWMs. However, it raises the question of why labour exports at arms length via the market and labour exports via the internal markets of TWMs coexist side by side.

The answer may be found in two factors: technology and management. When labour is exported from these countries, typically it is semi-skilled or skilled labour, less often managerial labour due to the high transactions and information costs involved in hiring managerial personnel at arm's length. These high costs arise from the nature of management itself: incomplete contracts, managerial discretion, and the difficulty of monitoring, evaluating and controlling managerial behaviour. TWMs, however, face these problems to a much lesser degree when they transfer their personnel abroad since they have had long-term, on-going relationships and experience with the managers they send abroad. One of the problems encountered by firms that hire workers from low-wage countries on a contract basis is that these workers, after accumulating enough money, often wish to return home prior to the end of the contract. Such labour turnover is highly disfunctional for a firm, especially if it occurs among its managers. Korean (or Philippine) construction firms can transfer abroad not only construction workers, but the entire management structure and hence be low-cost bidders on some types of contracts. As yet, TWMs in the construction industry do not have the ability to compete on very high technology construction contracts, but they are fast developing it. Moreover, they can, and have, joined construction consortia with firms based in high-income countries who can provide the technology to complement their skills.

TWMs in the banking industry have gone abroad for other reasons. Their FSAs rest in their knowledge of their customers in the home country. When their customers go abroad, through exports and FDI, they tend to follow them. As Wells (1983, pp. 107–17) points out, banks in low- and middle-income countries have access to banks abroad through their correspondent banking relationships. But for anything beyond routine transactions, the transactions and information costs of dealing through correspondent banks mount rapidly until it becomes more efficient to open a representative office or branch abroad. TWM banks are also motivated to go abroad by the entry of other multinational banks into their home country. These multinational banks based in high-income countries can offer local exporters world-wide financing and information services and possibly use these services as a wedge to serve local firms in their domestic operations as well. In response, TWM banks move to replicate the international services of their multinational competitors. In Hong Kong, for example, the trade orientation of the colony and its role as a major international financial centre have allowed local banks to develop a wide range of international trade and financial services, services that rival and in some instances surpass those of banks in high-income countries: electronic funds transfer and banking are notable examples. These high-technology FSAs then allow Hong Kong banks to compete head-on with other multinational and national banks both in Hong Kong and in other markets. Such TWM banks are also in a good position to service the needs of the rapidly expanding expatriot communities from South America, Asia, the Middle East, and to a much lesser extent Africa in high-income countries.

Of the 307 foreign banks with operations in New York, 9 are

Table 8.1: Foreign banks in New York

Group[a]	No.	Total staff	Staff of 10 or more	Staff of 20 or more	Top 500
Low-income economies	9	341	8	8	21
Lower middle-income economies	33	386	19	10	30
Upper middle-income economies	97	5,332	60	43	74
High-income oil exporters	15	152	16	15	25
Industrial market economies	138	13,745	105	93	324[b]
East Europe non-market economies	15	600	11	11	43

Notes: (a) This grouping uses the World Bank's classification of countries; (b) this includes 119 United States banks.

based in low-income countries and 130 in middle-income countries (Table 8.1.)[4] Of the 180 international banks with 20 or more employees in New York (indicating a substantial presence and operations), 61 (34 per cent) are based in low- and middle-income countries. Of the 500 largest banks in the world, 125 (25 per cent) are located in low- and middle-income countries. Using the dis-aggregated country data, the extent of a country's banking representation in New York is strongly related to the extent of its trade with, and the number of its citizens in, the United States.

Banking is one industry in which the 'downstream' nature of operations of TWMs is not necessarily observed, i.e., TWM banks follow the home country's trade and immigration patterns, they do not operate almost exclusively in 'downstream' countries with lower levels of per capita income and/or per capita manufacturing output. Some TWM banks also locate offices in major money centres such as New York and London as listening posts for information on financial developments world-wide and to gain access to advanced banking technology. According to the Bank of Korea, loans by subsidiaries and branches of Korean banks located abroad to customers were divided between Korean firms (57 per cent), Koreans abroad (14 per cent), foreign firms (5 per cent) and other financial institutions (24 per cent). The purpose of these loans was for trade financing (27 per cent), construction project financing (32 per cent), bill discount (23 per cent) and other (8 per cent). This data supports the conclusion that TWM banks service mainly firms from their home countries and home-country nationals residing abroad, and that their loans go mostly toward trade financing–facilitating and other service-type operations.

A roughly similar set of factors has motivated a small number of insurance firms in low- and middle-income countries to go abroad since insurance is an essential trade service. The Life Insurance Company of India, for example, has operations and offices world-wide to cater to the large expatriate Indian community abroad.

TWMs in the shipping industry have followed a similar pattern to that of TWMs in banking and insurance: they have followed their country's trade. For these firms, their FSAs originally lay in knowledge of the products and producers and the need for imports in their home country. Efficient shipping requires ships to operate at full capacity. Over time these firms have developed knowledge of trade patterns between other countries. Low wages for crew and officers (and often low-cost ships) allow these firms to be low-cost competitors on these routes. Some of these firms have also acquired or developed FSAs in the technology of shipping that allow them to compete head-on with other multinational shippers based on the quality and convenience of their services, and not just their low cost. Some of the largest shipping firms in the world, for example, the Pao and Tung groups in Hong Kong, are located in low- and middle-income countries. TWMs are also found in air transport, but, with a very few exceptions such as Cathay Pacific Airlines, these are government-owned, national-flag carriers.

There are also several TWMs in the construction industry. From 1970 to 1982 Korean construction firms had received approval to invest over $35 million abroad, roughly 15 per cent of Korea's total outward FDI. A Philippine company, CDCP, (with assets of $400 million) has undertaken major construction projects in the Middle East. In 1984, CDCP had to be bailed out by the government for losses and/or non-payment on contracts undertaken abroad. Several Taiwanese construction firms have undertaken major overseas construction projects. Brazilian construction and oil-drilling firms have extensive operations in Africa and often trade their services and supporting equipment for oil and other imports essential to Brazil. These TWM construction firms often form joint ventures with firms in the host country to increase their chances of winning contracts.

There are also TWMs in the hotel industry. Dunning and McQueen (1981) found that there were severalTWM hotel chains with more than one hotel located outside their home country. The ones with active management control by the parent in the home country were largely located in other low- and middle-income neighbouring countries (Dunning and McQueen 1982). Their FSAs lie in their ability to provide expertise in appropriate, low-cost construction, low-cost management and personnel who at the same time can provide quality service at international standards. These firms are motivated to go abroad by a saturated domestic market for international-class rooms, coupled, of course, with the impossibility of exporting hotel services produced in the home country. TWMs are also active in the trading sector. Chinese trading houses based in Hong Kong, Taiwan and Singapore through their affiliated and associated firms located at home and abroad control a significant part of the trade of Southeast Asia and between the Asia–Pacific Rim countries and North America and Europe. Indian trading houses operate extensively throughout South Asia, the Middle East and Africa. Several Indian trading companies are part of one of India's industrial houses so that in some respects they resemble mini Japanese trading houses. Korea's industrial conglomerates such as Dae Woo, Hyun Dai, Sam Sung and Sun Kyong also resemble mini Japanese trading houses, although as yet they do not engage in significant third-party or third-country trade.

It is also interesting to note the service industries in which few, if any, TWMs operate: many financial services (stock brokerage), media (television and radio, newspapers, advertising), travel and tourism, communications, power generation, restaurants, and health care. For these industries, although they are populated with MNEs from high-income countries, firms in low- and middle-income countries have not developed the advantages necessary for multinational operations.

8.4 SUMMARY AND CONCLUSION

Despite the outpouring of research on TWMs in the manufacturing sector over the past decade, from time to time a question has been raised as to whether their number, size and significance have justified so much attention. In service industries such as shipping, banking, hotels, international trade, and construction TWMs have become a significant force in certain regions and even world-wide: 30 per cent of all employees of foreign-owned banks in New York work for banks based in low- and middle-income countries. Sixty thousand Korean workers were employed by Korean construction firms in the Middle East in the late 1970s. The Pao and Tung groups based in Hong Kong have among the largest fleets in the world. Chinese trading firms control a significant percentage of Pacific trade. The Regent, Penninsula, and The Park Hotel groups operate throughout Asia.

The FSAs of these TWMs seem to have two characteristics: possession of a *package* of skilled but low-wage workers and managers who can be transferred abroad at low cost; and proprietary technology with which to produce an internationally acceptable level of services. In certain cases – shipping and some banking and construction services – some TWMs are at the fore front of the service technology in their industries. TWMs in the service industries have most often been drawn abroad to service domestic exporters (banking, trading and shipping) or to utilise undercapacity resources (construction, hotels). TWMs internalise their foreign operations within the boundaries of their firms since their FSAs are bound up in the human capital of their employees and their ability to manage them, or, as is the case in banking, when purchasing international banking services via the market would lead to high transaction costs and to a dissipation of their FSAs in client relations.

In the future, we might expect to see an increase in the number, size, scope, and geographical reach of TWMs in the service industries as the wage gap between low- and middle-income countries and high-income countries persists, as the human capital in these countries continues to be increased toward the levels in high-income countries, and as more and more low- and middle-income countries turn toward an outward-looking development strategy.

NOTES

1. Wells (1983) has collected a large data set on TWMs as part of the Harvard Multinational Enterprise Project. But this data set is far from complete.

2. See Panglaykim (1979) for a description of the 'known' interests of the Kwok Brothers.

3. See Vernon (1971), Chapter 1 for the methodology of the selection of the 187 firms in the Harvard Multinational Enterprise Project.

4. This classification of countries follows that of the World Bank.

Part Four

9

Policy Issues in International Trade and Investment in Services

Peter Enderwick

9.1 INTRODUCTION

The problem of restrictions on world trade and investment in services is currently at the very centre of international policy debate. For the first time service sector trade and investment issues are to form part of the remit of the General Agreement on Tariffs and Trade (GATT). Longstanding codes on the liberalisation of capital movements and invisibles have recently been reviewed and strengthened. Participation in lucrative service markets has been used by one nation as a bargaining lever in its attempts to obtain access to a heavily protected goods market in the service firm's source nation.

Liberalisation of international services may be seen as a logical extension of the domestic deregulation which has affected service sectors such as air transport, telecommunications and banking and finance in many of the advanced economies including the US, UK, Canada, Japan and Australia and which is now reaching a number of the developing nations including Malaysia, Taiwan and India. As shown in Chapter 1 both regulation and deregulation have important implications for competitive strengths, opportunities for the internationalisation of operations, industry structure and the degree of market competition. However, the easing of restrictions on world trade and investment in services raises a number of issues which may differ in both kind and degree from those associated with the liberalisation of domestic services.

The intention of this chapter is to examine the more important of these issues. The discussion is organised into eight sections. The first six deal with the liberalisation of service trade and investment. Section 9.2 outlines the case that has been made for restrictions. The pressures for a lowering of restrictions are considered in section 9.3. This is followed by an examination of restrictions in particular service sectors. The obstacles to achieving any meaningful liberalisation are the subject of section 9.5. Current and proposed agreements for a lowering of restrictions are discussed in section 9.6. Section 9.7 represents a switch in emphasis with an examination, from the perspective of the potential host economy, of the problems of attracting service investments. A summary is provided in section 9.8.

9.2 JUSTIFICATION FOR RESTRICTIONS ON TRADE AND INVESTMENT IN SERVICES

A variety of arguments have been put forward in defence of restrictions on services. Some represent the simple extension of a related case for the protection of tangible commodities. Others, specific to the service sector, are based on the particular characteristics of service outputs. There are five principal defences.

The first is one widely used in visible trade, the infant-industry argument. Here, restrictions offer protection from competitive pressure for emergent service industries. Protection, in theory provided only while the new industry establishes itself, allows high cost and inexperienced producers to coexist with more efficient competitors. As the industry becomes established it enjoys a lowering of unit costs (as scale increases or costs fall through learning curve effects) until eventually the industry can survive unprotected. The essence of the argument is that protection is temporary; experience suggests that in many cases the expectation of continued protection fosters inefficiency and high cost production resulting in the need for perpetual protection.

This argument has been used by some of the advanced economies in their desire to establish new service technologies but is most widely used in defence of developing country service industries. The principal defect of this argument is that infancy does not constitute necessary grounds for protection. An efficient capital market would fund an industry which was economically viable in the longer term by prudent weighting of changing cost conditions. If such an appraisal did indicate the need for assistance, financial subsidy would appear to be more appropriate than protection.

Subsidisation could be justified in three situations. The first is where capital market imperfections preclude adequate evaluation or the supply of funds. Subsidisation could form a second-best solution to this problem (the first-best solution being the restructuring of the capital market). Second, imperfections in the market for risk-taking may mean an insufficient supply of entrepreneurial skills. Again, subsidisation as a form of risk-underwriting could stimulate entrepreneurial talent. Paradoxically, protectionism by curtailing the inflow of such skills from overseas would do little to encourage the establishment of the infant industry. Finally, there may be positive externalities which accrue from the learning of particular service technologies. Again this argument is not one for protection, indeed it supports the case for opening up a market to the importation of such technologies perhaps through licensing or franchising. Subsidisation may be necessary if such technologies are offered on the external market on restrictive terms (Casson 1979).

The second defence of restrictions on services is to argue that governments may impose restrictions on the entry to, or scale of, services which could impose external costs. This could arise, for example, in road haulage, air transport or energy distribution where unrestricted competition could result in environmental damage through overcongestion, the impairment of safety standards, or wasteful duplication. This argument is not really one for restrictions on trade or investment in services, rather it indicates a possible case for public ownership or regulation.

A third, and related argument, is for the prevention of foreign participation in 'essential' service industries. The most widely cited example is the need to ensure domestic ownership of banks and other financial institutions if independence in monetary and credit policies is to be guaranteed. This argument again confuses the need for regulation of such institutions with the case for domestic (and often public) ownership. Further, it is based on the assumption that a nation enjoys a high degree of independence in its control of monetary aggregates. The growing interdependence of world financial markets and exchange rates casts doubt on the validity of such an assumption.

The fourth justification recognises the particular characteristics of some services, the most significant being the possibility of destructive competition and problems of market failure stemming from informational deficiencies. It is sometimes

217

argued that in the absence of regulation, service provision will address only the most lucrative market segments. Similarly, unrestricted competition may be pernicious in industries characterised by high fixed costs and fluctuating demand such as transport or communications. The lack of information on the part of service consumers is a widely-used justification for the regulation of service quality and occupational entry.

But as Hindley and Smith (1984) point out, this case for regulation only really applies when buyers' information needs and their likely responses are uniform and when information dissemination is costly. Whilst this argument has the merit of recognising the market failures likely to occur in the supply of certain services it errs in attributing such failures to ownership nationality or the extent of competition. Destructive competition is as likely in an unrestricted market where production is wholly undertaken by indigenous firms as where foreign ownership and participation are prevalent. Similarly, the entry of foreign suppliers may encourage the provision and dissemination of information to consumers as product differentiation and quality assurance based on branding increase.

Finally, there are a group of defensive arguments which have little substance. A number of developing countries limit foreign participation in service industries to minimise foreign exchange losses. This balance-of-payments rationale fails to recognise the potentially greater resource cost of inefficient import-substituting production. If lower-cost overseas suppliers are denied market access, the discriminatory government procurement policies or restrictions on the purchase of foreign exchange which favour higher-cost indigenous suppliers amount to a form of continuing subsidy. The costs of such a policy need to be weighed against the balance-of-payments effects of allowing the importation of services or the establishment of overseas-based suppliers. A related argument is the need for government intervention to ensure the 'balanced' development of the service sector. The economic reasoning behind such an argument is unclear. Efficient resource use and welfare maximisation imply specialisation according to comparative advantage. Efficient specialisation may not be compatible with some vague concept of 'balanced growth' (Griffiths 1975).

The final argument in this group is one of retaliation. A country imposes restrictions on service trade and investment because it believes that its own enterprises are subject to similar restrictions. Clearly, retaliation is an inefficient response from a global perspective, merely exacerbating restrictions on trade and investment.

As the above discussion suggests there are few real grounds for justifying the imposition of restrictions on world trade and investment in services. Many of the arguments confuse the need for some domestic regulation of services (minimum standards, entry qualifications etc.) with restrictions on imports or inward investment in service industries. There may be a strong case for some domestic regulation. Recent experience of deregulation suggests that the complete absence of regulation can result in negative consequences such as loss of service to rural areas or a fall in competition and standards as high-cost producers are absorbed by the more efficient. What is required is 'appropriate regulation' to maintain the standard of services offered on the market irrespective of where such services are produced (ISI 1987).

9.3 PRESSURES FOR THE EASING OF RESTRICTIONS ON TRADE AND INVESTMENT IN SERVICES

The now considerable pressures for an easing of restrictions on world services trade and investment derive from five principal sources. The first is the significance of world trade and investment in services. Official estimates suggest that trade in global services amounted to about $85 billion in the early 1970s and approached $400 billion in the mid-1980s. The volume of service exports doubled between 1960 and 1970 and again between 1970 and 1975 (US Office of the US Trade Representative 1983). Service trade is equal to around 20 per cent of the value of visible trade. Estimates of the value of FDI in services are even more problematic. Applying the average percentage of service-sector investment indicated in Table 1.6 (p. 13) to the 1980 stock of FDI suggests a stock value of overseas service investments of some $146 billion in 1980.

Both estimates are likely to understate the true value of global service trade and investment. One source suggests that US private service exports may have been undercounted by perhaps 38 per cent ($22.5 billion) in 1980 (Economic Consulting Services Inc. 1981). Granted their likely degree of understatement these estimates nevertheless indicate the significance of world services and the potential gains from an easing of restrictions on their international exchange.

The second source of stimulus to a lowering of restrictions is the growing incidence of such restrictions. An International Trade Administration report (1982) discovered that barriers to trade in services have grown in both their scope and incidence. The most severe barriers are to be found in the developing nations although the restrictions imposed by the advanced nations tend to have a greater trade impact. The widening scope of restrictions appears as controls applied to previously unfettered service industries and as new forms of restriction. This is particularly the case for emergent technologies in electronic communications and transborder data transmittal.

Third is the vigorous pressure for a lowering of restrictions displayed by the US authorities. As the dominant nation in service trade and investment the US interest is understandable. However, a number of recent developments have sharpened the incentives. One is the employment prospects offered by an expansion of the service sector. Three-quarters of US non-agricultural employment in 1985 was in services. Employment forecasts for the coming decade suggest that nine out of ten new jobs will be in services. Second, the recent deterioration in the US trade balance has focused attention on the balance-of-payments contribution of services. This contribution could be substantially increased with the creation of a more liberal world market for services. Finally, deregulation of a number of US service industries has resulted in many powerful service enterprises with both the means and inclination to expand their overseas operations. At the same time these firms are disadvantaged in facing competition in their domestic market from the enterprises of overseas nations unwilling to concede reciprocal access to their own economies.

The fourth source of pressure for liberalisation is technological change. Technology is having two major effects. The first is in the creation of completely new services. The integration of innovations in telecommunications, informatics and computer convergence has made possible digital satellite communications and local area networks creating, for example, new household database and access services. The second effect is the impact of new technology on the transportability of services. Some location-bound services are becoming increasingly tradable. There are increased opportunities for the substitution of services

Table 9.1: The likely impact of technological change on the internationalisation of selected services

Industry	Impact of technological change		US foreign presence index[a]
	Transportability	Type of technological change	
Accounting/ auditing	Increasing	Software programmes, remote data analysis	92%
Advertising	Increasing	Direct satellite broadcasting	85%
Banking	Increasing	Telebanking, 'out of hours' services	100%
Computer services and data processing	Increasing	Remote sales and maintenance	–
Construction	Increasing	CAD, remote entry	39%
Educational services	Increasing	Remote sales and teaching, high quality interactive programmes	2%
Engineering/ design	Increasing	Data bases, CAD/CAM, self diagnostic systems, remote maintenance	75%
Insurance	Increasing	Remote purchasing, interactive tailored packages	78%
Brokerage	Increasing	Direct terminal access, elimination of middle-man	84%
Tourism	Increasing	Video disc, video text, computer booking, teleconferencing	90%
Legal services	Increasing	National & international data bases, direct interrogation of bases	2%
Medical services	Increasing	Remote diagnosis and treatment, expert systems	39%
Films and TV	Increasing	DBS, video, cable	50%
Tele-communications	Increasing	Remote entry, Integrated Services Digital Networks (ISDN)	50%
Shipping	Modest increase	New logistic systems	39%
Airlines	Modest increase	Telecommunications-based route planning and control	39%

Notes: (a) Proportion of sales of US foreign affiliates to sales of foreign affiliates plus US exports.
Sources: Krommenacker (1986); US Office of Technology Assessment (1986).

for goods in, for example, the displacement of hard-copy data with electronic audiovisual transfer. Furthermore, these technological changes are affecting the mix between trade and investment in world services.

Table 9.1 provides an assessment of the likely impact of technological change on the transportability of a number of services. Also provided is a brief description of the type of technological advance likely to affect particular services. The final column provides an indication of the dominant mode of US overseas market servicing. A high percentage indicates a preference for FDI as opposed to the exporting of services. The table provides two significant findings.

The first is the universal effect of current and future technological advance in increasing the tradability of services. In the case of information-intensive services (accounting, banking, education, brokerage, legal and medical services) the increase in transportability will be very significant. To date the internationalisation of legal and educational services has been low. This could change as technology opens up new opportunities for exporting such services.

The second significant finding is the likely impact of these changes on the balance between FDI and export of services. In the case of US services many reveal a marked preference for FDI over exports. Seven of the services listed in Table 9.1 have a foreign presence index of 75 per cent or more. The thrust of technological change is likely to increase opportunities for exporting or remote market servicing. This is likely to be the case in accounting, engineering services and construction. Clearly, the growing internationalisation of service industries and new opportunities for trade as well as foreign investment will be responsive to a lowering of restrictions on world services.

The fifth incentive to an easing of restrictions are the potential efficiency gains from such a development. The potential benefits are likely to assume three forms. The first are the efficiency gains from an expansion in size and scale of service firms. Since many service firms enjoy a high degree of involvement in overseas markets, any lowering of barriers to such markets will stimulate the achievement of scale economies. Second, the lowering of protectionist barriers would allow a rationalisation of world service industries. Efficiency benefits could accrue from a more rational allocation of resources as suppliers reflect more closely patterns of comparative advantage. Third, indirect gains

222

could be enjoyed by manufacturing enterprises who, as major purchasers of services, would benefit from a more competitive supply sector.

In addition to these allocative efficiency gains liberalisation could result in qualitative benefits. The competitive stimulus provided by overseas service suppliers could lead to a rise in the quality of services available. In turn, this could stimulate innovation and a reduction in input use or cost (Gray 1983).

9.4 RESTRICTIONS ON PARTICULAR SERVICE SECTORS

International exchange of services is subject to a pattern of restrictions in many ways similar to those impeding goods. For all commodities the principal feature of recent years has been a growth in non-tariff barriers (NTBs). This growth has mirrored the decline in the importance of tariff barriers. Thus, the average US tariff rate was reduced through negotiations from 60 per cent in 1932 to around 5 per cent in 1980. NTBs only began to receive serious attention in the 1970s when there was a noticeable increase in their use, severity and variety. The Tokyo round of the GATT negotiations (1978) identified more than 800 NTBs in use.

The principal types of NTBs affecting services are as follows:

(i)   export subsidies and taxes;
(ii)   discriminatory procurement policies;
(iii)   selective indirect taxes;
(iv)   selective domestic subsidies and assistance;
(v)   restrictive technical and administrative regulations;
(vi)   controls over foreign investment;
(vii)   restrictive immigration policies;
(viii) selective monetary and exchange rate policies;
(ix)   quotas and restrictive trade policies.

The similarity of such barriers on both goods and services was revealed by a United States Department of Commerce Study (1976) which concluded that the problems faced by service suppliers were generally similar to those experienced by goods-producing firms, many were in fact industry specific. This suggests that it is not helpful to talk about a service industries problem; rather, restrictions are more usefully examined on an industry by industry basis.

The following brief discussions identify the principal restrictions experienced by the sixteen service industries examined in Table 9.1.

9.4.1 Accounting and auditing

In international accounting, an industry with a very high level of FDI, the principal obstacles are investment-based and include restrictions on the establishment of foreign branches, limits on the practice and licensing of non-nationals and the non-nationality qualified, and the remittance of earnings. Other difficulties result from discriminatory government procurement practices. The impact of these restrictions in favouring organisational forms which maintain national identity and expansion through acquisition are alluded to in Chapter 4.

9.4.2 Advertising

The global advertising industry reports an extensive range of restrictions. These arise from limits on national ownership (encouraging international associations and tie-ups), discriminatory licensing, taxes and restrictive technical agreements. Major difficulties have resulted from the widespread government ownership and control of broadcasting media. These difficulties are acute in some of the developing countries where fears of cultural imperialism prompt controls over advertising modes and content (UNCTC 1979).

9.4.3 Banking and brokerage

Restrictions on banking, brokerage and other financial institutions are pervasive. A number of countries impose restrictions on the operating forms of banks often prohibiting full branch status or circumscribing areas of legitimate business for foreign firms. Restrictions on personnel transfer (quota or delays in work permits) and the remittance of funds are common. Discriminatory controls include requirements for higher capitalisation of foreign banks, asset limits which constrain the expansion of foreign bank establishments and reciprocity requirements (OECD 1984; Pecchioli 1983). The growing incidence of financial liberalisation has led to an easing of some of these restrictions. For example, Australia has recently announced the opening up of its market to the entry of foreign banks. The principal impact of liberalisation is probably to reduce discriminatory restrictions and increase the likelihood of national treatment for all competing firms.

9.4.4 Computer services and data processing

Barriers to trade in computer services result from the significance of this industry in contemporary economic growth. Restrictions on the entry of foreign firms exist in both the developed (Japan, Italy) and developing (Brazil) countries. Widespread attempts to foster indigenous computer-software industries result in subsidisation, discriminatory purchasing practices, restrictions on licensing and controls on transborder data movements. In the developing countries overseas-based producers experience difficulties in enforcing patent and copyright protection as well as the repatriation of profits. Recent attempts (in Britain and Canada) to introduce tariffs on the value of software material could mean the growing importance of this type of barrier (Benz 1985).

9.4.5 Construction and engineering services

The significant labour content of construction and engineering services means that obstacles to the free movement of personnel will be a problem. A number of developing countries impose a legal requirement whereby the majority of employees must be nationals or that foreign workers obtain work permits. The cyclical nature of much of the industry is a temptation to discriminatory procurement practices and assistance to the domestic industry in the form of export subsidies, soft loans and risk insurance. As Chapter 6 revealed, the pressure on governments for assistance remains considerable. (See also Mansfield 1986.)

9.4.6 Educational, legal and medical services

This group of services has a relatively low international orientation, but this is expected to increase significantly in the future. All three are intensive in their use of skilled and professional labour. They are subject to the sorts of restrictions which many governments impose on professional occupations including entry requirements, restrictions on advertising and mandatory fee scales (OECD 1985). Internationally, these restrictions disallow or disadvantage foreigners. Other obstacles include restrictions on the importation of necessary materials (education) and hardware (medical) and discriminatory government regulation which tends to favour indigenous non-profit institutions.

9.4.7 Insurance

In common with other parts of the financial sector multinational insurance companies face restrictions on foreign ownership, the scope of permissible business activities and discriminatory legislation on requirements for reinsurance with state-owned companies (OECD 1983a).

9.4.8 Tourism

The restrictions on international tourism have led to significant changes in market servicing modes. The preference for FDI among hotel chains have given way to franchising and the sale of management services. This change has been prompted by difficulties in the importation of necessary supplies and in the remittance of profits. The international movem. :nt of tourists is impeded by visa requirements and currency restrictions (OECD 1983b).

9.4.9 Films and TV

This industry is one characterised by considerable exporting of services. Most overseas investment is in marketing and distribution facilities. In common with the international advertising

226

industry there are quantitative restrictions imposed by a number of countries, state monopolies and local work requirements. These restrictions are prompted in part by a desire to protect national cultures. Similar reasoning often lies behind the extensive subsidisation offered to national film producers. The advent of video and direct satellite broadcasting has created new problems of enforcing copyright and ensuring financial appropriation.

9.4.10 Telecommunications

Telecommunications is an international industry subject to very extensive restrictions. These manifest themselves primarily as restrictions on the entry of foreign operators, often because of the existence of state-owned monopolies, difficulties in the importation of necessary hardware and market fragmentation resulting from differing national standards. Government subsidies to the indigenous industry also discriminate against overseas suppliers. The extent of government involvement in this industry, particularly amongst the developing countries is brought out in Chapter 5.

9.4.11 Air transportation and maritime services

As Table 9.1 (pp. 221) reveals these industries have an important export component. Indeed, most overseas investment is in marketing and support facilities. The air transport industry is rife with both national and international regulation. At the national level overseas carriers face difficulties arising from discriminatory sales practices, discriminatory taxes and differential landing fees all of which tend to favour national airlines. At the international level cartel arrangements exist to allocate routes and set tariffs. The complexity of regulation of maritime services is comparable. Again taxes, government procurement decisions and the use of preferential cargo allocation schemes tend to work against overseas suppliers.

Table 9.2 provides a summary by industry of the major type of restriction encountered by US service firms. As the table reveals, predominantly investment-related difficulties were reported by firms in accounting, advertising, banking, health

Table 9.2: Restrictions experienced by US service industries in international markets

Industry	Investment						Trade/investment				
Accounting/auditing	x		x		x					x	
Advertising	x	x	x	x			x	x	x		
Banking/brokerage	x	x	x	x				x		x	
Comp. serv. and eng. serv.	x					x	x			x	x
Construct. and eng. serv.		x	x	x	x	x		x		x	x
Educ. serv.				x					x		
Legal serv.		x						x		x	
Med. serv.	x	x	x			x			x		
Insurance	x	x		x		x		x			x
Tourism	x		x		x	x			x		
Films & TV	x	x		x	x	x	x		x		
Telecomms		x	x			x				x	
Air trans.				x		x	x				x
Maritime services				x		x	x		x		x

Source: United States Department of Commerce (1976).

Remittance and repatriation restrictions

Ownership requirements

Personnel and employment restrictions

Taxes

Intellectual property

Government subsidies

Government-controlled facilities

Licensing

Duties and quotas

Standards

Restrictive government procurement

services and the hotel sector of tourism. Trade and investment restrictions affected telecommunications, computer services, construction and engineering services, education and legal services, films and TV and insurance.

Finally, there are two additional developments which may create further restrictions for some service industries. The first is the growing technological protectionism, in particular as practised by the USA. The rapid growth of restrictions in this area is affecting both technology imports and exports and more generally the terms on which technology is transferred. While the major impact of technological protectionism is on goods, some services will be affected particularly R&D facilities and repair and maintenance support infrastructure. Second, the mushrooming of joint venture arrangements is likely to distort patterns of market access as collaborating firms enjoy preference over non-collaborators. Such ventures already affect a large number of R&D programmes. The impact of these arrangements on competition is mixed (OECD 1986).

9.5 OBSTACLES TO THE LOWERING OF RESTRICTIONS

The extent of restrictions on international trade and investment in services outlined in the preceding section coupled with the potential benefits from a lowering of the same (section 9.3), suggest that considerable progress might be expected in the liberalisation of world services. However, the very limited progress which has been made is due in part to considerable opposition to liberalisation.

Obstacles to the lowering of restrictions on global services fall into two categories. The first are those indicating a lack of incentive to, or practical difficulties in, negotiation. The second represent outright opposition, particularly by developing countries, to any negotiations.

The first group comprises three substantive considerations. First, while the US has undoubtedly been the driving force in the present round of negotiations, the decline in American economic and political hegemony in recent years may make the process of eventual agreement on acceptable regulation more difficult (Miller 1985). The US position is further weakened by the general consensus that she has most to gain from any lowering of restrictions.

The second argument is based on the difficulties of demonstrating the economic gains from further liberalisation. The complexity of such a demonstration follows from the difficulties of defining and delineating services, data inadequacies, the extent of internal trade and uncertain economic conditions. The problems of defining service activity were alluded to in Chapter 1 where the two most popular approaches, that based on the characteristics, particularly the intangibility of services, and the residual approach were outlined. (For a fuller discussion of these problems the reader is referred to Hill 1977.) Valuation problems result from the difficulties of separating the measurement of service content from that of goods or people (Grubel 1987). These problems stem, in large part, from the absence of an adequate theory of service activity (Rugman 1987). In the international context the limitations are even greater.

Definitional problems lead to various forms of categorisation (see Boddewyn, Halbrich, Perry and Perry 1986). Data problems are compounded by national differences in the compilation of estimates and the tendency for balance-of-payments accounting procedures to include all invisible items within service-sector estimates. The inclusion of income or expenditure on items as diverse as food aid, military funds and investment income overstate the value of traded services.

Measurement problems are created by the fact that a large amount of service trade is intra-MNE trade. This means that both the extent of such trade and the terms of exchange (due to transfer pricing) are extremely problematic. The extent of internal service trade is not fully understood. Analysis of the world's leading manufacturing MNEs indicates that about 34 per cent of their total international trade is internal (Dunning and Pearce 1985). Incomplete estimates of US service trade suggest that in 1984 MNEs accounted for around $58 billion out of total service sales of $104 billion. Perhaps one-quarter of majority-owned affiliate sales went to the US parent or related affiliates (Whichard 1987).

If one accepts the arguments of Markusen (Chapter 2) that all MNEs, regardless of their industry classification, are in the business of trading services as they transfer intangible FSAs, the measurement and valuation problems appear insurmountable. Markusen points out some of the limitations of current approaches to the compilation of external accounts in the light of this definition of international services trade.

The calculation of potential economic gains from further liberalisation are not helped by the uncertain conditions prevailing in the world economy over the last few years. Uncertainty about the likely duration of a period of comparatively free trade in services compounds any cost-benefit analysis of liberalisation, and for nations facing probable costs of concession curtails the relevant benefit payback period (Aronson and Cowley 1985).

These measurement problems do not simply impede the demonstration of gains from a relaxation of trade and investment restrictions. They also hinder the process of monitoring acceptance of, and adherence to, any agreement. In the light of such apparent detection problems the incentive for cheating could be high. The expectation of widespread 'free-riding' by non-adherents reduces the estimated benefits for adherents compounding the problem of achieving initial agreement.

The third and final difficulty in achieving a freer environment for global services is the problem of merging any new proposals with existing agreements. Important agreements have been achieved within a number of forums including the OECD, the European Community and UNCTAD. The question that arises is whether further liberalisation is best achieved within existing agreements (and forums) or whether new initiatives and structures, e.g. GATT, are likely to be more successful. If a preference for the latter prevails the content and form of negotiations must take account of existing instruments.

Opposition to any further liberalisation has been expressed by a number of developing countries. Much of this opposition is based on arguments examined in section 9.2 as justifications for existing restrictions. Thus, a desire to protect infant service industries, a fear of balance-of-payments difficulties if the domestic market is easily accessible, and a wish to ensure national sovereignty over infrastructure activities deemed as crucial to development serve as arguments to both the imposition of restrictions and the retention of existing controls (Sapir 1985). Section 9.2 discussed the extent to which such arguments could be supported. Similar reservations would apply here. If, for example, certain service technologies are seen as central to economic development, it is incumbent upon policy-makers to obtain those technologies on the best possible economic terms. This may or may not imply indigenous ownership (or control).

More finely-focused opposition emphasises the present lack

of interest on the part of many developing economies in competing in any freer world market for services. Many have only reached the peak of their competitiveness in visible, particularly manufactured, goods and wish to see first a greater degree of transparency in the global market for these commodities. Contrasts between nations in the stage of economic development introduces similar contrasts in trade aspirations. The US, as the major instigator of new moves on liberalisation have also been accused of selectivity in such liberalisation. In particular it is claimed that the US is only really interested in increasing access to service industries in which they have a strong competitive profile such as educational, financial and business services. They are not as keen to see the same lowering of barriers in industries where developing country MNEs are competitive e.g. construction (see Chapter 8). Indeed, there has even been opposition to any lowering of restrictions from a number of US service firms who find themselves disadvantaged by the need to make substantial adjustment in the face of domestic deregulation.

The problem encountered in attempts to achieve such liberalisation of world services is that national governments view the potential costs and benefits from a distinctly nationalistic perspective. Globally, the lowering of barriers is not a zero-sum game (Sapir 1985). The probable benefits are likely to outweigh the costs. The difficulty is of course the differential incidence of costs and benefits and in devising suitable mechanisms for dealing with the problems of 'losers'.

9.6 APPROACHES TO THE LIBERALISATION OF TRADE AND INVESTMENT IN SERVICES

While the current GATT deliberations on the liberalisation of services trade are at the centre of the international stage it is important to note that there already exist a significant number of other instruments concerned with this issue.

In 1961 the OECD established two codes – the Code of Liberalisation of Current Visible Operations and the Code of Liberalisation of Capital Movement – whose objectives are to ensure that residents of different OECD member countries enjoy the same freedom to engage in business with each other as that enjoyed by the residents of a single country. Clearly, the achievement of this objective entails the elimination of barriers to cross-border trade in intangibles. The Invisibles Code, which covers a broad range of service operations, offers a detailed analysis of trade in sectors such as insurance, tourism and audiovisual works. The Capital Movements Code which deals with most medium- and long-term financial transactions encompasses direct investment in both service and non-service sectors.

The Codes, which have the legal status of Decisions of the Council of the OECD are binding on member countries. Despite this, the OECD forum inevitably results in some shortcomings. The first is that the OECD is really a consultative rather than a negotiating body (Ewing 1985). Its specialist committees make specific recommendations to member states, there is no substantive negotiation (OECD 1986b). Second, it is possible for member countries to avoid or evade aspects of the codes. The development of voluntary restraints or recommendations in the domestic market have a distortionary impact on services trade; an impact which may be difficult to quantify. Such measures often coexist with apparent adherence to the general body of recommendations since temporary exceptions are permitted if economic or financial circumstances justify them. Third, the OECD codes may be criticised for treating the symptoms (transactions) of a problem rather than the problem (restrictions on transactions) itself (Griffiths 1975). This criticism is increasingly being met with recent revisions to the Codes. The review process now focuses on the drawing up of an inventory of obstacles to trade and investment in a particular sector. The justifications for such restrictions are also examined. The OECD may recommend the removal or attenuation of restrictions which cannot be justified. Finally, the composition of the OECD, with its restriction to the most affluent industrialised nations, means that any recommendations will constitute only a partial solution. The characteristics of member nations also determine the service sectors most likely to receive attention. The recent review has concentrated on banking, insurance, tourism and audiovisual works. There has been no consideration of service industries like construction or engineering services where developing countries exhibit a growing competence.

The European Community Treaty embodies the right of establishment and freedom to provide services within the Community. The principal articles relating to services are Articles

52 and 59. The European Community has also enacted a number of consultative procedures which address the problems of service industries including shipping, air transport, insurance and banking. In addition to these EC Directives there also exist a large number of other sector-specific agreements. The importance and complexity of industries such as telecommunications, and air maritime transport have led to a wide range of agreements administered by international bodies such as the International Telecommunications Union, the International Civil Aviation Organisation and the International Maritime Organisation. The problem with such agreements, from the perspective of this chapter, is that they seek to address technical and regulatory issues and not the trade issues which are the focus here. Furthermore, their diversity results in the absence of any coherent framework which could be extended to other service sectors (Brock 1982).

It is because of these shortcomings that the US in particular was anxious to see the inclusion of services in the latest GATT round. The incorporation of services within the remit of GATT raises a number of significant questions, the most important of which concern the relevant content of any negotiations and the coverage of such negotiations. The question of content of the proposed GATT negotiations on services entails two subsidiary questions: the first is whether the negotiations should focus just on trade in services or whether they should also include direct investment in service industries; the second is whether service negotiations should or should not be linked to negotiations on other matters.

Rugman (1987) argues the need for a clear distinction between trade in services and FDI in services. This distinction is important for at least two reasons. First, as section 9.4 indicated, there are separate sets of restrictions affecting trade in services and investment in service industries. Their separation will clearly ease the task of bringing the type and extent of restrictions within manageable limits. Second, the experience and competence of GATT as a negotiating forum lies in the area of trade and not direct investment. The separation has now become firmly embodied in the GATT process. The Declaration which was issued on 20 September 1986 following a special session at Punta del Este (Uruguay) restricts negotiations to trade in services; there is no mention of investment in service industries.

With regard to the second question – whether or not service

negotiations should be tied to those over other issues – a variety of possibilities have been suggested. These include concessions to the developing countries over immigration controls in labour-intensive services such as construction, and a lowering of barriers to the importation of manufactured goods from the developing countries. The US, for one, has made clear its refusal to negotiate on the matter of immigration policies. While there is scope for tied negotiations, World Bank estimates suggest that about one-fifth of all manufactured goods exported from the developing to the developed nations in 1983 were subject to NTBs, both the advanced and developing countries are reluctant to tie negotiations over services to those over goods. Again, in practice the separation has been made. Following a compromise decision at Punta del Este, negotiations on services are to be conducted separately and outside the official GATT apparatus but in parallel to those on goods (Randhawa 1987).

The question of the coverage of GATT negotiations hinges on whether such negotiations would be more effective if they were based on the generalisation of successfully agreed bilateral treaties or whether the multilateralism of GATT can be invoked. The US in its national-study submission to GATT indicated the potential value of bilateral treaties.

While recognising that such agreements may be trade restrict-ing the US position is that they could serve as a model upon which multilateralism could build. The US has experience in this area, in particular its recent free-trade agreement with Canada. Indeed, bilateral agreements could offer a number of important lessons for the liberalisation of international services. Rugman (1987) makes the very important point that where internationally traded services are under the jurisdiction of MNEs they will be traded, to a large extent, internally.

Intra-firm trade is particularly high in the US–Canadian case (MacCharles 1985). Liberalisation of trade in services between these two nations would provide a very useful test of the prob-lems likely to be encountered elsewhere. The component ele-ments of such bilateral agreements do not draw a distinction between trade and investment issues but highlight the need for national treatment, minimum regulation, non-discrimination, right of access, transparency, due process and arbitration of disputes (see Malmgren 1985). Gray (1983) emphasises the need for non-discrimination and national treatment if investment issues are to be included. Merely allowing foreign firms the right to establishment will not ensure the full efficiency gains from a lowering of barriers on FDI; equality of treatment in the market place must also be assured.

While the US sees the merit of an incremental approach to the liberalisation of trade and investment in services the ultimate objective is a multilateral agreement. Indeed, if such an agreement is not eventually concluded there is a danger of resort to extraordinary unilateral rights which exist. Section 301 of the Trade Act of 1974 gives the US president a considerable range of retaliatory measures. The threat of such sanctions has already been invoked in two service sector disputes (Van Grasstek 1987).

Whether the desired multilateral agreement can be achieved within GATT has also been questioned. There may be problems in applying the most favoured nation (MFN) clause where economic considerations limit the desirable number of supplying firms, current dispute-settlement procedures which apply to goods may not be appropriate for services and there exist a variety of problems including customs valuation and the location of barriers (Aronson and Cowley 1985). Gray (1983) has argued for the restriction of service negotiations to the group of advanced industrialised economies since it is here that a similarity of interests sufficient to enable agreement may exist. Such a restriction would be contrary to the GATT forum.

More fundamental criticisms question whether any GATT-style agreement, if ever reached, would be enough. The analysis of Malmgren (1985) suggests that the policy focus on barriers to service trade is misplaced and will become increasingly so. As technological opportunities create new forms of services and new methods of delivery the object of concern should be the flow of information. While in theory this may be true, data limitations and the difficulties of defining and measuring service flows mean that at the present time it is a proposal with little merit. Concern about the appropriateness of the GATT forum has been further fuelled by the declaration at Punta del Este which introduced a subtle but significant shift in emphasis. The declaration reveals a new commitment to the expansion of trade in services and its attendant impact on economic development as the primary objective of the negotiations. This represents a notable shift from the goal of dismantling barriers to trade in services (Randhawa 1987).

The limited progress achieved within the GATT forum to date as well as the changing negotiating grounds which seems to result from a series of compromises necessary to achieve any momentum will hardly endear this form to policy-makers in the industrialised nations. The danger is that any agreement which eventually emerges will be ignored or neutralised by a spate of restrictive national regulations which may be respected by GATT.

9.7 POLICY IMPLICATIONS FOR POTENTIAL HOST NATIONS[1]

The second important policy area is the question of attracting service-sector MNEs. For a number of reasons a host nation is likely to derive considerable economic benefit from such investments.

It is now generally agreed that the existence of certain services, particularly producer services like finance, distribution, and research and development, can have a positive effect upon economic growth and performance. Where such services are in short supply all enterprises, both manufacturing and non-manufacturing, will be disadvantaged. Furthermore, such a shortage could encourage, within larger enterprises, the internal sourcing of services. For multi-locational enterprises this sourcing could occur outside the immediate host region or nation with a subsequent loss of economic activity.

Second, the establishment of service infrastructure will have a significant impact on an area's communications costs. In the absence of some of the wide range of comparatively sophisticated service technologies currently available, information capture, analysis and transmission costs are likely to be high. Cost disadvantages may mean the inability to attract additional service investment or to generate a sufficient volume of business to justify the more sophisticated technologies.

Third, the balance of manufacturing and non-manufacturing is the major determinant of the occupational structure of a region. This structure, in turn, is likely to exercise a major influence on new firm formation rates and employment performance. All other things being equal, those regions with an occupational structure favouring professional occupations display significantly higher rates of new firm formation (Storey and Johnson 1987). Similarly, studies for both the UK and US reveal a positive association between the performance of manufacturing firms and industries and their employment of non-production workers (Gudgin, Crum and Bailey 1979; Delehanty 1968).

Fourth, the level of business service provision in a nation may influence the adaptability of that nation's producers to changing economic conditions. This is of considerable importance in the present period of structural change as firms seek to rationalise and upgrade their products and plant.

For these reasons potential host governments need to understand the locational preferences and support needs of multinational service firms. Drawing upon the discussion of Chapter 1 which set out some of their likely characteristics we derive policy implications in four major areas: the targeting of investments; the bargaining position; the likely impact of service investments; and required infrastructure.

9.7.1 The targeting of service multinationals

In identifying potential service investors some changes in orientation will be required. There is evidence, certainly in the case of business services, that direct investment is often preceded by exports from the source nation (Dunning and Norman 1983, 1987). Some familiarity with the local market through initial servicing by export reduces investment risk, which is often significant in the case of services with the need to impose immediate and strict quality control or the attainment of minimum critical mass. Furthermore, investors appear to enjoy privileged access to some of their host-nation market where customers are affiliates of existing clients in the home market. This suggests that targeting should focus on those firms currently serving the local market through some non-equity mode (exporting, licensing etc.). If 'gradualism' in international operations applies to service industries, such firms are the key target group. In addition, where there exists a foreign-owned sector, investigation of parent company service purchases in the home market should be undertaken. There is likely to be a high degree of accordance between parent and affiliate loyalties in areas such as banking, accounting and advertising services.

Second, the attraction of foreign-based services should focus on the direct-investment mode. Although generalisations from the US experience with service affiliate sales dominating exports may be misleading (Sapir 1985) there are grounds for believing that service technologies supplied on a non-equity basis will be on restrictive terms. Technology transfer in services involves the transfer of skills rather than disembodied information. Its time-intensive nature means that the transferring organisation and transferee will seek to develop some form of long-term relationship. This is particularly likely in the case of differentiated services where buyer perceptions are based on the interaction of the firm's output, reputation and image e.g. construction (Chapter 6). In such a case buyers cannot separate the inputs and contribution of licensor and licensee. Underperformance by the licensee could impose significant external costs on the licensor.

Third, the geographical focus of investment attraction should shift. While the principal manufacturing investment source nations encompass the major service multinationals there are some differences. France, West Germany, the UK and USA together account for more than 40 per cent of 'other services'. Service multinationals appear to be of lesser significance in the case of Japan and the Netherlands. The Japanese case is the most interesting. While a large proportion of all outward Japanese investment, 85 per cent of all registered establishments in Europe (Loeve, De Vries and de Smidt 1985) is in commercial and service activities, these tend to be trade supporting and are unlikely to be self-reliant. Competitively, the Japanese are weak in services such as construction and software (Franko 1983). However, some services (insurance, securities) are being pulled overseas in the wake of Japanese manufacturing firms (Marsh 1984). Finally, a number of developing nations are rapidly achieving internationally competitive service industries particularly in banking, construction, shipping and trading (Chapter 8).

9.7.2 The bargaining position

To a degree, the economic impact of inward investment is dependent on the terms negotiated. Where host governments enjoy a strong bargaining advantage they are able to impose their preferences over such matters as local content, technology transfer and earnings remittance. In the case of multinational service firms there exist opposing influences on relative bargaining strength. The limited capital inflow, minimal technology transfer and marginal impact on labour market skills associated with traditional services places host governments, particularly those in the advanced nations, in a strong position (Cowell 1983). In addition, the riskiness of multinational service investments (demands of quality maintenance etc. and high rates of expropriation) means that investors are likely to prefer location in the advanced economies.

Offsetting these considerations, the difficulties of licensing some service technologies restrict the sources of supply to potential hosts. Furthermore, in many developing countries, the resource costs of cultivating indigenous service industries are so high in terms of committing scarce skilled labour resources to areas of relatively low value added and employment creation that such nations are likely to make considerable efforts to buy in services expertise. Clearly, relative bargaining strength is a pragmatic question requiring careful investigation.

9.7.3 The economic impact of service investments

In calculating investment incentives host governments need some assessment of the likely economic impact of inward investment. Service investments raise a number of interesting issues.

First, doubts have been cast on the propulsive effects of service industries. The small size of the producer services sector in most regions, its low export propensity, limited linkages and poor innovative record do not suggest the existence of characteristics conducive to the emergence of growth poles. Offsetting these arguments the possession of a vibrant producer services sector may be valuable in the diffusion of innovations (Antonelli 1985) and in the adjustment to structural change.

Second is their likely employment effects. For a number of reasons employment creation is unlikely to be very considerable. In the USA tradable services accounted for only 1.8 million jobs or 37 per cent of all export-related employment in 1982 (Benz 1985). Although tradeable services display higher labour content than manufacturers (Sapir and Schumacher 1984) the small average size of investing firms, their need for skilled labour and preference for entry by acquisition to ensure both more rapid entry and the achievement of critical mass, all militate against sizeable direct employment creation. Indirect employment creation depends on the ease with which service technologies are diffused and absorbed (Shelp 1985) and the extent to which multiplier effects are retained within the host economy. While precise estimates of these values are not available it is unlikely that multinational service-sector employment would approach the magnitudes associated with foreign-owned manufacturing firms.

Third, the export contribution of service multinationals may be low. In 1979 around 11 per cent of the UK's gross output of services was exported, compared to 33 per cent of the gross output of manufacturing. Existing evidence suggests that investments in business services (management consultancy, selection agencies, banking, insurance) are prompted by the desire to service mainly local markets (Dunning and Norman 1987). In the case of more readily exportable services (shipping, reinsurance) existing favoured locations (Liberia, Cyprus, Cayman Islands, Bermuda) appear to enjoy almost insurmountable advantages built around the virtual absence of regulation. There may be an indirect export impact from those services which enhance the competitiveness of the goods export sector (Miller 1985).

Fourth, there are grounds for concern over the likely durability of service investments. Narrow domestic markets mean that many service multinationals are dependent on overseas earnings. The rapid relative price rise (and poor productivity performance) of services encourages substitution of capital goods for increasingly uncompetitive services. Rapid innovation in high technology services has had a two-fold effect in displacing labour: capital-intensity has risen as 'new technology' has been applied; in addition, changes in the capital-component of output has reduced employment. For example, computer software products increased their market share from 12 per cent to 25 per cent between 1980 and 1985 at the expense of labour-intensive software services (Markusen 1985). Economies of scale in the provision of financial services is encouraging some large enterprises e.g. oil companies, to internalise these functions. Consideration of these factors suggests areas of potential vulnerability within service multinationals.

Fifth, the geographical impact of service multinationals is probably to accentuate national spatial inequalities. Their clustering within metropolitan centres of the most developed regions (Daniels 1982) suggests the possibility of dualistic

241

development. In the case of high technology business services offering wage levels often 50 per cent above the service-sector average, both spatial and wage inequality may be increased (Browne 1983).

Sixth, the contribution of service investments will be related to the existence and structure of non-service production. Clearly, in the case of producer services, suppliers will seek out potential clients in large and fast growing manufacturing sectors. But the relationship is more complex than this. The efficient provision of services to non-service firms may generate positive externalities for these firms enhancing their competitive edge (Miller 1985). But it is important to consider both the size and ownership structure of the goods sector. Where foreign ownership and entry by acquisition are significant, there is a higher probability of centralisation or external regional sourcing of service functions (Marquand 1983). This results from the propensity of acquiring firms to centralise and internalise their service functions both nationally and internationally (Cohen 1981; Marshall 1979).

Finally, there may be indirect benefits from the presence of service multinationals. The accumulation of host-government experience with such firms creates expertise which may be increasingly required in dealing with manufacturing firms pursuing appropriation through contractual and technical services. It is also possible that the existence of comprehensive and competitive business services may act as an inducement to mobile manufacturing firms, reinforcing the linkages between service and goods-producing industries (Marshall 1985).

9.7.4 Infra-structure support

The provision of appropriate infrastructure is a major element in the successful attraction of overseas investment. In the case of service multinationals support may assume novel forms. First, as highlighted at a number of points, there is a correlation between the existence of a vigorous goods sector and the likelihood of attracting service – particularly producer service multinationals. Complementarity appears to be absolutely crucial in the case of high technology services (Browne 1983). This does not necessarily imply close physical location. For a small nation inter-regional trade in business services is perfectly feasible.

Second, tangible infrastructure required by service multinationals is likely to differ from that normally offered. Service firms require a ready pool of highly educated labour. In the United States computer and management services industries 40 per cent of employees are in professional and technical occupations. This compares with an all industry average of 15 per cent (Browne 1983). Location appears to be a critical factor for service firms. Many seek close proximity to major education, communications and research centres (namely, Boston and Stanford in the USA, Cambridge and the 'M4 corridor' in England). More difficult to identify is the importance of intangible support in the form of an accommodative industrial policy encouraging collaboration between service users and suppliers (Gonenc 1984) and an atmosphere conducive to academic/industrial collaboration (Bullock 1983; Lowe 1985; Segal Quince 1985). Such centres may be a necessary, but not sufficient condition, for high technology services growth.

Third, there may be a case for public subsidy of key capital goods, particularly information-transmission systems. Their high initial capital and scale requirements suggest a possible barrier to entry. To date, only the very largest organisations (banks, oil companies, construction and consultancy firms and trading companies) have been able to establish private networks. The existence of industry (SWIFT in banking, airline information) and public data networks suggests that shared networks are both technically and economically feasible. The limited evidence on the adoption of international data telecommunications systems suggests that diffusion rates are fastest for the largest multinationals possessing in-house telecommunications skills. For smaller companies the existence of independent technical and service advisory companies are an important stimulus to adoption (Antonelli 1985).

The extent of financial assistance to the service sector is extremely limited in most nations. Within the European Community only Ireland has a service-specific financial-assistance policy. Stringent requirements on additionality, exportability, technological content and commercial viability meant that even here between 1979 and 1983 annual employment promoted averaged only 1640. A similar experience of limited job creation is also reported for countries like West Germany and Great Britain which have operated service assistance schemes (Bachtler 1987).

9.8 SUMMARY

This chapter has examined a variety of policy issues related to international trade and investment in services. Our discussion of justifications for restrictions (section 9.2) suggests that rarely can such arguments be defended on economic grounds. The growing importance of service trade and restrictions, the determination of the US authorities to achieve greater liberalisation, technological changes and potential efficiency gains all provide an important stimulus to an easing of restrictions (section 9.3). Restrictions on service industries can be grouped into those affecting trade and those affecting both trade and investment (section 9.4). The pattern of NTBs in the service sector is comparable to that evident in goods markets. Despite the considerable incentives to a lowering of restrictions little progress has been achieved. This is the result of both obstacles which exist (section 9.5) and the difficulties of agreeing an acceptable forum and agenda for negotiations (section 9.6).

Section 9.7 examined the implications for potential host nations attempting to attract service-sector multinationals. A re-examination of policies with regard to targeting, bargaining, evaluation of investment impact and assistance seems inevitable.

NOTES

1. This section draws on the more extensive discussion contained in Enderwick (1987).

10

Conclusions

Peter Enderwick

10.1 INTRODUCTION

This concluding chapter has two purposes. The first is to draw together some of the principal findings of the preceding chapters. The second is to highlight areas where further research is required. For ease of exposition the discussion focuses on nine primary areas of interest.

10.2 CONCEPTUAL AND DATA PROBLEMS

Problems of defining exactly what constitutes a service MNE has been a recurring theme in this volume. This problem hampers the collection of meaningful data on the extent of service output both nationally and internationally. It has also retarded attempts at creating a more liberal trading regime for services (Chapter 9). The lacuna in conceptualisation of service activity results in various classifications which provide one way of delineating the service sector. (For a typical listing see Schwamm and Merciai (1985).) The growing importance of services in both the national and international economy are sufficient justifications for further work in this difficult area. Similarly, empirical analysis is impeded by dependence on unsatisfactory data sources, the principal source being IMF balance-of-payments data. The purpose for which this data is compiled means that it is not suitable as a basis for examining international trade in services. Furthermore, the importance of FDI as a mode of overseas-market servicing means that trade data considerably understate the extent of global service transactions. The recent US initiatives

245

in filling some of these data gaps (Whichard 1987) are to be applauded and should be emulated by other nations. Problems of conceptualisation and measurement mean that we are unable to provide an accurate picture of the importance of, or trends in, services. Similarly, it is difficult to quantify the likely benefits (and costs) of further liberalisation.

One important implication of Chapter 2 is that even if these data deficiencies are remedied we will still be viewing global services from a highly restrictive perspective. The most significant service trade will occur within non-service-based multi-nationals in exploiting their competitive assets. The data requirements of this conceptualisation are immense necessitating detailed information on the determinants of the terms of such internal trade. A useful first step in the measurement of this broadened definition of global service trade is the US authorities' compilation of service sales by manufacturing MNEs. Again, this initiative should be taken up by other source nations.

10.3 HETEROGENEITY OF THE SERVICE SECTOR

In the same way that generalisations of the performance of manufacturing disguise significant contrasts between dynamic and more traditional component industries so our discussion must recognise a similar diversity within the service sector. Overall, the potential for service-sector MNEs is vast. As revealed in Chapter 1 most of the major industrial nations can be classified as post-industrial in the sense of their principal source of employment being the tertiary sector. The growing demand for and differentiation of services is coupled with low international penetration of service markets. US affiliates in the non-petroleum goods producing industries had 1974 sales equivalent to 16 per cent of the value of commodity production in the OECD nations (excluding the USA). The comparable figure for US service-industry affiliates was 3 per cent. At the same time the performance of many service firms has provided them with sufficient resources and resilience to consider overseas markets. Thus, between 1973 and 1983 the Fortune service 500 increased their profits at a rate 124 per cent in excess of the rise of the consumer price index. Their performance clearly out-ranked that of the 500 leading industrial corporations. Service firms enjoy a number of advantages during a difficult trading period. They tend to be less vulnerable to cyclical fluctuations, are often able to meet financing needs internally and the non-union status of many service firms yields benefits in a period of rapidly rising labour costs. In addition, as changing conditions have forced many manufacturing and extractive MNEs to accept non-majority ownership positions, service MNEs with their more recent take-off and heterogeneity of output are well placed to adapt their organisational form to meet the evolving demands.

This optimistic picture suppresses the variation which is apparent within the service sector. Some of the most dynamic industries, generally within business services, have been considered in Chapters 3 and 4. At the same time industries such as wholesale distribution, railways and sea transport actually experienced declining output between 1974 and 1984 in a number of countries.

Similar diversity is apparent in productivity levels and growth rates. Estimates for the UK suggest that between 1974 and 1984 annual productivity growth in internationally tradable services was more than three times that of non-tradable services (Ray 1986). The aggregate picture also conceals important differences between nations. While international productivity comparisons between service industries are fraught with tremendous difficulties some suggestive estimates are available. One survey (Economist 1985) suggested that productivity in the Japanese distributive sector was about half that of the US. Clearly, such differences may translate into similar differences in competitiveness. Considerably more disaggregated studies of individual service industries are required. It is only when we understand the differences that exist can any meaningful generalisations be made.

10.4 SERVICE-SECTOR SOURCE NATIONS

With regard to the major source nations for service-sector exports and foreign investment it is apparent that these coincide to a very large extent with those responsible for manufactured exports and MNEs. The OECD nations, and in particular the US, account for most international services. Some minor differences between service and manufacturing source nations are detectable. France holds a more significant position in services than in manufacturing. The opposite is true for Japan.

The potential role of Japanese service firms is perhaps the most widely discussed aspect of changes in the composition of source nations. Traditionally, Japanese service firms have been seen as disadvantaged in their overseas dealings. The source of this disadvantage has been attributed to distance from major export markets, the difficulties of communication which arise from the particular characteristics of the Japanese language and pervasive regulation of domestic service markets (Franko 1983). However, times are changing and any disadvantage is rapidly being eliminated. This is occurring as deregulation of the Japanese market is allowing the importation (and presumably diffusion to Japanese enterprises) of some of the skills necessary for successful overseas operations.

Internationalisation of Japanese enterprises, particularly financial institutions, has been facilitated by technological developments, the data-base strengths of the huge Japanese general trading companies, the continuing multinationalisation of Japanese manufacturing firms and the growing convergence of communications networks (Kakabadse 1987). The dynamism of deregulation is also encouraging the internationalisation of Japanese institutions. This occurs as the traditionally narrow business areas of financial organisations are relaxed encouraging competition at home and overseas and as internationalisation offers the necessary expertise required to compete in the increasingly liberalised home market (Burton and Saelens 1986). The spread of Japanese banks, securities houses and construction companies is likely to both continue and accelerate.

If these service firms attract the level of research which has been paid to their manufacturing counterparts our ignorance will be short-lived. Japanese service firms also raise a number of significant policy concerns, particularly their role in recycling the huge positive Japanese external balance and whether or not they will follow a competitive strategy of specialisation and domination. The position of Japanese banks (four in the world's top five in 1985) and securities houses (particularly Nomura, Daiwa, Nikko and Yamaichi) suggests that this cannot be ruled out. Internationalisation is spreading to the insurance sector, long-term credit banks and eventually perhaps management consultancy and advertising agencies. Japanese service firms represent the greatest potential threat to established service MNEs in a number of sectors.

The role of the developing countries as a source of international services is less clear. While Singapore currently ranks in the top 15 nations by service receipts it earns only one fifth that of the US. However, as Chapter 8 illustrates, in specialist market segments (retail banking, shipping, engineering and construction services, tourism) a handful of developing countries have achieved considerable progress. It is noteworthy that the success of a small number of developing countries in services is similar to the position that has occurred in manufactured goods. Indeed, the countries involved are in many cases identical. This suggests the inequality of development that will occur with a handful of Asian and Latin American countries broadening their economic base.

For Western service MNEs some comfort may be drawn from existing knowledge of the type and extent of restrictions which can be raised against successful manufacturing exporters in these nations. It is to be hoped that liberalisation of service markets prevents a similar pattern of obstacles being raised in these industries. Interestingly, the service investments from the Eastern bloc nations (Chapter 7) have taken a very different form. Most are trade based. Indeed, there is little cross-border manufacturing investment by these nations perhaps because of higher cost labour in the Western nations or a lack of techno-logical or marketing skills on the part of Eastern-bloc producers. Service investments from this area are likely to continue to focus on trade, export support and resource-based activities.

10.5 SERVICE SECTOR HOST NATIONS

There is a similar concentration of service investments within host nations. The overwhelming majority are in the OECD nations (Table 1.6). Exceptions occur in banking and news agencies where regional coverage must be high. Even here there is considerable selectivity with most service investments clustering into a relatively small number of developing economies. One implication of this is that the present pattern of market choice of service MNEs appears to offer little in the way of developmental potential to the majority of developing countries. Protection of home markets may be one factor explaining this inequality but is likely to be less important than the preference of investing firms for high income markets in the Western world.

Spatial inequality in the distribution of service activity is also apparent at the national level. A number of national studies have made clear the longstanding inequalities which exist in the distribution of service employment and output (Bannon 1985; Damesick 1987). Recent studies of overseas investment in industries such as banking suggest that FDI may exacerbate existing inequalities (Choi, Tschoegl and Yu 1986; Damanpour 1986; Daniels 1986). The role of agglomerative or location-specific factors in generating these patterns is an area requiring further research. To maximise the benefits from the presence of service-sector firms, policy-makers need to understand both the infrastructure needs of such firms and the extent to which viable location can be varied.

Service firms raise a number of other issues which need to be addressed. There has been some debate over the likely employment and labour-market effects of service investments. While in the US employment in business services increased by 530 per cent to more than 4.5 million between 1960 and 1984, employment creation in host nations has been much more modest. For example in Ireland, the only European country to operate a service-specific inducement policy, producer services still account for less than 12 per cent of all Irish service employment (Cogan 1986).

Employment quality and levels of remuneration in the service sector have also attracted considerable attention. In the same way that manufacturing MNE branch plants have been criticised for their limited growth potential where they display standardised products, low-skill content, limited linkages and questionable employment stability so low-paid, low-skilled non-union service jobs may become a contentious issue. This is particularly likely where mergers and takeovers have created very large multinational employers in service industries such as cleaning (Landor 1986) or where labour turnover among young non-union workers exceeds 200 per cent per annum as in fast foods (Lamb and Percy 1987). More research is called for in understanding the economic benefits which such investments bring and ways in which marginalised employees can be best protected.

10.6 CORPORATE SYNERGY IN THE SERVICE SECTOR

The degree of product specialisation, and diversification, of service firms is a further area highlighted at a number of points in this book. As suggested in Chapters 1 and 5, product specialisation can be a competitive strength where impartiality forms a positive attribute for clients or where quality is enhanced (Chapter 6). However, extreme specialisation can also create potential vulnerabilities as market changes or advances in technologies disrupt traditional business patterns. Reuters, whose primary business is the collection and transmission of news, now dominates the UK market for financial services providing business information to over 17,000 subscribers. Diversification is also apparent within financial services, accounting firms and advertising agencies.

Within banking, technological progress and internationalisation have provided access to new methods of financing and the development of non-financial services. Competition is now provided by non-banking organisations such as American Express and Merrill Lynch who are striving to provide a complete range of financial services. Accounting firms are rapidly diversifying into areas like management consultancy as traditional business areas (tax, auditing) stagnate. In fact, seven of the top twelve management consulting firms are accounting firms. A similar trend is apparent within advertising agencies who are diversifying into market research, business information and management consultancy.

At the same time there are opposing forces which are curbing the drive for diversification. The high costs of dedicated communications networks are encouraging the growth of firm size, concentration and in some cases specialisation. The failure of several synergistic combines have resulted in divestments as, for example, airlines have sold off hotel groups or car rental divisions. Sometimes these sales have increased specialisation e.g. Pan Am's sale of the Intercontinental hotel chain to Grand Metropolitan; in others new goods/services combines have emerged e.g. possible purchase of a car rental firm by a major car producer. Increased competition within management consultancy is encouraging the search for specialisation in areas such as information technology. Fast-growing firms like Bain and Co. have developed new market niches with their dedicated partner system (close and continuing links with a single competitor in an industry).

The net impact of these opposing trends is not clear. For specialist service firms narrow domestic markets mean a dependence on overseas earnings. For example, overseas affiliate revenues within the advertising industry are equivalent to almost 13 per cent of US domestic earnings. The comparable figure for banking is nearly 20 per cent. In these cases the economic well-being of the source nation industry is closely related to its performance in overseas markets.

For such firms a potential threat exists in the diversification programmes of much larger industrial corporations. This danger has been accentuated by recent developments. The impact of new information technology with its potential for joint use by companies pursuing related activities has created new economic clusterings orbiting around major high-technology firms. Service firms may find themselves absorbed within, and technologically dependent upon such groupings. Furthermore, the economies of scale available in many service areas means that internal demand may result in residual service capacity within clusters. In seeking outside business these traditionally industrial corporations now constitute a new source of competition to service-based companies. A good example is provided by the US giant General Electric. In 1980 23 per cent of corporate earnings were derived from the sale of services. By 1985 this had risen to 38 per cent.

The economics of synergistic combines and economies of scope within service industries are areas where our understanding is both limited and rapidly outdated. Work in this area would yield considerable benefits.

10.7 CORPORATE STRATEGY IN THE SERVICE SECTOR

While the chapters in this collection have touched upon the growth and competitive strategies of service MNEs we still lack anything in the way of a coherent body of thought on the likely strategies of such firms. The discussion of Chapter 1 suggested a number of distinctive features of service MNEs including the importance of branding, specialisation, incremental innovation, differential regulation, and economies of scale, scope, agglomeration and coordination. Other writers cite the importance of factors such as responsiveness to market needs, clear identity, adaptation to local conditions and operational control (Kakabadse 1987). There also exist a number of excellent studies of the ways in which service enterprises market their output

(Cowell 1983) and manage their operations (Heskett 1986).

What is now required is a synthesis of this knowledge with the distinctive features of many global services (e.g. oligopolistic competition, easily imitated technological advantages) to derive some general principles of corporate strategy in the service sector. In addition, research needs to address questions such as the impact of new technologies including networking on the management of internal markets, the determinants of novel market-servicing forms within services (Dunning 1987), the extent to which technological change and liberalisation are reinforcing the competitive position of established service MNEs *vis-à-vis* new entrants, and the links between strategy and structure (Channon 1978). Such work would greatly assist both policy-makers and industry participants in understanding the dynamics of the service sector.

10.8 POLICY ISSUES IN THE SERVICE SECTOR

The service sector generates a number of policy-related issues. Policy changes, particularly deregulation, have had a major impact on the service sector. Deregulation has affected operations in a number of ways. First, it creates new opportunities for market entry and internationalisation. This has been most obvious in financial, medical and transportation services in recent years. Second, it affects the creation and application of competitive advantages. Enterprises based in unregulated areas have been at the forefront in entering related overseas markets when deregulation has occurred. The success of US-based hospital chains in entering the UK and other markets is a prime example. Third, the immediate aftermath of deregulation is often a substantial restructuring of the industry. For innovative, adaptive competitors there are substantial opportunities; for others there may be elimination or acquisition. The experience of the US airline industry in recent years is a salutary one.

Protective policies have in many cases fragmented domestic markets and may have acted to the detriment of indigenous suppliers. For example, legislation favouring domestic firms has ensured that half of the Japanese market for auditing services is in the hands of indigenous firms. The comparable figure in France is perhaps as high as two-thirds. The 'Big Eight' have not been able to achieve anything like the penetration apparent in other countries (see Chapter 4). On the other hand, protectionism within the insurance markets of several European nations have prevented large-scale clients achieving economies of single sourcing and have actually encouraged in-house provision with a resultant loss of business to national insurers (Kakabadse 1987). Careful evaluation of such policies is obviously required.

More sophisticated analyses of policy issues are called for in the international arena. Chapter 9 suggested that there was opposition on the part of many developing nations to a further liberalisation of global services as it was generally felt that US service MNEs would be the principal beneficiaries of such a development. This view appears a little simplistic when one recognises that for services subject to sizeable economies of scale (i.e. many information-based services) the integration of markets brings significant gains to suppliers located in small nations (McCulloch 1987). Considerably more research is needed on these areas of dynamic policy change.

10.9 INNOVATION AND NEW TECHNOLOGY IN THE SERVICE SECTORS

Innovation in the service sector is a further area of rapid change. Innovations may occur in a variety of ways arising in related service or commodity industries or resulting from the hybrid combination of novel service activities. The speed of this change and its diffusion necessitate close monitoring. Good examples are provided by the short product life cycle of the computer software industry and the implications of cross-border data transmission.

Service firms are also undertaking major expenditures on new technologies. One estimate suggested that the leading US banks spent $7 billion on electronic banking technology between 1980 and 1985 and devoted between 11 and 15 per cent of their non-interest expenditure to automation. French banks appear to be spending a comparable amount (Economist 1986). While some research has been undertaken on aspects of new technology, particularly employment displacement, in the international context more work is required on its likely impact on methods of overseas-market servicing, organisational forms and infrastructure needs. While technological forecasting is neither easy nor particularly accurate, it is necessary (see Netherlands Economic Institute 1985).

10.10 CONTRASTS BETWEEN MANUFACTURING AND SERVICE MNEs

There is now a vast body of work on the activities of multinationals, particularly manufacturing MNEs. If this knowledge is to be of value in explaining the activities of service firms we need to be aware of any differences which exist between the two sectors. The evidence of this volume is that the eclectic theory of the MNE does appear to offer a useful explanatory framework for investigating service firms.

In analysing the determinants of internationalisation of service firms we are not yet in a position to judge whether or not traditional economic variables such as size or nationality, which have been successful in explaining the growth of manufacturing MNEs (Buckley, Dunning and Pearce 1978), will prove as useful when applied to service MNEs (but see Tschoegl 1983).

Both similarity and diversity of experience with goods-producing MNEs have been noted on a number of occasions in this book. Commonality of experience is most apparent in the case of restrictions on overseas operations where there was no evidence of a service-sector problem *per se*.

Complementarity is apparent in other areas. The overseas affiliates of source-nation manufacturing MNEs constitute an important customer group for many intermediate service MNEs in accounting and contracting for example. Furthermore, the development of specialist service firms may have enhanced the overseas competitive profile of non-service MNEs. Where there are significant economies of agglomeration high technology manufacturers and business service firms are often found together (Browne 1983). In a number of areas there are marked differences between service and non-service MNEs. These include degrees of multinationality and risk, growth strategies, size and specialisation. These contrasts suggest caution when applying recommendations on 'best practice' derived from analysis of manufacturing MNEs.

Bibliography

Accountancy (1975) 'Accountants on the move', *Accountancy* March, p. 22.
—— (1980) 'Touche Ross's International's talk of growth', *Accountancy* April, p. 9.
—— (1981) 'People and firms', *Accountancy* September, p. 32.
—— (1983) 'People and firms', *Accountancy* February, p. 36.
Accountant (1975) 'Notes and notes', *The Accountant* 15 May, p. 651.
—— (1978) 'Notice board', *The Accountant* 6 July, p. 31.
—— (1979) 'Notice board', *The Accountant* 2 August, p. 199.
—— (1981a) 'Professional notices', *The Accountant* 29 January, p. 167.
—— (1981b) 'Notice board', 9 July, p. 51.
Advertising Age (1984) 'World brands', *Advertising Age* 25 June, pp. 49–74.
Agarwal, R.G. (1975) 'Joint ventures among developing Asian countries', UNCTAD TC/B/AC.19/R.7.
—— (1981) 'Third-World joint ventures: Indian experience', in Kumar and McLeod (1981), pp. 115–32.
—— and Khera, I.P. (1983) 'Strategic planning for Western direct investment in developing countries", *Mid-Atlantic Journal of Business,* Summer, pp. 13–30.
—— and Weekly J.K. (1982) 'Foreign operations of Third World multinationals: a literature review and analysis of Indian companies', *The Journal of Developing Areas*, vol. 17.
Agmon, T. and Kindleberger C.P. (eds) (1977) *Multinationals from small countries*, MIT Press, Cambridge, Mass.
Aliber, R.Z. (1985) 'A survey of multinational banking', *Journal of Money, Credit and Banking*, vol. 16, pp. 661–72.
Antonelli, C. (1985) 'The diffusion of an organisational innovation: international data telecommunications and multinational industrial firms', *International Journal of Industrial Organisations*, vol. 3, pp. 109–18.
Aronson, J.D. and Cowley, P.F. (1985) 'Services trade: a case for open markets', *Economic Impact*, vol. 50, pp. 11–17.
Arthur Andersen (1963) *The first fifty years, 1913–1963*, Arthur Andersen, New York.

256

—— (1985) 'Personnel by Divisions', booklet, Arthur Andersen, New York.

Arthur Young (1985) *The firm and its services*, Arthur Young, London.

Bachtler, J. (1987) 'Regional incentive policy and the service sector', *Journal of Regional Policy*, vol. 1, pp. 21–35.

Baer, W. and Samuelson, L. (1982) 'Toward a service-oriented growth strategy', *World Development*, vol. 9, p. 6.

Balakrishnan, K. (1976) 'Indian joint ventures abroad: geographic and industry patterns', *Economic and Political Weekly* (Review of Management), May.

Ballance, R.H. and Sinclair, S. (1983), *Collapse and survival: industry strategies in a changing world*, Allen and Unwin, London.

Bannon, M. (1985) 'Service activities in national and regional development: trends and prospects for Ireland', in M. Bannon and S. Ward (eds), *Services and the new economy: implications for national and regional development*, Regional Studies Association (Irish Branch), Dublin, pp. 38–61.

Barker, B.L. (1981) 'A profile of US multinational companies in 1977', *Survey of Current Business*, vol. 63, no. 10 (October), pp. 38–57.

Barna, T. (1983) 'Process plant contracting: a competitive new European industry' in G. Shepherd, F. Duchene and C. Saunders (eds), *Europe's industries: public and private strategies for change*, Frances Pinter, London, pp. 167–85.

Barnes, P. (1984) 'The wire services from Latin America', *Nieman Reports*, vol. XVIII, p. 1.

Bavishi, V.B. and Wyman, H.E. (1983) *Who audits the world?*, School of Business Administration, University of Connecticut, Storrs, Conn.

Bayley, E.R. (1981) *Joe McCarthy and the press*, University of Wisconsin Press, Madison.

Beaudreau, B. (1986) 'Managers, learning and the multinational firm: theory and evidence', unpublished PhD thesis, University of Western Ontario.

Belli, R.D. (1981) 'US business enterprises acquired or established by foreign direct investors in 1980', *Survey of Current Business*, vol. 61, p. 8.

Benz, S.F. (1985) 'Trade liberalisation and the global service economy', *Journal of World Trade Law*, vol. 19, no. 2, pp. 95–120.

Bertrand, O. and Noyelle, T. (1986) *Changing technology: skills and skill formation in French, German, Japanese, Swedish and US financial services firms*, OECD, Paris.

Blackaby, F. (ed.) (1979) *De-industrialisation*, Heinemann, London.

Bluestone, B.F. and Harrison, B. (1982) *The de-industrialisation of America*, Basic Books, New York.

Boddewyn, J.J., Halbrich, Perry M.B. and Perry A.C. (1986) 'Service multinationals: conceptualisation, measurement and theory', *Journal of International Business Studies*, vol. 16, pp. 41–57.

Bohdanowicz, J. (1984) *Who audits the UK?*, Financial Times Business Information, London.

Boyd-Barrett, J.O. (1976), 'The world-wide news agencies: development, organisation, competition, markets and product, unpublished

PhD thesis, Open University, British Library Microfilm D317 37/80.
—— (1977) 'The collection of foreign news in the national press', in J.O. Boyd-Barrett, J. Seymoure-Ure and J. Tunstall, *Studies on the press*, HMSO, London, pp. 7–44.
—— (1980a), *The international news agencies*, Sage, London; Constable, Beverly Hills.
—— (1980b), 'A four-point plan for the news agencies' *InterMedia*, vol. 8, no. 5 (September) pp. 8–11, reprinted in *Vidura* (1980), October, pp. 305–12.
—— (1985) *Assessment of news agency and foreign broadcast monitoring services as information sources*, Consultant Report, STC CR-54, (NATO Unclassified), SHAPE Technical Centre, The Hague.
—— and Palmer, M. (1981) *Le Traffic des Nouvelles*, Alain Moreau, Paris.
British Calibration Service (1984) *Approved Laboratories and their Measurement*, September.
Brock, W.E. (1982) 'A simple plan for negotiating on trade in services', *The World Economy*, vol. 5, pp. 229–40.
Browne, L.E. (1983) 'High technology and business services,' *New England Economic Review*, July–August, pp. 5–17.
Buckley, P.J. and Casson, M. (1976) *The future of the multinational enterprise*, Macmillan, London.
—— and Casson, M. (1985) *The economic theory of the multinational enterprise*, Macmillan. London.
—— Dunning, J.H. and Pearce, R.D. (1978) 'The influence of firm size, industry, nationality and degree of multinationality on the growth of the world's largest firms, 1962–1972', *Weltwirtschaftliches Archiv*, vol. 114, no. 2, pp. 243–57.
Bullock, M. (1983) *Academic enterprise, industrial development and the development of high technology financing in the US*, Brand Brothers, New York.
Burstein, M.L. (1960a) 'The economics of tie-in sales', *Review of Economics and Statistics*, vol. 42, pp. 68–73.
—— (1960b) 'A theory of full-line forcing', *Northwestern University Law Review*, vol. 55, pp. 62–95.
—— (1984) 'Diffusion of knowledge-based products: applications to developing countries', *Economic Inquiry*, vol. 22, pp. 612–33.
Burton, F. and Saelens, F. (1986) 'The European investments of Japanese financial institutions', *Columbia Journal of World Business*, vol. 21, pp. 27–33.
Business Asia (1980a) 'Indian companies as foreign investors', *Business Asia*, 19 December, pp. 404–5.
—— (1980b) 'Indian multinationals spring fresh drive into Asian Markets', *Business Asia*, 19 December, pp. 404–5.
Business India (1979) 'The new multinationals', *Business India*, 20 August, pp. 33–5, and 2 September, pp. 44–7.
Busjeet, V. (1980) 'Foreign investors from less developed countries', unpublished PhD thesis, Harvard Business School.
C & L Journal (1979) '125th Anniversary Issue, *C & L Journal*, vol. 31 (June).
Cairns, D., Lafferty M., and Mantle, P. (1984) *IAB summary of*

accounts and accountants 1983–84, Lafferty Publications, London.

Carman, J.M. and Langeard, E. (1979) *'Growth strategies for service firms'*, paper presented to the Eighth Annual Meeting of the European Academy for Advanced Research in Marketing, Groningen, April.

Casas-Gonzalez, A. (1975a) 'Joint ventures among Latin American Countries', UNCTAD TD/B/AC.19/R.2, 22 October.

—— (1975b), 'Regional multinational firms in Latin America', UNCTAD, Division of Trade Expansion and Economic Integration, October.

Casson, M. (1979) *Alternatives to the Multinational Enterprises*, Macmillan, London.

—— (1982a) 'The theory of foreign direct investment', in J. Black and J.H. Dunning (eds), *International capital movements*, Macmillan, London, pp. 22–57.

—— (1982b) 'Transaction costs and the theory of the multinational enterprise', in A.M. Rugman (ed.), *New theories of the multinational enterprise*, Croom Helm, London, pp. 24–43.

—— (1985) 'Horizontal and vertical integration in the construction industry', unpublished paper.

—— (1987) *The firm and the market: studies on transactions costs and the strategy of the firm*, MIT Press, Cambridge.

Caves, R.E. (1971) 'International corporations: the industrial economics of foreign investment', *Economica*, vol. 38, pp. 1–27.

—— (1982) *Multinational enterprise and economic analysis*, Cambridge University Press, Cambridge.

—— and Murphy II, W. (1976) 'Franchising: firms, markets and intangible assets', *Southern Economic Journal*, vol. 42, pp. 572–86.

Central Statistical Office (1983) *United Kingdom balance of payments, 1982 edition*, HMSO, London.

Channon, D.F. (1978) *The service industries: strategy, structure and financial performance*, Macmillan, London.

Chaudry, N.G. (1980) 'Joint ventures abroad', *Indian and Foreign Review*, April, 4.

Chen, E.K.Y. (1981) 'Hong Kong multinationals in Asia: characteristics and objectives', in Kumar and McLeod 1981, pp. 79–99.

Choi, S-R., Tschoegl, A. and Yu, C-M. (1986) 'Banks and the world's major financial centers 1970–80', *Weltwirlschaftliches Archiv*, vol. 122, pp. 48–64.

Chung, W.K. (1978), 'Sales by majority-owned foreign affiliates of US companies, 1976', *Survey of Current Business*, vol. 58, no. 3 (March), pp. 31–40.

Clairmonte, E. and Cavanagh, J. (1984) 'Transnational corporations and services: the final frontier', *Trade and Development*, vol. 5, pp. 215–73.

Cogan, D. (1986) 'The services sector revisited: an analysis of job creation potential', *Journal of Irish Business and Administrative Research*, vol. 8, no. 2, pp. 58–68.

Cohen, R.B. (1981) 'The new international division of labour, multinational corporations and urban hierarchy', in M.J. Dear and A.J. Scott (eds), *Urbanisation and urban planning in capitalist society*,

Methuen, London, pp. 287–315.

Committee on Invisible Exports (1983), *World invisible trade*, Committee on Invisible Exports, London.

Conklin, David (1987) *Canada's trade in high technology: the case of information technology*, Institute for Research on Public Policy, Ottawa.

Cooper Brothers & Co. (1954) *A history of Cooper Brothers & Co. 1854–1954*, Cooper Brothers & Co., London.

Coopers & Lybrand (1986) *International directory*, Coopers & Lybrand, London.

Cordeiro, C.A. (1978) 'Internalization of Indian firms: a case for direct foreign investment from a less developed country', unpublished undergraduate honours thesis, Department of Economics, Harvard College.

Council for Mutual Economic Assistance (1980), *1979 yearbook of the member countries of the Council for Mutual Economic Assistance*, Statistika, Moscow.

Cowell, D.W. (1983) 'International marketing of services', *The Service Industries Journal*, vol. 3, pp. 308–28.

Curhan, J.P., Davidson, W.H. and Suri, R. (1977) *Tracing the multinationals: a sourcebook on US-based enterprises*, Ballinger, Cambridge, Mass.

Damanpour, F. (1986) 'A survey of market structure and activities of foreign banking in the US', *Columbia Journal of World Business*, vol. 21, pp. 35–56.

Damesick, P.J. (1987) 'Regional economic change since the 1960s', in P.J. Damesick and P.A. Wood (eds), *Regional problems, problem regions and public policy in the United Kingdom*, Oxford University Press, Oxford, pp. 19–41.

Daniels, P.W. (1982) *Service industries: growth and location*, Cambridge University Press, Cambridge.

—— (1986) 'Foreign banks and metropolitan development: a comparison of London and New York', *Tijdschrift voor Econ en Soc Geografie*, vol. 77, no. 4, pp. 269–87.

—— Leyshon, A. and Thrift, N.J. (1986) 'UK producer services: the international dimension', *Working Papers on Producer Services, 1*, St David's University College, Lampeter and University of Liverpool.

Dare, O. (1983) 'The news agency of Nigeria: a study of its impact on the flow of news and the role conceptions of its staffers, unpublished PhD thesis, Indiana University, University Microfilms International, DA8406788.

David, K. (1984) 'Home government policy and international competitive performance of Third World corporations: a study of Indian and Korean service industries', in Thomas Brewer (ed.), *Studies of political risks in international business*, Praeger, New York.

Davidson, W.H. (1980) *Experience effects in international investment and technology transfer*, UMI Research Press, Ann Arbor.

—— and McFetridge, D. (1984) 'International technology transaction and the theory of the firm', *Journal of Industrial Economics*, vol. 32, pp. 253–64.

Delehanty, G.F. (1968) *Non-production workers in US manufacturing*, North Holland, New York.

Deloitte, Plender, Griffiths & Co. (1958) *Deloitte & Co: 1845–1956*, Deloitte, Plender, Griffiths & Co., London.

Department of Environment (1985) *Housing and construction statistics 1974–84*, HMSO, London.

Department of Trade and Industry (1980) *Overseas trade statistics of the UK*, HMSO, London.

Diaz-Alejandro, C. (1977) 'Foreign direct investment by Latin America', in T. Agmon and C.P. Kindleberger (eds), *Multinationals from small countries*, MIT Press, Cambridge, Mass.

Dilullo, A.J. (1981) 'Service transactions in the US international accounts, 1979–80', *Survey of Current Business*, vol. 61, no. 11, pp. 29–46.

Doyle, P. and Corstjens, M. (1983) 'Optimal growth strategies for service organisations', *Journal of Business*, vol. 56, no. 3, pp. 389–405.

Dunning, J.H. (1977) 'Trade, location of economic activity and MNE: a search for an eclectic approach', in B. Ohlin, P.O. Hesselborn and P.M. Wijkman (eds), *The international allocation of economic activity*, Macmillan, London.

—— (1981a) 'Explaining outward investment in developing countries: in support of the eclectic theory of international production', in Kumar and McLeod (1981), pp. 1–22.

—— (1981b) *International production and the multinational enterprise*, Allen and Unwin, London.

—— (1985) *Multinational enterprises, economic structure and international competitiveness*, John Wiley & Sons, Chichester.

—— (1987) *Transnationals and the growth of service sectors: some conceptual and theoretical issues*, mimeo.

—— and McQueen, M. (1981) *Transnational corporations in the international hotel industry*, UNCTC, New York.

—— and McQueen, M. (1982) 'The eclectic theory of the multinational enterprise and the international hotel industry', in A.M. Rugman (ed.), *New theories of the multinational enterprise*, St Martin's Press, New York, pp. 79–106.

—— and Norman, G. (1983) 'The theory of the multinational enterprise: an application to multinational office location', *Environment and Planning*, Series A, 15, pp. 675–92.

—— and Norman, G. (1987) 'The location choice of offices of international companies', *Environment and Planning*, Series A, vol. 19, pp. 613–31.

—— and Pearce, R.D. (1985) *The world's largest industrial enterprises 1962–1983*, Gower, Aldershot.

Eastman, H. and Stykolt, S. (1967) *The tariff and competition in Canada*, Macmillan, Toronto.

Economic Consulting Services Inc. (1981) *The international operations of US service industries: current data collection and analysis*, Economic Consulting Services Inc., New York.

Economist (1978) 'Italy's world builders', *The Economist*, 11 November, pp. 80–1.

Economist (1985) 'Japan survey', *The Economist*, 7 December.

Economist (1986) 'International banking survey', *The Economist*, 22 March.

Encarnation, D.J. (1982) 'The political economy of Indian joint industrial ventures abroad: a study of domestic policies and transnational linkages', *International Organization*, vol. 21, pp. 31–59.

Enderwick, P. (1985) *Multinational business and labour*, Croom Helm, London.

—— (1987) 'The strategy and structure of service sector multinationals: implications for potential host regions', *Regional Studies*, vol. 21, no. 3, pp. 215–23.

Ewing, A.F. (1985) 'Why freer trade in services is in the interest of developing countries', *Journal of World Trade Law*, vol. 19, no. 2, pp. 147–69.

Feketekuty, G. and Hauser, K. (1985) 'Information technology and trade in services,' *Economic Impact*, vol. 52, pp. 22–8.

Fleming, M.C. (1980) 'Construction', in P.S. Johnson (ed.), *The structure of British industry*, Granada, London.

Franklin, D.E. (1982) 'Dealing with East European importing organisations: a survey of UK exporters' experience', *European Journal of Marketing*, vol. 16.

Franko, L. (1983) *The threat of Japanese multinationals — how the West can respond*, John Wiley and Sons, Chichester.

—— (1984) 'The pattern of Japanese multinational investment', *Multinational Business*, 1.

Fuchs, V.R. (1968) *The service economy*, National Bureau of Economic Research, New York.

Gemmell, N. (1982) 'Economic development and structural change: the role of the service sector', *The Journal of Development Studies*, vol. 19, p. 1.

Gershuny, J. (1983) *Social innovation and the division of labour*, Oxford University Press, Oxford.

—— and Miles, I. (1983) *The new service economy: the transformation of employment in industrial societies*, Frances Pinter, London.

Ghymn, K.I. (1980) 'Multinational enterprises from the Third World', paper presented to the 1980 meeting of the Academy of International Business, mimeograph.

Goldberg, L.G. and Saunders, A. (1981) 'The growth of organizational forms of foreign banks in the United States', *Journal of Money, Credit and Banking*, vol. 13, pp. 365–74.

Goldman, M.L. (1980) *The enigma of Soviet petroleum: half full or half empty?*, Allen and Unwin, London.

Gonenc, R. (1984) 'Software – a new industry', *OECD Observer*, vol. 131, pp. 20–3.

Gordon, D.M. (1979) *The working poor: towards a state agenda*, The Council of State Planning Agencies, Washington, DC.

Gray, H.P. (1983) 'A negotiating strategy for trade in services', *Journal of World Trade Law*, vol. 17, no. 5, pp. 377–88.

Griffiths, B. (1975) *Invisible barriers to invisible trade*, Macmillan, London.

Grubel, H.G. (1974) 'Taxation and the rates of return from some US asset holdings abroad 1960–69', *Journal of Political Economy*, vol.

82, pp. 469–87.

—— (1977), 'A theory of multinational banking', *Banca Nazionale del Lavoro Quarterly Review*, vol. 123, pp. 349–63.

—— (1983) 'The new international banking', *Banca Nazionale del Lavoro Quarterly Review*, vol. 144, pp. 263–84.

—— (1987) 'Traded services are embodied in materials or people', *The World Economy*, vol. 10, no. 3, pp. 319–30.

Gudgin, G., Crum, R.E. and Bailey, S. (1979), 'White collar employment in UK manufacturing industry', in P.W. Daniels (ed.), *Spatial patterns of office growth and location*, John Wiley and Sons, London.

Hall, P. (1983) 'What's all the fuss about inter press?', *Columbia Journalism Review*, January/February, pp. 53–7.

Heenan, D.A. and Keegan, W.J. (1979) 'The rise of third world multinationals', *Harvard Business Review*, January/February, pp. 101–9.

Heskett, J. (1986) *Managing the service economy*, Harvard Business School Press, Cambridge, MA.

Hill, M.R. (1983a) *East–West trade, industrial co-operation and technology transfer*, Gower Press, Aldershot.

—— (1983b) *'Soviet and East European multinational activity in the United Kingdom and Republic of Ireland'*, report submitted to the Institute for Research and Information on Multinationals (IRM), Geneva.

—— (1983c) *'Soviet and East European multinational activity in Sweden – a preliminary study'*, report submitted to the Institute for Research and Information on Multinationals (IRM), Geneva.

Hill, P. (1977) *Les Proies des Multis Rouges, Vision*, Fevrier, pp. 44–8.

Hill, T.P. (1977) 'On goods and services', *The Review of Income and Wealth*, vol. 23, pp. 315–38.

Hillebrandt, P.M. (1984) *Analysis of the British construction industry*, Macmillan, London.

Hindley, B. and Smith, A. (1984) 'Comparative advantage and trade in services', *The World Economy*, vol. 7, pp. 369–89.

Hollander, S.C. (1970) *Multinational retailing*, Michigan State University, East Lansing.

Hoogvelt, A.M.M. (1982) *The Third World in global development*, Macmillan, London.

Horstmann, I. and Markusen, J. (1987a) 'Strategic investments and the development of multinationals', *International Economic Review*, vol. 28, pp. 109–21.

—— and Markusen, J. (1987b) 'Licensing versus direct investment: a model of internalization by the multinational enterprise', *Canadian Journal of Economics*, vol. 20, no. 3, pp. 464–81.

Howenstein, N.G. (1982) 'Growth of US multinational companies 1966–77', *Survey of Current Business*, 62, 4 (April), pp. 34–46.

Indian Institute of Foreign Trade (1978) *India's joint ventures abroad*, Indian Institute of Foreign Trade, New Delhi.

Indian Investment Centre (1970) *Joint ventures abroad*, Indian Investment Centre, New Delhi.

Institute of Chartered Accountants (1975) *List of members, 1975/76*, ICAEW, London.

—— (1985), *List of members, 1985/86*, ICAEW, London.

Institute of Soviet and East European Studies (1983), *East–West business directory: a listing of companies in the West with Soviet and East European equity participation*, Carleton University, Ottawa, Duncan Publishing, London.

Inter Company Comparisons (ICC) Limited (1981), *Industrial performances analysis: a financial analysis of UK industry and commerce*, ICC Business Ratios Division, London.

—— (1982), *Industrial performances analysis: a financial analysis of UK industry and commerce*, ICC Business Ratios Division, London.

International Accounting Bulletin (1984), 'France's big league: the first detailed analysis, *International Accounting Bulletin*, March, pp. 16–18.

—— (1986), 'Arthur Andersen first through a new barrier', *International Accounting Bulletin*, March, p. 3.

International Labour Organisation (1981) *Employment effects of multinational enterprises in industrialised countries*, International Labour Office, Geneva.

International Monetary Fund (1983) *International Monetary Fund annual report*, International Monetary Fund, Washington.

International Trade Administration (1982) *Services and US trade policy*, Center for Strategic and International Studies, Georgetown University, Washington.

IPTC News (1985) (newsletter of the International Press Telecommunications Council), no. 58 (March), p. 6.

ISI (1987) *Bulletin*, 1, September, International Services Institute, Arizona.

ITI (1983) *Success in invisibles*, British Overseas Trade Board/British Consultants Bureau Report, London.

Jo, S.H. (1981) 'Overseas direct investment by South Korean firms: direction and pattern', in Kumar and McLeod (1981), pp. 53–77.

Johnson, H.G. (1970), 'The efficiency and welfare implications of the multinational corporation', in C.P. Kindleberger (ed.), *The international corporation: a symposium*, MIT Press, Cambridge, Mass., pp. 35–56.

Jones, E. (1981) *Accountancy and the British economy 1840–1980: The evolution of Ernest & Whinney*, Batsford Books, London.

Kakabadse, M.A. (1987) *International trade in services: prospects for liberalisation in the 1990s* (Atlantic Paper 64), Croom Helm, London.

Kenward, L. (1983) 'On employment in the major industrial countries', *Finance and Development*, vol. 2.

Kindleberger, C.P. (1969) *American business abroad*, Yale University Press, New Haven.

Knirsch, P. (1983) *East European firms in the Federal Republic of Germany and Austria*, report submitted to the Institute for Research and Information on Multinationals (IRM), Geneva.

Kobrin, S.J. (1984) 'Expropriation as an attempt to control foreign firms in LDCs: trends from 1960 to 1979', *International Studies Quarterly*, vol. 28.

Kojimi, K. and Ozawa, T. (1984) *Japan's general trading companies: merchants of economic development*, OECD Development Centre Studies, Paris.

Krommenacker, R.J. (1986) 'The impact of information technology on trade interdependence', *Journal of World Trade Law*, vol. 20, no. 4, pp. 381–400.

Kumar, K. (1981) 'Multinationalization of Third-World public-sector enterprises', in Kumar and McLeod (1981), pp. 187–201.

—— (1983) 'Foreign direct investment by Korean firms in manufacturing sector', *Asian Finance*.

—— and McLeod, M.G. (eds) (1981) *Multinationals from developing countries*, Lexington Books, Lexington, Mass.

—— and Schive, C. (1987) 'The Third World multinationals: a study of Taiwanese firms', East–West Centre, Hawaii.

—— and Kim, K.Y. (1984) 'The Korean manufacturing multinationals', *Journal of International Business Studies*, vol. 15, no. 1, pp. 45–61.

Lall, S. (1982) 'The emergence of Third World multinationals: Indian joint ventures overseas', *World Development*, vol. 10, pp. 127–46.

—— (1982) 'The export of capital from developing countries: India', in J. Dunning and J. Black (eds), *International capital movements*, Macmillan, London.

—— and Siddharthan, N.S. (1982) 'The monopolistic advantages of multinationals: lessons from foreign investment in the US', *Economic Journal*, vol. 92, pp. 668–83.

—— (1983), *The new multinationals*, John Wiley & Sons, New York.

Lamb, H. and Percy, S. (1987) *Working for Big Mac*, Transnational Information Centre, London.

Landor, J. (1986) *Beyond the pail*, Transnational Information Centre, London.

Lawrenson, J. and Barber, L. (1985), *The price of truth: the story of the Reuters £££ millions*, Mainstream Publishing, Edinburgh.

Lecraw, D.J. (1976) 'Choice of technology in low-wage countries', unpublished PhD Thesis, Harvard University, Cambridge, Mass.

—— (1977) 'Direct investment by firms from less developed countries', *Oxford Economic Papers*, November, pp. 442–57.

—— (1980), 'Intra-Asian direct investment: theory and evidence from the ASEAN region', *UMBC Economic Review*, vol. 2.

—— (1981a) 'Technological activities of LDC-based multinationals', *The Annals of the American Academy of Political and Social Sciences*, November, pp. 163–74.

—— (1981b) 'Internationalization of firms from LDCs: evidence from the ASEAN region', in Kumar and McLeod 1981, pp. 37–51.

—— (1983) 'Performance of Transnational Corporations in less developed countries', *Journal of International Business Studies*, vol. 14, no. 1, pp. 15–33.

Lees, F.A. (1974) *International banking and finance*, Macmillan, London.

Leyshon, A., Daniels, P.W. and Thrift, N.J. (1987) 'Large accountancy firms in the UK: operational adaptation and spatial development', *Working Papers on Producer Services 2*, St David's University College, Lampeter, and University of Liverpool.

Loeve, A., De Vries, J. and Smidt, M. de (1985), 'Japanese firms and the gateway to Europe', *Tijdschrift voor Econ en Soc Geographie*, vol. 7, pp. 2–10.

London Chamber of Commerce and Industry (1980) *Trade contacts in Eastern Europe*, London Chamber of Commerce and Industry, London.

Lowe, J. (1985) 'Science parks in the UK', *Lloyds Bank Review*, vol. 156, pp. 31–42.

MacCharles, D.C. (1985) 'Increased competition and Canada's domestic and international trade flows', *Canadian Journal of Administrative Sciences*, December.

McCulloch, R. (1987) *International competition in services*, National Bureau of Economic Research, Working Paper 2235, Cambridge, MA.

McMillan, C.H. (1978) *Direct Soviet and East European investment in the industrialised Western economies*, Institute of Soviet and East European Studies, Carleton University, Ottawa.

—— (1979a) 'Growth of external investments by the Comecon countries', *The World Economy*, vol. 2, no. 3, pp. 363–86.

—— (1979b) 'Soviet investment in the industrial Western economies and in the developing economies of the Third World', in US Congress Joint Economic Committee, *Soviet Economy in a Time of Change, 2*, US Government Printing Office, Washington, DC.

Malmgren, H.B. (1985) 'Negotiating international rules for trade in services', *The World Economy*, vol. 8, no. 1, pp. 11–26.

Management Accounting (1985) 'Change of name for Thomson McLintock', *Management Accounting*, January, p. 10.

Mannisto, M. (1981) 'Hospital management companies expand foreign operations', *Journal of the American Hospital Association*, vol. 55, no. 3, pp. 52–6.

Mansfield, E. and Romeo, A. (1980) 'Technology transfer to overseas subsidiaries by US based firms', *Quarterly Journal of Economics*, vol. 94, pp. 737–50.

—— Romeo, A. and Wagner, S. (1979) 'Foreign trade and US research and development, *Review of Economics and Statistics*, vol. 61.

Mansfield, N.R. (1986) 'Some international issues from the early 1980s facing British consulting engineers', *Proceedings of Institute of Civil Engineers*, Part 1, vol. 80, pp. 1211–31.

Mantel, I.M. (1975) 'Sources and uses of funds for a sample of majority-owned foreign affiliates of US companies, 1966–72', *Survey of Current Business*, vol. 55, no. 7, pp. 29–52.

Markusen, A.R. (1985) 'High-technology jobs, markets and economic development prospects: evidence from California' in P. Hall and A.R. Markusen (eds), *Silicon landscapes*, George Allen and Unwin, Hemel Hempstead, pp. 35–48.

Markusen, J. (1987) 'Intra-firm trade by the multinational enterprise', Institute for Research on Public Policy, University of Western Ontario, mimeo.

—— and Melvin, J. (1985) *The theory of international trade and its Canadian applications*, Butterworths, Toronto.

Marquand, J. (1983) 'The changing distribution of service employment', in J.B. Goddard and A.G. Champion (eds), *The urban and regional transformation of Britain*, Methuen, London, pp. 99–134.

Marsh, F. (1984) 'Future trends in Japanese overseas investment',

Multinational Business, vol. 2, pp. 1–11.

Marshall, J.N. (1979) 'Ownership, organisation and industrial linkage', *Regional Studies*, vol. 13, pp. 531–58.

—— (1985) 'Business services: the regions and regional policy', *Regional Studies*, vol. 19, pp. 352–63.

Matthews, P. (1984) *Report of the Committee to Consider the Structure, Function and Status of the Export Credits Guarantee Department*, HMSO, London.

Meyer, H.E. (1977) 'The communist internationale has a capitalist accent', *Fortune*, February, pp. 134–48.

Miller, R.R. (1985) *International Competition in Services: An American Perspective* Strathclyde International Business Unit, Working Paper 85/5, University of Strathclyde, Glasgow.

Momigliano, F. and Siniscalco, D. (1982) 'The growth of service employment: a reappraisal', *Banca Nazionale Del Lavoro Quarterly Review*, 3.

Morgan, B. (1979) *Directory of Soviet and East European companies in the West*, Institute of Soviet and East European Studies, Carleton University, Ottawa.

Nambudiri, C.D.S., Lyandi, O. and Akkinus, D.M. (1981) 'Third-World-Country firms in Nigeria' in Kumar and McLeod (1981), pp. 145–53.

Nelson, P. (1970) 'Information and consumer behaviour', *Journal of Political Economy*, vol. 78.

Netherlands Economic Institute (1985), *The service sector and technological developments*, Netherlands Economic Institute, Rotterdam.

Nicholas, S. (1983) 'Agency contracts, institutional modes, and the transition to foreign direct investment by British manufacturing multinationals before 1939', *Journal of Economic History*, vol. 43, pp. 375–686.

Nioisi, J. (1985) *Canadian multinationals*, Between the Lines, Toronto.

Nordic Bank (1981) *A reader's guide to Swedish financial statements*, Custodia AB, Stockholm.

Norton, D. (1984) 'Public policy for private sector services', *Journal of Irish Business and Administrative Research*, vol. 6, no. 2, pp. 84–105.

Noyelle, T.J. (1983) 'The implications of industry restructuring for spatial organisation in the United States', in F. Moulaert and P.W. Salinas (eds), *Regional analysis and the new international divison of labour*, Kluwer, Nijhoff, Boston, pp. 113–33.

—— (1986) *New technologies and services: impacts on cities and jobs*, University of Maryland, Institute for Urban Studies Washington, DC.

—— and Dutka, A. (1986) *Business services in world markets: lessons for trade negotiations*, AEI Press, Washington, DC.

—— and Dutka, A. (1987) *Business services in world markets: accounting, advertising, law and management consulting*, Ballinger, Cambridge, Mass.

O'Brien, P. (1980a) 'The internationalisation of the Third World industrial firms', *Multinational Business*, vol. 4, pp. 1–8.

—— (1980b) 'The new multinationals: developing country firms in international markets', *Futures*, pp. 303–16.

—— (1980c) 'Third World industrial enterprises: export of technology and investment', *Economic and Political Weekly*, special issue, October.

Okibgo, P.J.C. (1975), 'Joint Ventures among African countries', UNCTAD TD/B/AC.19/R.3, 2 October.

OECD (1980) National accounts of OECD countries 1961–78, OECD, Paris.

—— (1981) *Recent international direct investment trends*, OECD, Paris.

—— (1983a) *Trade in international services: insurance*, OECD, Paris.

—— (1983b) 'The obstacles to international trade in services: tourism', *OECD Observer*, vol. 126, pp. 14–15.

—— (1984) 'Obstacles to international trade in services: banking', *OECD Observer*, vol. 128, pp. 21–4.

—— (1985) 'Competition in the professions', *OECD Observer*, Vol. 132, pp. 21–4.

—— (1986a) *Competition policy and joint ventures*, OECD, Paris.

—— (1986b) 'Liberalisation of trade and investment in the services sector: the role of the OECD codes', *OECD Observer*, vol. 139, pp. 25–7.

Oman, C. (1984) *New forms of international investment in developing countries*, OECD, Paris.

Ozawa, T. (1982), 'A newer type of foreign investment in Third World resource development', *Rivista Internazionale di Scienze Economiche et Commerciali*, vol. 29, pp. 1133–51.

Panglaykim, J. (1979) *Emerging enterprises in the Asia-Pacific region*, CSIS, Jakarta.

—— (1981) 'Multinational corporations in ASEAN/South Korea/Hong Kong: a descriptive picture', paper presented to a conference on 'Third World Multinationals', East-West Centre, Honolulu, 12–18 September.

Peat Marwick (1985) *Peat Marwick international annual review 1985*, Peat Marwick, London.

Pecchioli, R.M. (1983) *The internationalisation of banking: the policy issues*, OECD, Paris.

Pollard, S. (1979) 'The rise of the service industries and white-collar employment' in Bo Gustafsson (ed.), *Post-industrial society*, Croom Helm, London.

Pratten, C.F. (1976) *A comparison of the performance of Swedish and UK companies*, Department of Applied Economics Occasional Paper 47, Cambridge University Press.

Price, R. (1980) *Masters, unions and men: work control in building and the rise of labour 1830–1914*, Cambridge University Press, Cambridge.

Price Waterhouse (1984), *Price Waterhouse annual review 1983–84*, Price Waterhouse, London.

—— (1985), 'Some significant events in the history of the firm', typescript, London.

Rabino, S. (1984) 'Foreign competition for the US banking world', *Long Range Planning*, vol. 17, no. 3, pp. 115–22.

Raju, M.K. (1980) *Internationalization of Indian business*, Forum of Free Enterprise, Bombay.

—— and Prahalad, C.K. (1982) *The emerging multinationals-Indian experience in the ASEAN region*, M.K. Raju Consultants Private Ltd, Madras.

Randhawa, P.S. (1987) 'Punta del Este and after: negotiations on trade in services and the Uruguay round', *Journal of World Trade Law*, vol. 21, no. 4, pp. 163–71.

Ray, G. (1986) 'Productivity in services', *National Institute Economic Review*, vol. 115, February, pp. 44–7.

Read, R. (1983) 'The growth and structure of multinationals in the banana export trade', in M. Casson (ed.), *The growth of international business*, George Allen and Unwin, London, pp. 180–213.

Richards, A.B. (1981) *Touche Ross & Co 1899–1981*, Touche Ross & Co., London.

Richards, G.E. (1950) *History of the firm: the first fifty years 1850–1900*, typescript.

Rimmer, T. (1981) 'Foreign news on UPIs "A" wire in the USA', *Gazette*, vol. 28, pp. 35–49.

Rugman, A.M. (1979) *International diversification and the multinational enterprise*, Lexington Books, Lexington, Mass.

—— (1981) *Inside the multinationals: the economics of internal markets*, Croom Helm, London, and Columbia University Press, New York.

—— (1985) 'Internationalization is still a general theory of foreign direct investment', *Weltwirtschaftliches Archiv*, vol. 121, pp. 570–5.

—— (1987) 'Multinationals and trade in services: a transaction cost approach, *Weltwirtschaftliches Archiv*, vol. 123, pp. 651–67.

Salmon, J.W. (1984) 'Organising medical care for profit', in J.B. McKinlay (ed.), *Issues in the political economy of health care*, Tavistock, London, pp. 143–86.

Sapir, A. (1985) 'North–south issues in trade in services', *The World Economy*, vol. 8, pp. 27–42.

—— and Schumacher, D. (1984) *The employment impact of shifts in the composition of commodity and services trade*, OECD, Paris.

Scheman, R.L. (1973) 'The multinational in a new mode: ownership by the developing countries', *International Development Review*, vol. 15, no. 2, pp. 22–4.

Schramm, W. and Atwood, E. (1981) *Circulation of news in the Third World*, Chinese University Press, Hong Kong.

Schwamm, H. and Merciai, P. (1985) *The multinationals and the services*, IRM Multinational Reports, 6, Geneva.

Segal, N. (1985) 'The Cambridge phenomenon', in 'New Technology and the Local Economy', *Regional Studies*, vol. 19, pp. 563–78.

Segal Quince Wicksteed (1985), *The Cambridge phenomenon. The growth of high technology industry in a university town*, Segal Quince Wicksteed, Cambridge.

Seymour, H., Flanagan, R. and Norman, G. (1985) 'International investment in the construction industry: an application of the eclectic approach', unpublished paper.

Shelp, R.K. (1981) *Beyond industrialisation: ascendancy of the global service economy*, Praeger, New York.

—— (1985) 'Service technology and economic development', *Economic Impact*, vol. 52, pp. 8–13.

Shihata, I.F.I. (1975) *Joint Ventures among Arab Countries*, UNCTAD, TD/B/AD.19/R.5, October.

Singh, D. (1977) 'Capital budgeting and Indian investments in foreign countries', *Management International Review*, vol. 1.

Smith, A.D. (1972) *The measurement and interpretation of service output changes*, National Economic Development Office, London.

Sobell, V. (1984) *The Red market: industrial co-operation and specialisation in Comecon*, Gower Press, Aldershot.

Somarajiwa, R. (1984) 'Third-World entry to the world market in news: problems and possible solutions', *Media, Culture and Society*, vol. 6, pp. 119–36.

Statistics Canada (1986) *Canada's International Trade in Services – 1969–84*, Minister of Supply and Services, Ottawa.

Stevenson, R.L. and Cole, R. (1980) *Foreign news and the 'New world information order' debate*, part 2, Foreign News in Selected Countries (Office of Research, International Communications Agency), Washington, DC.

Storey, D.J. and Johnson, S. (1987) 'Regional variations in entrepreneurship in the UK', *Scottish Journal of Political Economy*, vol. 34, no. 2, pp. 161–73.

Svenska Handelsbanken (1980) *Starting a business in Sweden*, Svenska Handelsbank, Stockholm.

Teece, D.J. (1977) *Technology transfer by multinational firms*, Ballinger, Cambridge, Mass.

—— (1981) 'The market for know-how and the efficient international transfer of technology', *The Annals of the Academy of Political and Social Science*, vol. 458, pp. 81–96.

—— (1986) *The multinational corporation and the resource cost of international technology transfer*, Ballinger, Cambridge.

Telser, L.G. (1960) 'Why should manufacturers want fair trade', *Journal of Law and Economics*, vol. 3, pp. 86–105.

—— (1979) 'A theory of monopoly of complementary goods', *Journal of Business*, vol. 52, pp. 211–30.

Thee, K.-W. (1981) 'Indonesia as a host country to Indian joint ventures' in Kumar and McLeod (1981), pp. 133–44.

Ting, W.-L. (1980a) 'A comparative analysis of the management technology and performance of firms in newly industrialising countries', *Columbia Journal of World Business*, Fall, pp. 83–91.

—— (1980b) 'New wave multinationals now compete with their Western technology, marketing mentors', *Marketing News* vol. 1, (17 October), p. 12.

—— (1980c) 'NIC multinationals and the transfer of technology', a paper presented at the Economic Seminar in Greater Taipei Area, April.

—— and Schive, C. (1981) 'Direct investment and technology transfer from Taiwan', in Kumar and McLeod (1981), pp. 101–14.

Tschetter, J. and Lukasiewicz, J. (1983) 'Employment changes in construction: secular, cyclical and seasonal', *Monthly Labor Review*, vol. 106, pp. 11–17.

Tschoegl, A. (1983), 'Size, growth and transnationality among the

World's largest banks', *Journal of Business*, vol. 56, no. 2, pp. 187–201.

Tunstall, J. (1981) 'Worldwide news agencies – private wholesalers of public information', in J. Richstad and M.H. Anderson (eds), *Crisis in international news*, Columbia University Press, New York, pp. 258–67.

UNCTC (1979) *Transnational corporations in advertising*, United Nations, New York.

United Nations (1978) *Transnational corporations in world development: a re-examination*, UN Publications, New York.

—— (1983) *Transnational corporations in world development third survey*, United Nations Publications, New York.

United States Department of Commerce (1976) *US service industries in world markets: current problems and future policy development*, Washington, DC.

United States Department of State (1971) *Nationalisation, expropriation and other takings of United States and certain foreign property since 1960*, Bureau of Intelligence and Research.

US Office of Technology Assessment (1986) *Trade in services: exports and foreign revenues*, Government Printing Office, Washington, DC.

US Office of the US Trade Representative (1983) *US national study on trade in services: a submission by the United States Government to the General Agreement on Tariffs and Trade*, Government Printing Office, Washington, DC.

Van Grasstek, C. (1987) 'Trade in services: obstacles and opportunities', *Economic Impact*, vol. 58, pp. 46-51.

Vernon, R. (1966) 'International investment and international trade in the product cycle', *Quarterly Journal of Economics*, vol. 80, pp. 190–207.

—— (1971) *Sovereignty at bay: the multinational spread of US enterprises*, Basic Books, New York.

Villa, P. (1981) 'Labour market segmentation and the construction industry in Italy', in F. Wilkinson (ed.) *The dynamics of labour market segmentation*, Academic Press, London, pp. 133–49.

Wells, L.T., Jr (1977) 'The internationalization of firms from the developing countries', in Agmon and Kindleberger (1977).

—— (1978) 'Foreign investment from the Third World: the experience of Chinese firms from Hong Kong', *Columbia Journal of World Business*, vol. xiii, pp. 39–49.

—— (1980a) 'Strategies of multinational firms: new Third World multinationals', *Tatung Life*, January 1.

—— (1980b) 'Third World multinationals', *Multinational Business*, vol. 1.

—— (1981) 'Foreign investment from the Third World', in Kumar and McLeod (1981).

—— (1983) *Third World multinationals*, MIT Press, Cambridge, Mass.

—— and Warren, V. (1979) 'Developing country investors in Indonesia', *Bulletin of Indonesian Economic Studies*, March, pp. 69–84.

Whichard, O.G. (1982), 'Employment and employee compensation of US multinational corporations in 1977', *Survey of Current Business*, vol. 62, no. 2 (February), pp. 37–60.

—— (1987) 'US sales of services to foreigners', *Survey of Current Business*, vol. 67, no. 1, pp. 22–41.

White, E. (1981) 'The international projection of firms from Latin American countries', in Kumar and McLeod (1981), pp. 155–86.

White, R. (1984) 'Multinational retailing: a slow advance?', *Retail and Distribution Management*, vol. 12, no. 2, pp. 8–13.

Wilkins, M. (1974) *The maturing of multinational enterprise: American business abroad from 1914 to 1970*, Harvard University Press, Cambridge, Mass.

Wilson, R. (1977) 'The effect of technological environment and product rivalry on R & D effort and licensing of inventions', *Review of Economics and Statistics*, vol. 59, pp. 171–8.

Winsbury, R. (1977) *Thomson McLintock & Co – the first hundred years*, Thomson McLintock, London.

Wise, T.A. (1981) *Peat Marwick Mitchell & Co: 85 years*, Peat Marwick Mitchell, New York.

Withers, R. (1985) *Overseas projects board: 4th report*, British Overseas Trade Board, London.

World Bank (1984) *World development report 1984*, Oxford University Press, New York.

Yannopolous, G.B. (1983) 'The growth of transnational banking', in M. Casson (ed.), *The growth of international business*, George Allen and Unwin, London, pp. 236–57.

Yu, B.T. (1984) 'A contractual remedy to premature innovation: the vertical integration of brand-name specific research', *Economic Inquiry*, vol. 22, pp. 660–7.

Zaleski, E. (1984) 'Socialist multinationals in developing countries', report submitted to the Institute for Research and Information on Multinationals (IRM), Geneva.

Zurawicki, L. (1979) *Multinational enterprises in the West and East*, Sijthoff and Hoordhoff, Alphen ad Rijn.

Index

For Product Safety Concerns and Information please contact our EU
representative GPSR@taylorandfrancis.com Taylor & Francis Verlag GmbH,
Kaufingerstraße 24, 80331 München, Germany

Batch number: 08153780

Printed by Printforce, the Netherlands